Mobil

Travel Guide®

COASTAL
SOUTHEAST

ACKNOWLEDGMENTS

We gratefully acknowledge the help of our representatives for their efficient and perceptive inspections of the lodging and dining establishments listed, the establishments' proprietors for their cooperation in showing their facilities and providing information about them, and the many users of previous editions who have taken the time to share their experiences. Mobil Travel Guide is also grateful to all the talented writers who contributed entries to this book.

Front and back cover images: ©iStockPhoto.com

All maps: created by Mapping Specialists

ISBN: 9-780841-61126-9   Manufactured in Canada

10 9 8 7 6 5 4 3 2 1

TABLE OF CONTENTS

WRITTEN IN THE STARS   4

STAR RATINGS   6

INTRODUCTIONS   9

COASTAL SOUTHEAST

GEORGIA   10-79

NORTH CAROLINA   80-154

SOUTH CAROLINA   155-198

3

COASTAL SOUTHEAST

★
★
★
★
★

INDEX   199

WRITTEN IN THE STARS

Because time is precious and the travel industry is ever-changing, having accurate, reliable travel information at your fingertips has never been more important. With this in mind, Mobil Travel Guide has provided invaluable insight to travelers through its Star Rating system for more than 50 years.

The Mobil Corporation (known as Exxon Mobil Corporation since a 1999 merger) began producing the Mobil Travel Guide books in 1958 following the introduction of the U.S.-interstate highway system in 1956. The first edition covered only five Southwestern states. Since then, our books have become the premier travel guides in North America, covering all 50 states and Canada, and beginning in 2008, international destinations such as Hong Kong and Beijing.

Today, the concept of a "five-star" experience is one that permeates the collective conciousness, but few people realize it's one that originated with Mobil. We created our star rating system to give travelers an easy-to-recognize quality scale for choosing where to stay, dine and spa. Based on an objective process, we make recommendations to our readers that we believe will enhance the quality and value of their travel experiences. Our trusted Mobil One- to Five-Star rating system is the oldest and most respected lodging and restaurant inspection and rating program in North America. Most hoteliers, restaurateurs and industry observers favorably regard the rigor of our inspection program and understand the prestige and benefits that come with receiving a Mobil Star rating.

The Mobil Travel Guide process of rating each establishment includes unannounced inspections, incognito evaluations and a review of unsolicted comments from the general public. We inspect more than 500 attributes at each property we visit, from cleanliness to the condition of the rooms and public spaces, to employee attitude and courtesy. It's a system that rewards those properties that strive for and achieve excellence each year. And the very best properties raise the bar for those that wish to compete with them.

Only facilities that meet Mobil Travel Guide's standards earn the privilege of being listed in the guide. Properties are continuously updated, and deteriorating, poorly managed establishments are removed. We wouldn't recommend that you visit a hotel, restaurant or spa that we wouldn't want to visit ourselves.

★★★★★The Mobil Five-Star Award indicates that a property is one of the very best in the country and consistently provides gracious and courteous service, superlative quality in its facility and a unique ambience. The lodgings and restaurants at the Mobil Five-Star level consistently continue their commitment to excellence, doing so with grace and perseverance.

★★★★The Mobil Four-Star Award honors properties for outstanding achievement in overall facility and for providing very strong service levels in all areas. These award winners provide a distinctive experience for the ever-demanding and sophisticated consumer.

★★★The Mobil Three-Star Award recognizes an excellent property that provides full services and amenities. This category ranges from exceptional hotels with limited services to elegant restaurants with a less formal atmosphere.

★★The Mobil Two-Star property is a clean and comfortable establishment that has expanded amenities or a distinctive environment. These properties are an excellent place to stay or dine.

★The Mobil One-Star property is limited in its amenities and services but provides a value experience while meeting travelers' expectations. The properties should be clean, comfortable and convenient.

We do not charge establishments for inclusion in our guides. We have no relationship with any of the businesses and attractions we list and act only as a consumer advocate. We do the investigative legwork so that you won't have to.

Restaurants and hotels—particularly small chains and stand-alone establishments—change management or even go out of business with surprising quickness. Although we make every effort to continuously update information, we recommend that you call ahead to make sure the place you've selected is still open.

COASTAL SOUTHEAST

STAR RATINGS

MOBIL RATED HOTELS

Whether you're looking for the ultimate in luxury or the best bang for your travel buck, we have a hotel recommendation for you. To help you pinpoint properties that meet your needs, Mobil Travel Guide classifies each lodging by type according to the following characteristics.

★★★★★The Mobil Five-Star hotel provides consistently superlative service in an exceptionally distinctive luxury environment. Attention to detail is evident throughout the hotel, resort or inn, from bed linens to staff uniforms.

★★★★The Mobil Four-Star hotel provides a luxury experience with expanded amenities in a distinctive environment. Services may include automatic turndown service, 24-hour room service and valet parking.

★★★The Mobil Three-Star hotel is well appointed, with a full-service restaurant and expanded amenities, such as a fitness center, golf course, tennis courts, 24-hour room service and optional turndown service.

★★The Mobil Two-Star hotel is considered a clean, comfortable and reliable establishment that has expanded amenities, such as a full-service restaurant.

★The Mobil One-Star lodging is a limited-service hotel, motel or inn that is considered a clean, comfortable and reliable establishment.

For every property, we also provide pricing information. The pricing categories break down as follows:

$ = Up to $150

$$ = $151-$250

$$$ = $251-$350

$$$$ = $351 and up

All prices quoted are accurate at the time of publication; however, prices cannot be guaranteed.

MOBIL RATED RESTAURANTS

Every restaurant in this book has been visited by Mobil Travel Guide's team of experts and comes highly recommended as an outstanding dining experience.

★★★★★The Mobil Five-Star restaurant offers one of few flawless dining experiences in the country. These establishments consistently provide their guests with exceptional food, superlative service, elegant décor and exquisite presentations of each detail surrounding a meal.

★★★★The Mobil Four-Star restaurant provides professional service, distinctive presentations and wonderful food.

★★★The Mobil Three-Star restaurant has good food, warm and skillful service and enjoyable décor.

★★The Mobil Two-Star restaurant serves fresh food in a clean setting with efficient service. Value is considered in this category, as is family friendliness.

★The Mobil One-Star restaurant provides a distinctive experience through culinary specialty, local flair or individual atmosphere.

Because menu prices can fluctuate, we list a pricing category rather than specific prices. The pricing categories are defined as follows, per diner, and assume that you order an appetizer or dessert, an entrée and one drink:

       $ = $15 and under

       $$ = $16-$35

       $$$ = $36-$85

       $$$$ = $86 and up

MOBIL RATED SPAS

Mobil Travel Guide's spa ratings are based on objective evaluations of hundreds of attributes. About half of these criteria assess basic expectations, such as staff courtesy, the technical proficiency and skill of the employees and whether the facility is clean and maintained properly. Several standards address issues that impact a guest's physical comfort and convenience, as well as the staff's ability to impart a sense of personalized service. Additional criteria measure the spa's ability to create a completely calming ambience.

★★★★★The Mobil Five-Star spa provides consistently superlative service in an exceptionally distinctive luxury environment with extensive amenities. The staff at a Mobil Five-Star spa provides extraordinary service beyond the traditional spa experience, allowing guests to achieve the highest level of relaxation and pampering. These spas offer an extensive array of treatments, often incorporating international themes and products. Attention to detail is evident throughout the spa, from arrival to departure.

★★★★The Mobil Four-Star spa provides a luxurious experience with expanded amenities in an elegant and serene environment. Throughout the spa facility, guests experience personalized service. Amenities might include, but are not limited to, single-sex relaxation rooms where guests wait for their treatments, plunge pools and whirlpools in both men's and women's locker rooms, and an array of treatments, including a selection of massages, body therapies, facials and a variety of salon services.

★★★The Mobil Three-Star spa is physically well appointed and has a full complement of staff.

INTRODUCTION

If you've been a reader of Mobil Travel Guides, you may have noticed a new look and style in our guidebooks. Since 1958, Mobil Travel Guide has assisted travelers in making smart decisions about where to stay and dine. Fifty-one years later, our mission has not changed: We are committed to our rigorous inspections of hotels, restaurants and, now, spas, to help you cut through all the clutter, and make easy and informed decisions on where you should spend your time and budget. Our team of anonymous inspectors are constantly on the road, sleeping in hotels, eating in restaurants and making spa appointments, evaluating hundreds of standards to determine a property's star rating.

As you read these pages, we hope you get a flavor of the places included in the guides and that you will feel even more inspired to visit and take it all in. We hope you'll experience what it's like to stay in a guest room in the hotels we've rated, taste the food in a restaurant or feel the excitement at an outdoor music venue. We understand the importance of finding the best value when you travel, and making the most of your time. That's why for more than 50 years, Mobil Travel Guide has been the most trusted name in travel.

If any aspect of your accommodation, dining, spa or sightseeing experience motivates you to comment, please contact us at Mobil Travel Guide, 200 W. Madison St., Suite 3950, Chicago, IL 60606, or send an email to info@mobiltravelguide.com Happy travels.

COASTAL SOUTHEAST

GEORGIA

THINK SWEET TEA AND PEACHES. THINK CIVIL WAR *AND* CIVIL RIGHTS HISTORY. THINK MILES of golf, fishing, hiking and hunting—and antebellum gentility. With Georgia on your mind (and a tip of the hat to Ray Charles), there's no limit to the travel experiences offered up by the Peach State.

Tourism is one of Georgia's primary industries, and the state boasts many wonders, from its Blue Ridge vacation lands in the north—where Brasstown Bald Mountain rises 4,784 feet—to the deep "trembling earth" of the ancient Okefenokee Swamp bordering Florida. Stone Mountain, a giant hunk of rock that rises from the plain near Atlanta, is the world's largest granite exposure. The coastal Golden Isles, set off by the Marshes of Glynn, feature moss-festooned oaks that grow down to the white sandy beaches.

Historical attractions also abound, from the world's largest brick fort near Savannah to the Martin Luther King Jr. Historical District in Atlanta. There is the infamous Confederate prison at Andersonville and the still lavish splendor of the cottage colony of 60 millionaires of the Jekyll Island Club, now a state-owned resort. Most towns in the state have historical homes and museums offering perspective on Native Americans as well as Revolutionary and Civil War efforts and artifacts.

The state of Georgia holds a storied place in America's past, beginning with the founding of the Georgia Colony in the early 1700s by James Oglethorpe and named for King George II of England. Georgia's barrier islands not only sheltered the fledgling colony, they provided a bulwark on the Spanish Main for English forts to oppose Spanish Florida and help end the centuries-old struggle for domination among the Spanish, French and English along the South Atlantic Coast.

The state was one of the country's original 13 colonies and the fourth state to join the Union (January 2, 1788), but the fifth of the 11 Confederate states to secede during the Civil War. Georgia's lot in the Civil War was a harsh one from the time Sherman opened his campaign on May 4, 1864, until he achieved the Union objective of splitting the South from the Mississippi to the sea. Reconstruction ushered in a long, slow recovery, but today Georgia's capital city, Atlanta, is the center of the New South, alive with culture and history and teeming with business—the city boasts headquarters for Coca-Cola, Delta Airlines and Home Depot, among others. The state is the nation's largest producer of peanuts, pecans and peaches and is also heavy in paper and wood pulp production.

Information: www.georgia.org

10

GEORGIA

★
★
★
★
★

 FUN FACTS

The *Savannah* was the first American steamship to cross the Atlantic Ocean in 1819.

Famous Georgia natives include Julia Roberts, Martin Luther King Jr., Jimmy Carter and Kim Basinger.

The first big American gold strike took place in Georgia in 1828.

Coca-Cola was invented in Columbus, Georgia, in 1885.

Georgia doctor Crawford Long first used ether as an anesthetic in 1842.

GEORGIA'S BLUE RIDGE FOOTHILLS

Whether you're looking for a leisurely, scenic drive or a weekend of family attractions, try the Blue Ridge Mountains and the Chattahoochee National Forest, both just two hours north of Atlanta.

For a perfect 200-mile loop, head north on Highway 400 (a toll road) and drive 50 miles toward Dahlonega. Highway 19 leads you the rest of the way into town. Named from the Cherokee word *talonega* (meaning "yellow money"), Dahlonega (dah-LON-ah-ga) was the site of the nation's first gold rush in the 1830s. In 1838, the federal government built a branch of the U.S. Mint here, stamping the town's name on $6 million worth of gold coins before the operation was shut down at the onset of the Civil War. The Dahlonega Gold Museum is now housed in the old courthouse building. In the surrounding square, you'll find a colorful assortment of shops and restaurants, including an old-fashioned general store that sells penny candy. Attractions include gold mine tours and even a small (but fruitful!) gold panning station beside the visitor center. On the south side of the square, the landmark **Smith House** *(84 S. Chestatee St., 706-867-7000, 800-852-9577; www.smithhouse. com)* has served all-you-can-eat family-style Southern meals for more than 80 years. They also offer overnight lodging.

From Dahlonega, follow Highway 19 north to Highway 129 east about 25 miles to Cleveland, the birthplace of the Cabbage Patch dolls. Take a tour and watch the dolls "grow" here in a "hospital" outside of town. Then continue north on Highway 75 to Helen, a modest mountain town that transformed itself into a Bavarian village. Dig into bratwurst and Heineken, and dance with dirndl- and lederhosen-clad locals during Oktoberfest. A museum in the castle on Main Street (706-878-3140) tells the full story. A scenic stretch of the Chattahoochee River cuts through the town, and local outfitters shuttle people upstream for leisurely float trips back down.

Return south on Highway 75, turning east onto Highway 17, which rolls through a quieter stretch of the foothills to Clarkesville. Antique shops and cafés make this small town worthy of a stop before heading south on Highway 441-365 to Atlanta. *Approximately 200 miles.*

GEORGIA

★
★ ★
★ ★
★

ALBANY

Southwestern Georgia is home to the Plantation Trace region, famous for its woodlands, rivers and its rich farm and history. Albany and surrounding Dougherty County are no exception. Known as the "Pecan Capital of the World," the area is renowned for its quail hunting and is home to a massive 800-acre animal park. The town was founded by Colonel Nelson Tift, a Connecticut Yankee who led a party up the Flint River from Apalachicola, Florida and constructed the first log buildings. Settlers followed when the Native Americans were moved to western lands.

Information: Convention and Visitors Bureau, 225 W. Broad Ave.,
229-434-8700; www.albanyga.com

WHAT TO SEE AND DO

ALBANY MUSEUM OF ART

311 Meadowlark Drive, Albany, 229-439-8400; www.albanymuseum.com

The museum's collection of sub-Saharan African art is particularly strong. About 15 other permanent and changing exhibits feature both local and regional artists. Tuesday-Friday 10 a.m.-5 p.m.

THE PARKS AT CHEHAW

105 Chehaw Park Road, Albany, 229-430-5275; www.parksatchehaw.org

The creeks, streams and cypress swamps of this 800-acre park are home to all sorts of wildlife, including deer, beavers, tortoises, alligators and a variety of birds. Nature trails allow visitors to see the animals up close, and an old-style locomotive takes visitors on a 20-minute train ride through a restored area. Don't miss the fantastic children's park and farm or the wild animal park, designed by famed naturalist Jim Fowler, which features rhinos and the only cheetah population in Georgia. Admission: adults $2, children under 12 $1, seniors adults over 62 and military $1. Daily 9 a.m.-5 p.m. Zoo hours: 9:30 a.m.-5 p.m. Admission: adults $7, children under 12 $4, senior adults over 62 and military $4 (includes park pass).

HOTELS

★COMFORT SUITES

1400 Dawson Road, Albany, 229-888-3939, 888-726-3939; www.comfortsuites.com

62 rooms. Complimentary continental breakfast. Wireless Internet access. Fitness room. Outdoor pool. Pets not accepted. $

★
★
★
★
★

★HAMPTON INN AT ALBANY MALL

806 N. Westover Blvd., Albany, 229-883-3300, 800-426-7866;
www.hamptoninn.com

82 rooms. Complimentary full breakfast. Bar. Wireless Internet access. Business center. Fitness room. Outdoor pool, whirlpool. Pets not accepted. $

★★QUALITY INN

1500 Dawson Road, Albany, 229-435-7721, 888-462-7721; www.merryacres.com

110 rooms. Restaurant, bar. Complimentary full breakfast. High-speed Internet access. Fitness room. Outdoor pool. Complimentary airport shuttle. $

★REGENCY INN

911 E. Oglethorpe Expressway, Albany, 229-883-1650

151 rooms. Restaurant, bar. Complimentary full breakfast. Outdoor pool. $

AMERICUS

Americus is at the center of an area once known as the "granary of the Creek nations," so called because Native Americans living in the area were known for their agriculture, particularly corn. The town was supposedly named for either new world explorer Amerigo Vespucci or for the settlers themselves, who were referred to as "merry cusses" because of their reputed happy-go-lucky ways. The town flourished in the

1890s and many Victorian and Gothic Revival buildings remain from that period. Today the town has the headquarters for International Habitat for Humanity, which has built more than 225,000 homes around the world for those in need.

Information: Americus-Sumter County Chamber of Commerce, Tourism Division, 400 Lamar St., 229-924-2646, 888-278-6837; www.americus-sumterchamber.com

WHAT TO SEE AND DO

HABITAT FOR HUMANITY—GLOBAL VILLAGE AND DISCOVERY CENTER

121 Habitat South, Americus, 229-924-6935, 800-422-4828; www.habitat.org

See life-size replicas of houses around the world and exhibits on poverty. Learn about the organization's impact globally and experience hands-on what it's like to construct compressed earth blocks and clay roof tiles just as Habitat volunteers do in Asia and Africa.

HOTELS

★★WINDSOR HOTEL

125 W. Lamar St., Americus, 229-924-1555, 888-297-9567;
www.windsor-americus.com

53 rooms. Restaurant, bar. Wireless Internet access. Spa. $

1906 PATHWAY INN BED & BREAKFAST

501 S. Lee St., Americus, 229-928-2078, 800-889-1466;
www.1906pathwayinn.com

For a small-town getaway, this English colonial bed and breakfast offers guests Old South charm. Six rooms. Complimentary full breakfast. Wireless Internet access. $

RESTAURANT

★★★GRAND DINING ROOM

125 W. Lamar St., Americus, 229-924-1555;
www.windsor-americus.com

Located in the Windsor Hotel, this restaurant offers traditional Southern favorites along with cuisine from different regions of the country. A charming Victorian setting completes the dining experience. American menu. Dinner. Bar. $$

ATHENS

This ultimate college town is the site of the University of Georgia, which was chartered in 1785. The landscape here is stunning—set on a hill beside the Oconee River, enhanced by towering oaks and elms, white-blossomed magnolias, old-fashioned boxwood gardens and many well-preserved and still-occupied antebellum houses. But what makes Athens worth mentioning is the university's claim as one of the best college experiences in America and the town's lively (some lists even rank it among the top 10) music scene. Bands like REM, the B-52s and the Indigo Girls among others all got their start here. Whether you're looking for music festivals, college sports or antebellum history, the home of the Georgia Bulldogs offers up an active mix.

Information: Athens Convention & Visitors Bureau, 300 N. Thomas St., Athens, 706-357-4430, 866-653-0603; www.athenswelcomecenter.com

GEORGIA

★
★
★
★
★

WHAT TO SEE AND DO
CHURCH-WADDEL-BRUMBY HOUSE
280 E. Dougherty St., Athens, 706-353-1820; www.visitathensga.com
Restored 1820 Federal-style house thought to be the oldest residence in Athens. Houses the Athens Welcome Center, which has information on self-guided tours of other historic houses and buildings. Monday-Saturday 10 a.m.-6 p.m., Sunday from noon.

STATE BOTANICAL GARDEN
2450 S. Milledge Ave., Athens, 706-542-1244;
www.uga.edu/botgarden
Approximately 300 acres with natural trails, wildlife and special collections. Gardens October-March daily 8 a.m.-6 p.m.; April-September daily 8 a.m.-8 p.m. Visitor Center & Conservatory Tuesday-Saturday 9 a.m.-4:30 p.m., Sunday 11:30 a.m.-4:30 p.m. Closed on University of Georgia holidays.

TAYLOR-GRADY HOUSE
634 Prince Ave., Athens, 706-549-8688; www.taylorgradyhouse.com
Restored 1844 Greek Revival mansion surrounded by 13 columns said to symbolize 13 original states; period furniture. Monday-Friday 9 a.m.-1 p.m., 2-5 p.m.

THE UNIVERSITY OF GEORGIA
College Station and East Campus Roads, Athens, 706-542-0842; www.uga.edu
Consisting of 16 schools and colleges, the main campus extends more than two miles south from the Arch, College Avenue and Broad Street. Nearby are farms managed by the College of Agriculture, a forestry preserve and University Research Park. Historic buildings from the 1800s include Demosthenian Hall; chapel; Old College, the oldest building, designed after Connecticut Hall at Yale; Waddel Hall and Phi Kappa Hall.

SPECIAL EVENTS
NORTH GEORGIA FOLK FESTIVAL
Sandy Creek Park, 400 Bob Holman Road, Athens, 706-208-0985;
www.athensfolk.org
This annual festival showcases music that has roots in the region. Genres include bluegrass, gospel and more. Early October. $$

SPRING TOUR OF HOMES
489 Prince Ave., Athens, 706-353-1801, www.achfonline.org
Celebration of Athens architecture held by the Athens-Clarke Heritage Foundation. May.

HOTELS
★BEST WESTERN COLONIAL INN
170 N. Milledge Ave., Athens, 706-546-7311, 800-592-9401; www.bestwestern.com
70 rooms. Complimentary continental breakfast. High-speed Internet access. Pets accepted, fee. Pool. $

★★HOLIDAY INN ATHENS

197 E. Broad St., Athens, 706-549-4433, 800-465-4329;
www.holidayinn.com
307 rooms. High-speed Internet access. Airport transportation available. Health and fitness center, spa. Indoor pool. **$**

★HOLIDAY INN EXPRESS ATHENS

513 W. Broad St., Athens, 706-546-8122, 800-465-4329;
www.holidayinn.com
160 rooms. Complimentary continental breakfast. High-speed Internet access. Airport transportation available. Health and fitness center. Pets not accepted. **$**

RESTAURANTS
★★HARRY BISSETT'S NEW ORLEANS CAFÉ AND OYSTER BAR

279 E. Broad St., Athens, 706-353-7065; www.harrybissetts.net
The Cajun-Creole menu features fresh flown-in seafood daily. Lunch, dinner, brunch, bar. Casual attire, reservations recommended, outdoor seating. Lunch, 11:30 a.m.-3 p.m. Saturday Brunch, 11:30 a.m.-3:30 p.m. Sunday Brunch, 11:30 a.m.-3:30 p.m. Dinner (Sunday-Thursday) 5:30-10 p.m. Dinner (Friday-Saturday) 5:30-11 p.m. **$$**

★THE VARSITY

1000 W. Broad St., Athens, 706-548-6325; www.thevarsity.com
American fare. Lunch, dinner; casual attire, outdoor seating. **$**

ATLANTA

"An old city that feels new," is how one traveler describes this capital of the New South. Indeed, the real story of Atlanta is not its Civil War past but its present. While Atlanta proper has a population of only 429,500 due to policies that prevent annexation, the metro area is closer to 5 million. And those millions have supported the growth of Atlanta into a world-class city that offers culture (the famed Alliance Theatre), sports (four professional teams, a NASCAR speedway, numerous golf courses and an Olympic Park), 19 colleges and universities (from the Georgia Institute of Technology to Emory University to Spelman and Morehouse Colleges) and yes, some pretty spectacular history.

Atlanta began as "Standing Pitch Tree," a Native American Creek settlement until 1813 when the military built a fort and white settlers followed, making it an important trading post. After Georgia's secession from the Union on January 19, 1861, the city became a manufacturing, storage, supply and transportation center for the Confederate forces—and the last real barrier on General William Tecumseh Sherman's "March to the Sea." Although Atlanta had quartered 60,000 Confederate wounded, it was untouched by actual battle until Sherman began the fierce fighting of the Atlanta Campaign on May 7, 1864. When Union forces seized the railroad 20 miles south at Jonesboro on September 1, General Hood evacuated Atlanta, and the mayor surrendered the city the next day. The 117-day siege razed 90 percent of its buildings and homes. Many citizens returned to the city by early 1865, and Atlanta became the federal headquarters for Reconstruction. Railroad lines led the way—by 1872, Atlanta was on its way to becoming an expanded rail center for the country. Georgia is

GEORGIA

still a center for paper and wood pulp, peaches, peanuts and pecans and some mining, but Atlanta's role as the business hub of the South has really launched the region. From Coca-Cola, developed in response to Prohibition and first served at Jacob's Pharmacy on May 8, 1886, to Home Depot and Delta Airlines, Atlanta is home to many international corporate giants.

Atlanta has also been a historical center for black enterprise and culture. Martin Luther King Jr. was born here, the annual National Black Arts Festival is the largest of its kind and the city is home to more than five historically black colleges and universities.

Cultural and historical attractions thrive on Peachtree Street, Atlanta's equivalent to New York's Broadway. Peach blossoms are few. Instead, the busy thoroughfare is lined with the city's most important skyscrapers, luxury shops and hotels.

Information: Convention and Visitors Bureau, 233 Peachtree St., Northeast, 404-521-6600, 800-285-2682; www.atlanta.net

WHAT TO SEE AND DO

ATLANTA BOTANICAL GARDEN

1345 Piedmont Ave., Atlanta, 404-876-5859; www.atlantabotanicalgarden.org

Features 15 acres of outdoor gardens: Japanese, rose, perennial and others. The Fuqua Conservatory has tropical, desert and rare plants from around the world. There's also a special exhibit area for carnivorous plants. Tuesday-Sunday, April-October, 9 a.m.-7 p.m.; May-October, Thursdays until 10 p.m.; November-March 9 a.m.-5 p.m. Closed Mondays except Monday holidays such as Labor Day and Memorial Day.

16

GEORGIA

ATLANTA BRAVES (MLB)

Turner Field, 775 Hank Aaron Drive, Atlanta, 404-522-7630; www.atlantabraves.com

Major League Baseball team.

ATLANTA CYCLORAMA

Grant Park, 800 Cherokee Ave. S.E., Atlanta, 404-658-7625; www.atlantacyclorama.org

This theater in the round tells the story of the 1864 Battle for Atlanta as the studio revolves around a massive painting and diorama completed in 1885. Tuesday-Sunday 9 a.m.-4:30 p.m.

ATLANTA FALCONS (NFL)

Georgia Dome, 1 Georgia Dome Drive, Atlanta, 404-223-8444; www.atlantafalcons.com

Professional football team.

ATLANTA HAWKS (NBA)

Philips Arena, 1 Philips Drive, Atlanta, 404-878-3800; www.hawks.com.au

Professional basketball team.

ATLANTA HISTORY CENTER

130 W. Paces Ferry Road, Atlanta, 404-814-4000; www.atlantahistorycenter.com

The center consists of five major structures and 33 acres of woodlands and gardens. Exhibits range from basic state history to regional folk art to even Georgia golf legend Bobby Jones. Monday-Saturday 10 a.m.-5:30 p.m., Sunday noon-5:30 p.m. (gardens and grounds close at 5:15 p.m.).

CENTENNIAL OLYMPIC PARK

265 Park Ave., West, Atlanta, 404-223-4412; www.centennialpark.com

This 21-acre park was constructed for the 1996 Summer Olympics and serves as Atlanta's downtown centerpiece. It features the Fountain of Rings (where water shoots up in the shape of Olympic rings), an amphitheater and Great Lawn for festivals and concerts, a visitor center and a memorial to the two people killed in the bombing here during the Games. Daily 7 a.m.-11 p.m.

CNN STUDIO TOUR

1 CNN Center, Atlanta, 404-827-2300, 877-426-6868; www.cnn.com

Tour the studio, view a recreation of the main control room, visit an interactive exhibit of top news stories or learn the secrets of working a weather map. The 45-minute tours leave every 20 minutes; reservations recommended. Daily 9 a.m.-5 p.m.

FERNBANK MUSEUM OF NATURAL HISTORY

767 Clifton Road N.E., Atlanta, 404-929-6300; www.fernbank.edu

Exhibits at this monumental four-story museum include the Earth's formation, the dinosaur era, the first European settlers in North America and more. An IMAX theater shows nature-themed films on its giant screen and hosts "Martinis & IMAX" every Friday night. Monday-Saturday 10 a.m.-5 p.m., Sunday noon-5 p.m.

FERNBANK SCIENCE CENTER

156 Heaton Park Drive N.E., Atlanta, 678-874-7102; www.fernbank.edu

The center includes an exhibit hall, an observatory, a planetarium and a science library. The grounds also contain a 65-acre forest area with marked trails. Monday-Wednesday 8:30 a.m.-5 p.m., Thursday-Friday 8:30 a.m.-10 p.m., Saturday 10 a.m.-5 p.m., Sunday 1-5 p.m.

GEORGIA

★
★
★
★
★

FOX THEATRE

660 Peachtree St. N.E., Atlanta, 404-881-2100;
www.foxtheatre.org

One of the most lavish movie theaters in the world, the Fox was conceived as a Shriners' temple with a more than 4,000-seat auditorium, and hosts performances by the Atlanta Ballet, Broadway shows, a summer film festival, a full spectrum of concerts, theatrical events, plus trade shows and conventions. Guests in the theater (built in 1929) sit in an Arabian courtyard under an azure-painted sky with hundreds of 11-watt bulbs fixed in crystals, twinkling like stars. With 3,622 pipes, the colossal organ is the second-largest theater organ in the United States. Tours Monday, Wednesday-Thursday 10 a.m.; Saturday 10 a.m. and 11 a.m.

GEORGIA AQUARIUM

225 Baker St., Atlanta, 404-581-4000; www.georgiaaquarium.org

This three-year-old aquarium is the world's largest and most up-to-date. The site holds more than 8 million gallons of fresh and salt water and more animals than any other aquarium in existence. On display are rare whale sharks, beluga whales, penguins, eels, seals and just about any kind of fish imaginable. Sunday-Friday 10 a.m.-5 p.m., Saturday 9 a.m.-6 p.m. Thanksgiving Holiday, November 26-29 8 a.m.-8 p.m.

GEORGIA STATE FARMERS' MARKET

16 Forest Parkway, Forest Park, 404-675-1782;
www.agr.state.ga.us

Owned and operated by the state and covering 150 acres, this is one of the largest farmers' markets of its kind in the Southeast. Tuesday-Saturday.

HIGH MUSEUM OF ART

1280 Peachtree St. N.E., Atlanta, 404-733-4444;
www.high.org

African sculpture; European, American and contemporary painting and sculpture; decorative art; photography. Rotating exhibits. Tuesday-Saturday 10 a.m.-5 p.m., Thursday 10 a.m.-8 p.m., Sunday noon-5 p.m.

JIMMY CARTER LIBRARY AND MUSEUM

441 Freedom Parkway, Atlanta, 404-865-7100; www.jimmycarterlibrary.org

This museum has exhibits on life in the White House, major events during the Carter administration and the life of President Carter. It includes a full-scale replica of the Oval Office. Museum: Monday-Saturday 9 a.m.-4:45 p.m., Sunday noon-4:45 p.m.; Library: Monday-Friday 8:30 a.m.-4:30 p.m.

MARGARET MITCHELL HOUSE

990 Peachtree St., Northeast, Atlanta, 404-249-7015; www.gwtw.org

Home of the famous Atlanta native and author of *Gone with the Wind*, which was written here in a cramped basement apartment. The museum displays a portrait of Scarlett O'Hara from the movie, the original door from Tara, Scarlett's home and a great collection of movie posters. Hour-long guided tours. Monday-Saturday 9:30 a.m.-5:30 p.m., Sunday noon-5 p.m.

MARTIN LUTHER KING, JR. NATIONAL HISTORIC SITE

450 Auburn Ave., Atlanta, 404-331-5190; www.nps.gov/malu

A two-block area in memory of the famed leader of the Civil Rights movement and winner of the Nobel Peace Prize. Features include the Freedom Hall Complex, Chapel of All Faiths, King Library and Archives and the reflecting pool. Films and slides on Dr. King's life and work may be viewed in the screening room. The National Park Service operates an information center. Guided tours of King's boyhood home are conducted by park rangers. Daily 9 a.m.-5 p.m. Memorial Day weekend-Labor Day until 6 p.m.

SIX FLAGS OVER GEORGIA

7561 Six Flags Parkway, Austell, 770-739-3400;
www.sixflags.com/parks/overgeorgia

A family theme park featuring Georgia's history under the flags of England, France, Spain, the Confederacy, Georgia and the U.S. More than 100 rides, shows and attractions, including the Georgia Cyclone roller coaster. Mid-May-early September daily; early March-mid-May and early September-October weekends only.

STATE CAPITOL

214 State Capitol, Atlanta, 404-656-2844; www.sos.state.ga.us

The dome, topped with native gold, is 237 feet high. Inside are historical flags, statues and portraits. Monday-Friday 8 a.m.-5:30 p.m. Tours 10 a.m., 11 a.m., 1 p.m. and 2 p.m.

STONE MOUNTAIN PARK

Highway 78 E., Stone Mountain, 770-498-5690; www.stonemountainpark.com

This 3,200-acre park surrounds the world's largest granite monolith, which rises 825 feet from the plain. The top of the mountain is accessible by foot or cable car. Surrounding the sculpture are Memorial Hall, a Civil War museum, an antebellum plantation featuring 19 buildings restored and furnished with 18th- and 19th-century heirlooms. An antique Auto and Music Museum houses cars dating from 1899 and an antique mechanical music collection; riverboat *Scarlett O'Hara* provides scenic trips around a 363-acre lake; full-size replicas of Civil War trains make a 5-mile trip around the base of the mountain. Also, a 45-minute laser show is projected onto the north face of the mountain mid-May-Labor Day nightly, April-mid-May and after Labor Day-October, Saturday. A 732-bell carillon plays concerts Saturday-Sunday daily 6 a.m.-midnight. Attractions daily 10 a.m.-5 p.m.

SYMPHONY HALL

1280 Peachtree St., Atlanta, 404-733-4900; www.atlantasymphony.org

The permanent home of the Atlanta Symphony Orchestra, Chorus and Youth Orchestra; performances. September-May and mid-June-mid-August.

UNDERGROUND ATLANTA

50 Upper Alabama St. S.W., Atlanta, 404-523-2311;
www.underground-atlanta.com

This underground mall features shops, pushcart peddlers, restaurants and nightclubs, street entertainers and various attractions. The six-block area was created in the 1920s when several viaducts were built over existing streets at second-story level to move traffic above multiple rail crossings. Merchants moved their shops to the second floors, relegating the first floors to oblivion for nearly half a century. Today visitors descend onto the cobblestone streets of a Victorian city in perpetual night. On lower Alabama Street, the shops are housed in the original, once-forgotten storefronts. Monday-Saturday 10 a.m.-9 p.m., Sunday 11 a.m.-6 p.m.; open later in summer; restaurant and club hours may vary.

GEORGIA

★
★
★
★
★

THE WORLD OF COCA-COLA

101 Baker St., Atlanta, 404-676-5151; www.wocacatlanta.com

This recently renovated and expanded tribute to the world's most popular soft drinks has a 4D theater and interactive displays and exhibits that trace the history of Coca-Cola from its introduction in 1886 at Jacob's Pharmacy Soda Fountain on Atlanta's Peachtree Street to the present. The tasting room of more than 70 different Coke products is the main draw. September-May, Monday-Saturday 9 a.m.-5 p.m., Sunday 11 a.m.-5 p.m.; June-August, Monday-Saturday 9 a.m.-6 p.m., Sunday 11 a.m.-5 p.m.

WREN'S NEST

1050 Ralph D. Abernathy Blvd., Southwest, Atlanta, 404-753-7735

Eccentric Victorian house of Joel Chandler Harris, journalist and transcriber of the Uncle Remus stories. Original family furnishings, books, photographs. Tours Tuesday-Saturday 10 a.m.-2:30 p.m.

ZOO ATLANTA

Grant Park, 800 Cherokee Ave. S.E., Atlanta, 404-624-5600; www.zooatlanta.org

Features natural habitat settings and is known for its primate center, aviary and representative Southeastern habitats exhibits. The giant panda exhibit is a major draw. Daily 9:30 a.m.-5:30 p.m., ticket booths close at 4:30 p.m.

SPECIAL EVENT

ATLANTA DOGWOOD FESTIVAL

887 W. Marietta St., Atlanta, 404-817-6642; www.dogwood.org

This springtime festival in celebration of the blooming of Atlanta's dogwood trees features an artists' market, a kids' village full of activities and live music. Early April.

HOTELS

★★★ATLANTA MARRIOTT MARQUIS

265 N.E. Peachtree Center Ave., Atlanta, 404-521-0000, 888-855-5701; www.marriott.com

This polished convention hotel has a 50-story atrium and unlimited views of the city. The guest rooms are elegantly appointed, and the hotel has 120,000 square feet of meeting space. 1,663 rooms. Four restaurants, two bars. High-speed Internet access. Spa. $$

★★EMBASSY SUITES BUCKHEAD

3285 Peachtree Road N.E., Atlanta, 404-261-7733, 800-362-2779; www.atlantabuckhead.embassysuites.com

316 rooms, all suites. Restaurant, bar, Complimentary full breakfast. Wireless Internet access. Spa. Pets not accepted. $$

★★EMBASSY SUITES HOTEL AT CENTENNIAL OLYMPIC PARK

267 Marietta St., Atlanta, 404-223-2300, 800-362-2779; www.embassysuites.com

321 rooms, all suites. Two restaurants, bar, Complimentary full breakfast. Wireless Internet access. Fitness room. Pool. Pets not accepted. $$

★
★
★
★
★

MARTIN LUTHER KING JR. HISTORIC DISTRICT

East of downtown Atlanta is a small neighborhood named Sweet Auburn. Established in the late 19th century, the neighborhood, centered around Auburn Avenue, was a thriving community of black businesses and culture, isolated from the rest of Atlanta by segregation laws. Martin Luther King Jr. was born in Sweet Auburn on January 15, 1929, in an upstairs bedroom in a two-story Victorian house at 501 Auburn Avenue. Since his death and entombment here, much of the neighborhood has been declared a National Historic District. His father, Reverend Martin Luther King, and mother, Alberta Williams, had been married in the house three years earlier, and all three of their children were born here. The nine-room Queen Anne style house has been restored and furnished to reflect how it looked during MLK's childhood.

The best way to approach the district from downtown Atlanta is to start at the central Five Points MARTA station. Go north on Peachtree Street, the city's main artery, to pick up Auburn Avenue on the far side of Woodruff Park. Follow Auburn Street east to the King Center, about a mile. On the way, you will pass many landmarks such as the modern **Auburn Avenue Research Library** (101 Auburn), which maintains a special collection on African-American history and heritage. **The APEX Museum** (135 Auburn) has an exhibit on the development of the neighborhood, including a short video, along with displays of African art. The Southern Christian Leadership Conference continues to work for social change out of its offices in the **Prince Hall Masonic Building** (332 Auburn).

The **Ebenezer Baptist Church** (407 Auburn), the 1922 sanctuary where Dr. King, his father and his grandfather preached, is the heart of the community. It is so popular with visitors that the congregation built a much larger sanctuary across the street and maintains the original 750-seat building for special services. Adjacent to the small sanctuary is the **King Center for Nonviolent Social Change** (449 Auburn), where the crypt of Martin Luther King Jr. remains set behind an eternal flame in a reflecting pond in the plaza, visible 24 hours a day. The Center, founded by Dr. King's widow, Coretta Scott King, and now chaired by his son Dexter King, maintains exhibits displaying personal effects and mementos, including one on Mahatma Gandhi, who inspired King's dedication to nonviolence. Across the street at the **Martin Luther King Jr., Historic Site visitor center** (450 Auburn), the National Park Service has displays about the Nobel Peace Prize winner and screens a 30-minute film with historical footage from the Civil Rights era. The National Park Service also leads guided walking tours of the district.

GEORGIA

★
★ ★
★ ★
★
★

★★★★★FOUR SEASONS HOTEL ATLANTA

75 14th St., Atlanta, 404-881-9898, 800-332-3442; www.fourseasons.com

This Neoclassical tower rises over Atlanta's Midtown, where world-class culture, flourishing businesses and enticing stores line the streets. Well-suited for both business and leisure travelers, this hotel offers its guests fine accommodations and flawless, intuitive service. Earth tones and polished woods set a relaxed elegance in the rooms and suites. The state-of-the-art fitness center is complete with an indoor pool and sun terrace. Park 75's fresh approach to American cuisine earns praise from locals and hotel guests alike. 244 rooms. Restaurant, bar. High-speed Internet access. Business center. Fitness room. Indoor pool, whirlpool. Spa, Pets accepted, some restrictions. $$$$

★★★GEORGIA TECH HOTEL AND CONFERENCE CENTER

800 Spring St. N.W., Atlanta, 404-347-9440, 800-706-2899;
www.gatechhotel.com

This Midtown hotel offers state-of-the-art conveniences such as flatscreen TVs to the business travelers who frequent it. The contemporary guest rooms are comfortable and feature marble bathrooms. 252 rooms. Restaurant, two bars. Wireless Internet access. Airport transportation available. Health club. Indoor pool. $$

★★★THE GLENN HOTEL

110 Marietta St. N.W., Atlanta,
404-521-2250, 866-404-5366; www.glennhotel.com

Situated at the intersection of Marietta and Spring Streets, the Glenn Hotel has a convenient downtown location. The Philips Arena and CNN are nearby, and restaurants, shops and businesses are within walking distance. The hotel is modern and cozy at the same time. Rooms have plasma TVs, large work desks with Herman Miller Aeron chairs, rain showers and Gilchrist & Soames bath amenities. 110 rooms. Restaurant, two bars. Wireless Internet access. Airport transportation available. $$$

★★★GRAND HYATT ATLANTA

3300 Peachtree Road N.E., Atlanta,
404-237-1234, 888-591-1234; www.atlanta.hyatt.com

Handsomely appointed accommodations, impeccable service and access to fashionable Buckhead dining and shopping make this city hotel a popular choice. 438 rooms. Restaurant, bar. Wireless Internet access. Fitness center, sauna. $$$

★HAMPTON INN

3398 Piedmont Road N.E., Atlanta,
404-233-5656, 888-537-1091; www.hamptoninn.com

154 rooms. Bar. Complimentary full breakfast. Wireless Internet access. Pool. Pets not accepted. $$

★★★HILTON ATLANTA AIRPORT AND TOWERS

1031 Virginia Ave., Atlanta, 404-767-9000, 800-445-8667; www.hilton.com

Conveniently located near the airport as well as the zoo, Stone Mountain and Six Flags. Amenities include an Olympus Gym, Jacuzzi and 24-hour room service. 504 rooms. Restaurant, bar. Pool. Pets accepted. Complimentary airport transportation available. $$

★★★HILTON ATLANTA AND TOWERS

255 Courtland St. N.E., Atlanta, 404-659-2000, 800-445-8667; www.hilton.com

With five restaurants, three bars, a fitness center with a jogging track, tennis courts and billiard rooms, guests don't need to leave. The contemporary rooms include comfortable working areas and large bathrooms. 1,226 rooms. Five restaurants, three bars. Wireless Internet access. Fitness center. Pets accepted. **$$**

★HOLIDAY INN EXPRESS

505 Pharr Road, Atlanta, 404-262-7880, 800-465-4329; www.hiexpress.com

87 rooms, all suites. Complimentary full breakfast. Wireless Internet access. Health and fitness center, spa. Outdoor pool. **$**

★★HOTEL INDIGO

683 Peachtree St. N.E., Atlanta, 404-874-9200; www.midtownatlantahotel.com

140 rooms. Restaurant, bar. Wireless Internet access. Airport transportation available. Pets accepted. **$$**

★★★HYATT REGENCY ATLANTA

265 Peachtree St. N.E., Atlanta, 404-577-1234, 800-591-1234; www.hyatt.com

Located downtown, this 23-story atrium hotel successfully combines convenience with superb accommodations and first-class amenities, including a state-of-the-art fitness center. Minutes away are the Atlanta Market Center, Georgia Dome, Underground Atlanta and Centennial Olympic Park. 1,260 rooms. Two restaurants, two bars. Wireless Internet access. Fitness center. Outdoor pool. **$$**

★★★★INTERCONTINENTAL BUCKHEAD

3315 Peachtree Road N.E., Atlanta,
404-946-9000, 800-972-2404; www.intercontinental.com

Recognized as one of the leading business hotels in the area, the InterContinental Buckhead is also great for leisure travelers. Lenox Square, the largest shopping mall in the Southeast, and the upscale Phipps Plaza are within walking distance. It also boasts the only day spa in an Atlanta hotel. Vast and lovely grounds add to the experience. 422 rooms. Restaurant, bar. Complimentary breakfast. Wireless Internet access. Health and fitness center, spa. **$$$**

★★★JW MARRIOTT HOTEL BUCKHEAD ATLANTA

3300 Lenox Road N.E., Atlanta, 404-262-3344, 800-613-2051; www.marriott.com

The upscale JW Marriott Hotel Buckhead has a prime location near the city's top shopping malls and best restaurants. Rooms have luxury bedding and pillow top mattresses, as well as marble bathrooms and soaking tubs. 367 rooms. Restaurant, bar, coffee shop. High-speed Internet access. **$$$**

★★★★THE MANSION ON PEACHTREE

3376 Peachtree Road, Atlanta, 404-995-7500;
www.rwmansiononpeachtree.com

Opened in May 2008, this 127-room luxury spot in the heart of Buckhead is the tallest hotel in the neighborhood. Made from limestone and cast stone, the structure soars 580 feet over the traffic on Peachtree Road. Guests are catered to by a staff of

GEORGIA

★
★
★
★
★

professionally trained butlers, each of whom is assigned to guests in their comfortably appointed rooms full of mirrors, modern furnishings and marble bathrooms. With daily fresh flowers and housekeeping service twice a day, this hotel is the newest destination for travelers with the most discriminating tastes. A 15,000-square-foot spa is on site and the Tom Colicchio-owned restaurant Craft is set to open here in late 2008.

★★★MARRIOTT DOWNTOWN ATLANTA

160 Spring St. N.W., Atlanta, 404-688-8600, 866-316-5959;
www.marriott.com

Ideal for business travelers, this contemporary hotel has ample meeting space, a friendly staff and a location near Olympic Park, CNN Center and the Georgia World Congress Center. 312 rooms. Restaurant, bar. Wireless Internet access. $$

★★★OMNI HOTEL AT CNN CENTER

100 CNN Center N.W., Atlanta, 404-659-0000, 888-444-6664;
www.omnihotels.com

Located in downtown Atlanta and conveniently connected to the CNN Center and the Georgia World Congress Center, this hotel offers guests spacious rooms and good service. Take a stroll through Centennial Olympic Park located across the street or enjoy the 50,000-square-foot, state-of-the-art Turner Athletic Club. 1,067 rooms. Restaurant, bar. Wireless Internet access. Spa. $$

★★REGENCY SUITES HOTEL

975 W. Peachtree St. N.E., Atlanta, 404-876-5003, 800-642-3629;
www.regencysuites.com

96 rooms, all suites. Complimentary continental breakfast. High-speed Internet access. Airport transportation available. $$

★★★THE RITZ-CARLTON, ATLANTA

181 Peachtree St. N.E., Atlanta, 404-659-0400, 800-241-3333;
www.ritzcarlton.com

Its prime downtown location, makes this cosmopolitan hotel convenient to businesses, government offices and sporting arenas. The rooms are handsomely decorated and offer views of the city skyline. Many suites have kitchenettes, and some feature baby grand pianos. Twice-daily housekeeping and a technology butler service are available. The clubby Atlanta Grill serves updated Southern cooking. 444 rooms. Restaurant, bar. High-speed Internet access. $$$

★★★★THE RITZ-CARLTON, BUCKHEAD

3434 Peachtree Road N.E., Atlanta, 404-237-2700, 800-241-3333;
www.ritzcarlton.com

This hotel is in one of the city's most fashionable neighborhoods and offers a warm and luxurious experience. The hotel underwent a complete renovation in 2008. Rooms have antique furnishings and sublime amenities like pillow-top mattresses and flatscreen TVs. Bay windows showcase views of the downtown skyline. The fitness center appeals to athletic-minded visitors, as does the indoor pool and sundeck. Afternoon tea in the Lobby Lounge is a Georgia tradition, especially after

★
★
★
★

a day of perusing the area's shops. The Café is a popular gathering place for casual fare. The Dining Room, also renovated in 2008, serves award-winning cuisine. 517 rooms. Restaurant, bar. Wireless Internet access. Airport transportation available. Business center. Fitness room. Indoor pool, whirlpool. Pets accepted, some restrictions; fee.

★★★SHERATON ATLANTA HOTEL

165 Courtland St., Atlanta, 404-659-6500, 800-325-3535;
www.sheratonatlantahotel.com

Three restaurants, business conveniences and a full range of amenities make this hotel a good option for business travelers. Close to CNN Center, the Georgia Dome and Centennial Park. 760 rooms. Restaurant, bar. Wireless Internet access. **$$**

★★★TWELVE HOTEL & RESIDENCES

361 17th St. N.W., Atlanta, 404-961-1212;
www.twelvehotels.com

The 26-story Twelve Hotel & Residences is located in Atlanta's recently constructed Midtown at Atlantic Station. Many shops, restaurants, a grocery store and a movie theater are just steps away. The large lobby is modern and relaxed, with floor-to-ceiling windows. Guest suites feature full kitchens, walls adorned with local artwork and LCD TVs. 101 rooms, all suites. Restaurant, bar. Wireless Internet access. Airport transportation available. **$$**

★★★W ATLANTA AT PERIMETER CENTER

111 Perimeter Center West, Atlanta, 770-396-6800, 888-625-5144;
www.whotels.com

Located near the Perimeter mall, this hotel has contemporary guest rooms and a lively lounge scene in the downstairs bar. 275 rooms. Restaurant, bar. High-speed Internet access. **$$$**

★★★THE WESTIN BUCKHEAD ATLANTA

3391 Peachtree Road N.E., Atlanta, 404-365-0065, 800-937-8461;
www.westin.com/buckhead

Located in Buckhead and adjacent to the city's best shopping malls, this 22-story hotel is a landmark. All guest rooms are spacious and decorated with Biedermeier-style furnishings. Nearby attractions include Zoo Atlanta and the Fernbank-Museum of Natural History. 365 rooms and 11 suites. Restaurant, bar. Wireless Internet access. Airport transportation available. Fitness center. Sauna. spa. **$$$$**

★★★THE WESTIN PEACHTREE PLAZA

210 Peachtree St. N.W., Atlanta, 404-659-1400, 800-937-8461;
www.westin.com/peachtree

As if the gracious service and spacious guest rooms with views of downtown weren't enough, this hotel also offers special touches such as signature luxury bedding and bath products. Dine at either of the two restaurants, enjoy a workout in the fitness center or just relax at the indoor pool. 1,068 rooms. Two restaurants, two bars. High-speed Internet access. Fitness center. Spa. Indoor pool. **$$**

GEORGIA

★
★
★
★
★

★★★WYNDHAM PEACHTREE CONFERENCE CENTER HOTEL

2443 Highway 54 W., Peachtree City, 770-487-2000, 877-999-3223;
www.wyndham.com

Surrounded by 19 wooden acres this comfy hotel provides large rooms with pillow-top mattresses. You can also enjoy an array of activities onsite, including racquetball, tennis and volleyball. Or get in a game of golf at the adjacent course. Casual dining is available at the Terrace Restaurant. 250 rooms. Two restaurants, bar. Wireless Internet access. Tennis. Airport transportation available. $

SPECIALTY LODGINGS

GASLIGHT INN BED & BREAKFAST

1001 St., Charles Ave., N.E., Atlanta, 404-875-1001; www.gaslightinn.com

Located in the Virginia Highlands area, with easy access to rapid transit, the free-way, shopping and dining, this bed and breakfast is popular for its cozy guest rooms and great location. Eight rooms. Restaurant. Complimentary full breakfast. Wireless Internet access. $$

KING-KEITH HOUSE BED & BREAKFAST

889 Edgewood Ave. N.E., Atlanta, 404-688-7330, 800-728-3879; www.kingkeith.com

Six rooms. High-speed Internet access. $

LAUREL HILL BED & BREAKFAST

1992 McLendon Ave., Atlanta, 404-377-3217; www.laurelhillbandb.com

Six rooms. Complimentary full breakfast. Wireless Internet access. No children under age 12. $

SERENBE BED & BREAKFAST

10950 Hutcheson Ferry Road, Palmetto, 770-463-2610; www.serenbe.com

This inn, built in 1901, is located on a farm where guests can feed animals, go on hay-rides, have marshmallow roasts or paddle canoes and view nearby waterfalls. Seven rooms. Complimentary full breakfast. $

SHELLMONT INN

821 Piedmont Ave. N.E., Atlanta, 404-872-9290; www.shellmont.com

This beautifully restored Victorian masterpiece is filled with antiques (some original to the house). Five rooms and one carriage house. Children under 12 in carriage house only. Complimentary full breakfast. $$

SUGAR MAGNOLIA

804 Edgewood Ave. N.E., Atlanta, 404-222-0226; www.sugarmagnoliabb.com

Located in Atlanta's historic Inman Park neighborhood, this elegant Victorian bed and breakfast built in 1892 features six fireplaces and cozy guest suites decorated with period furnishing. Four rooms. Complimentary full breakfast. $

RESTAURANTS

★★★ANTHONY'S

3109 Piedmont Road N.E., Atlanta, 404-262-7379; www.anthonysfinedining.com

Set back from the road on a three-acre wooded lot, Anthony's is housed in a plantation house built in 1797. The 12 different dining rooms and seven working fireplaces in the main dining room make for an intimate experience—perfect for special occasion and group dining. The New American menu offers classics, like veal Anthony (scallopine stuffed with lobster) and pumpkin seed- and coriander-crusted grouper. American menu. Lunch and dinner. Closed Sunday. Bar. Business casual attire. Reservations recommended. Valet parking. $$$

★★★ARIA

490 E. Paces Ferry Road, Atlanta, 404-233-7673; www.aria-atl.com

Once a private library in upscale Buckhead, Aria has been transformed into a contemporary restaurant. Leather walls, metal curtains and an eclectic chandelier all help to lure sophisticated diners in for chef Gerry Klaskala's Southern-inspired American cuisine. There is also a private table in the wine cellar downstairs, but you'll have to call ahead—those in-the-know book three months in advance. American menu. Dinner. Closed Sunday. Bar. Business casual attire. Reservations recommended. Valet parking. Outdoor seating. $$$

★★★ATLANTA FISH MARKET

265 Pharr Road, Atlanta, 404-262-3165;
www.buckheadrestaurants.com

Tucked away from the bustle of Buckhead (but hard to miss with its giant outdoor fish statue), this large, family-friendly seafood restaurant is a favorite among locals. The restaurant features several airy, comfortable dining rooms and menus printed twice daily to update customers with the freshest seafood choices. The open kitchen showcases the chefs at work. Seafood menu. Lunch, dinner. Bar. Children's menu. Casual attire. Reservations recommended. Valet parking. Outdoor seating. $$

★★★AU PIED DE COCHON

3315 Peachtree Road N.W., Atlanta, 404-946-9070,
888-424-6835; www.aupieddecochonatlanta.com

This popular, 24-hour French brasserie is located in the Intercontinental Buckhead hotel. The American-French menu is available around the clock. A raw bar features fish flown in daily. Jazz five nights a week up the ante on Au Pied's offerings. American, French menu. Breakfast, lunch, dinner, late-night, brunch. Bar. Children's menu. Business casual attire. Valet parking. Outdoor seating. $$$

★★BABETTE'S CAFÉ

573 N. Highland Ave., Atlanta, 404-523-9121;
www.babettescafe.com

International menu. Dinner, Sunday brunch. Closed Monday. Bar. Children's menu. Casual attire. Reservations recommended. Valet parking. Outdoor seating. $$

★★★★BACCHANALIA

1198 Howell Mill Road, Atlanta, 404-365-0410; www.starprovisions.com

Set in a renovated factory complex, this urban dining room has a sleek, industrial feel. The dramatic vaulted ceiling and exposed brick-trimmed factory windows of the dining room nicely contrast the long, low-lit, sexy bar of this former meat-packing plant. Chefs Anne Quatrano and Clifford Harrison create vibrant, seasonal American menus that change daily based on whatever organic and small-farm produce is available. Plates are presented with little fuss but lots of flavor. American menu, bar, business casual attire. Reservations recommended. Outdoor seating. Dinner Monday-Saturday from 6 p.m.

★BASIL'S MEDITERRANEAN CAFÉ

2985 Grandview Ave., Atlanta, 404-233-9755; www.basilsinbuckhead.com

Mediterranean menu. Lunch, dinner, brunch. Bar. Business casual attire. Reservations recommended. Outdoor seating. **$$**

★★★BLUEPOINTE

3455 Peachtree Road, Atlanta, 404-237-9070; www.buckheadrestaurants.com

This popular restaurant is located in the Pennacle office building next to Lenox Square Mall. The modern décor, featuring chrome railings, eclectic tile floors, an open display kitchen, oversized windows and blue velvet and leather booths, perfectly complements the inventive Pacific Rim-Pan-Asian cuisine prepared by executive chef Doug Turbush. Lunch, dinner. Bar. Sushi bar. Business casual attire. Reservations recommended. Valet parking. **$$$**

★★★BONE'S RESTAURANT

3130 Piedmont Road N.E., Atlanta, 404-237-2663; www.bonesrestaurant.com

The masculine décor match the juicy steaks and sides. Huge portions and high prices attract a power lunch, cigar-smoking crowd. The homemade steak sauce and shortbread cookies are worth a return trip. Steak menu. Lunch, dinner Monday-Friday. Bar. Business casual attire. Reservations recommended. Valet parking. **$$$**

★★★THE CAFÉ

3434 Peachtree Road N.E., Atlanta,
404-237-2700, 800-241-3333; www.ritzcarlton.com

Chef Christophe LeMetayer takes his cue from his native France for the menu of this all-day restaurant in the Ritz-Carlton, Buckhead hotel. Sunday brunch is a particular treat, with more than 100 dishes offered. American menu. Breakfast, lunch, Sunday brunch. Bar. Children's menu. Business casual attire. Reservations recommended. Valet parking. Outdoor seating. **$$**

★★★CANOE

4199 Paces Ferry Road N.W., Atlanta, 770-432-2663; www.canoeatl.com

Right on the banks of the Chattahoochee River, this casual but sophisticated restaurant serves delicious American cuisine prepared by executive chef and seventh generation Atlantan Carvel Grant Gould. The eclectic menu ranges from slow roasted beef short ribs to seared Georgia Mountain Trout. A canoe-like ceiling, wrought iron paddle table legs, overstuffed chairs, art by local artists and a brick display kitchen with a copper hood add to the experience. American menu. Lunch, dinner, Sunday brunch. Bar. Business casual attire. Reservations recommended. Valet parking. Outdoor seating. **$$$**

★
★
★
★
★

★★★CHOPS

70 W. Paces Ferry Road, Atlanta, 404-262-2675;
www.buckheadrestaurants.com

Chops is really two restaurants in one. Upstairs, power diners chomp on delicious prime-aged beef in a clubby steakhouse atmosphere (dark mahogany paneling, black leather booths with burgundy seats and an open display kitchen). Downstairs in the Lobster Bar, diners sit in white stucco grottos and savor delicate seafood creations. Steak and seafood menu. Lunch, dinner. Bar. Business casual attire. Reservations recommended. Valet parking. **$$$**

★★★CITY GRILL

50 Hurt Plaza, Atlanta, 404-524-2489; www.citygrillatlanta.com

Located in an office building that once housed the Federal Reserve Bank, this sophisticated restaurant features regional American cuisine in an elegant environment. Lunch, dinner. Closed Sunday. Bar. Children's menu. Business casual attire. Reservations recommended. Valet parking. **$$$**

★THE COLONNADE

1879 Cheshire Bridge Road, Atlanta, 404-874-5642

American menu. Lunch, dinner. Bar. Casual attire. Outdoor seating. No credit cards accepted. **$$**

★COWTIPPERS

1600 Piedmont Ave., Atlanta, 404-874-3751; www.cowtippersatlanta.com

Tex-Mex-American menu. Lunch, dinner. Bar. Children's menu. Casual attire. Outdoor seating. **$$**

★★DAILEY'S

17 International Blvd., Atlanta, 404-681-3303; www.daileysrestaurant.com

American menu. Lunch, dinner. Bar. Casual attire. **$$**

★★DANTE'S DOWN THE HATCH

3380 Peachtree Road N.E., Atlanta, 404-266-1600;
www.dantesdownthehatch.com

Fondue menu. Great for group events. Live jazz six nights a week. Dinner. Bar. Business casual attire. Reservations recommended. **$$**

★★★★★THE DINING ROOM

3434 Peachtree Road N.E., Atlanta, 404-237-2700,
800-241-3333; www.ritzcarlton.com

Prepare for an extraordinary experience when dining in the masterful hands of chef Arnaud Berthelier, who creates menus influenced by the lively flavors of France, Spain and Northern Africa at the Dining Room in the Ritz-Carlton, Buckhead. Dishes served in the classically elegant room (think deep, tufted banquettes cloaked in Victorian green silk) include sweetbread kebobs with tomato confit, lobster and citrus cocotte or truffle-stuffed guinea hen. After dessert and a cheese course, sample the petit fours, which arrive in numbers. French menu. Dinner. Closed Sunday-Monday. Jacket required. Reservations recommended. Valet parking. **$$$$**

★DUSTY'S BARBECUE

1815 Briarcliff Road, Atlanta, 404-320-6264; www.dustys.com

Barbecue menu. Lunch, dinner. Children's menu. Casual attire. $

★★★ECCO

40 Seventh St., Atlanta, 404-347-9555; www.ecco-restaurant.com

Ecco, located in Midtown Atlanta, offers fresh selections of meats and cheeses, abundant small plates and main courses. The seasonal European cuisine—with Spanish, Italian and French influences—includes dishes such as roasted chicken breast with rapini, olives, lemon and sage or fig-glazed lamb loin with warm potatoes and chicory. Enhance the experience with any of the unique cocktails served. International menu. Dinner. Bar. Casual attire. Reservations recommended. Valet parking. Outdoor seating. $$

★★FIRE OF BRAZIL CHURRASCARIA

118 Perimeter Center West, Atlanta, 770-551-4367; www.fireofbrazil.com

Brazilian steak menu. Lunch, dinner. Bar. Casual attire. Reservations recommended. Outdoor seating. $$$

★FLYING BISCUIT CAFÉ

1655 McLendon Ave., Atlanta, 404-687-8888; www.flyingbiscuit.com

American menu. Breakfast, lunch, dinner. Children's menu. Casual attire. Reservations recommended. $$

★★★THE FOOD STUDIO

887 W. Marietta St., Studio K 102, Atlanta,
404-815-1178; www.thefoodstudio.com

Inside a century-old renovated factory lies this hidden gem of a restaurant. With dishes such as seared sea scallops with edamame succotash and smoked tomato vinaigrette, and an organic heirloom tomato salad with grilled cornbread and lemon mayonnaise, this restaurant celebrates the wide array of regional flavors found across America. American menu. Dinner. Bar. Business casual attire. Reservations recommended. Valet parking. Outdoor seating. $$$

★★FRITTI

309 N. Highland Ave., Atlanta, 404-880-9559; www.frittirestaurant.com

Traditional brick-oven pizza, Italian menu. Lunch, dinner. Bar. Children's menu. Casual attire. Reservations recommended. Valet parking. Outdoor seating. $$

★GEORGIA GRILLE

2290 Peachtree Road, Atlanta, 404-352-3517; www.georgiagrille.com

Southwestern fare. Dinner. Closed Monday. Bar. Casual attire. Reservations recommended. $$$

★HAVELI

225 Spring St., Atlanta, 404-522-4545

Indian cuisine. Lunch and dinner. Bar. Casual attire. Reservations recommended. $$

★★HORSERADISH GRILL

4320 Powers Ferry Road, Atlanta,
404-255-7277; www.horseradishgrill.com

American/Southern menu. Lunch, dinner, Sunday brunch. Bar. Children's menu. Business casual attire. Reservations recommended. Valet parking. Outdoor seating. $$

★★HSU'S GOURMET CHINESE

192 Peachtree Center Ave., Atlanta, 404-659-2788; www.hsus.com

Chinese menu. Lunch, dinner. Bar. Children's menu. Casual attire. Reservations recommended. $$

★★IMPERIAL FEZ

2285 Peachtree Road N.E., Atlanta, 404-351-0870; www.imperialfez.com

Mediterranean, Moroccan menu. Dinner. Children's menu. Casual attire. Reservations recommended. Valet parking. $$

★★★JOËL

3290 Northside Parkway, Atlanta, 404-233-3500; www.joelrestaurant.com

Executive chef and owner Joël Antunes was the former executive chef at the Ritz-Carlton Buckhead restaurant. In 2005 he won the James Beard award for best chef Southeast, so one can likely count on the fare at Joël to be delicious. And it is. Sample dishes include lobster risotto with asparagus and artichokes and braised beef short ribs in red wine sauce. Lunch, dinner. Closed Sunday. Bar. Business casual attire. Reservations recommended. Valet parking. Outdoor seating. $$$

★★★KYMA

3085 Piedmont Road, Atlanta, 404-262-0702; www.buckheadrestaurants.com

True to its name, the atmosphere at Kyma ("wave" in Greek) brings to mind the crisp, clean seascape colors of the Greek Islands. The restaurant specializes in classic Greek dishes, especially fresh seafood. Greek menu. Dinner. Closed Sunday. Bar. Business casual attire. Reservations recommended. Valet parking. Outdoor seating. $$$

★★★LA GROTTA

2637 Peachtree Road N.E., Atlanta, 404-231-1368; www.lagrottaatlanta.com

There are two outposts of this upscale Italian restaurant (this one in Buckhead and a sister property in Dunwoody), both of which are decorated in traditional Italian décor. The menu includes homemade pastas such as goat cheese ravioli and entrées like grilled salmon. Italian menu. Dinner. Closed Sunday; also last week in June and first week in July. Bar. Business casual attire. Reservations recommended. Valet parking. Outdoor seating. $$$

★MARY MAC'S TEA ROOM

224 Ponce de Leon Ave. N.E., Atlanta, 404-876-1800; www.marymacs.com

Southern menu. Lunch, dinner. Closed Christmas-New Year's. Bar. Children's menu. Casual attire. Reservations recommended. $

31

GEORGIA

★★★MCKENDRICK'S

4505 Ashford Dunwoody Ave., Atlanta, 770-512-8888; www.mckendricks.com

This upscale steak house restaurant is located near the Perimeter shopping mall and is a great place for business dinners. The atmosphere is clubby, the steaks thick and the seafood fresh (try the lobster). The 350-strong wine list has won critical acclaim. Steak menu. Lunch, dinner. Bar. Business casual attire. Reservations recommended. Valet parking. $$$

★★MCKINNON'S LOUISIANE

3209 Maple Drive, Atlanta, 404-237-1313; www.mckinnons.com

Cajun/Creole menu. Dinner. Bar. Live music. Business casual attire. Reservations recommended. $$

★★NAKATO JAPANESE RESTAURANT

1776 Cheshire Bridge Road N.E., Atlanta, 404-873-6582; www.nakatorestaurant.com

Sushi-Japanese menu. Dinner. Bar. Children's menu. Casual attire. Reservations recommended. Valet parking. $$

★★★NAVA

3060 Peachtree Road, Atlanta, 404-240-1984; www.buckheadrestaurants.com

The Southwestern décor (terra cotta stone floor, log-beamed ceilings, cow hide-covered bar seats) complements the food, which is full of bold flavors, vibrant colors and exotic textures. Signature margaritas, Ancho chili grilled flatiron steak, jalapeno grilled shrimp, garlic chipotle mashed potatoes and Serrano roasted lamb rack are just some of the authentic offerings from chef Jesse Perez. Southwestern menu. Lunch, dinner. Bar. Casual attire. Reservations recommended. Valet parking. Outdoor seating. $$$

★★NICKIEMOTO'S

990 Piedmont Ave., Atlanta, 404-253-2010; www.nickiemotosmidtown.com

Sushi/Pan-Asian menu. Lunch, dinner. Bar. Casual attire. Reservations recommended. Valet parking. Outdoor seating. $$

★★★NIKOLAI'S ROOF

255 Courtland St., Atlanta, 404-221-6362, 800-445-8667; www.nikolaisroof.com

Located at the Hilton in downtown Atlanta, this French-Russian restaurant delivers a panoramic view along with chilled vodka and Russian classics like borscht and piroshkis, foie gras and boar tenderloin. The restaurant also offers the largest single malt collection in the city. Choose from an eight-course prix fixe dinner or an à la carte menu. Wine pairings from the award-winning wine list are also offered. International menu. Dinner. Closed Sunday. Bar. Children's menu. Business casual attire. Reservations recommended. Valet parking. $$$

★★★ONE MIDTOWN KITCHEN

559 Dutch Valley Road, Atlanta, 404-892-4111; www.onemidtownkitchen.com

Located off the beaten path near Piedmont Park, this Midtown restaurant serves a changing menu of small plates and dishes such as pork dumplings with hominy, braised lamb shank with red pepper grits and port-anise poached pear. Wines can

★
★
★
★

be enjoyed four ways from five price tiers—this list changes nightly, too. Dessert by noted pastry chef Jonathan St. Hilaire is a must. American menu. Dinner. Bar. Casual attire. Reservations recommended. Valet parking. Outdoor seating. $$

★★★PANO'S & PAUL'S

1232 W. Paces Ferry Road, Atlanta, 404-261-3662; www.buckheadrestaurants.com

Don't let the strip mall location of this restaurant fool you. Locals say this upscale restaurant defines Buckhead fine dining. Executive chef Gary Donlick's American-Continental menu includes fried lobster tail and other contemporary specialties. An extensive wine list, weekend piano music and friendly service complete the experience. American, Continental menu. Dinner. Closed Sunday. Bar. Business casual attire. Reservations recommended. $$$

★★★★PARK 75

75 14th St. N.E., Atlanta, 404-253-3840, 800-332-3442; www.fourseasons.com

Located in the Four Seasons Hotel, Park 75 is a classic choice for tranquil and comfortable fine dining. The serene, pale-yellow dining room is warmed by iron candelabras, custom lighting and oversized watercolor murals. The cross-cultural menu offers seasonal local vegetables, meats and fish. The signature Park 75 surf and turf, for example, puts a twist on the classic by combining butter-braised Maine lobster with milk-fed veal filet and foie gras. The wine list is mostly American, with some boutique and international selections. For a special treat, reserve the chef's table and enjoy an eight-course menu with wines to match. American menu. Breakfast, lunch, dinner, Sunday brunch. Bar. Children's menu. Business casual attire. Reservations recommended. Valet parking.

★★PETITE AUBERGE

2935 N. Druid Hill Road, Atlanta, 404-634-6268; www.petiteauberge.com

Continental, French menu. Lunch, dinner. Closed Sunday. Bar. Business casual attire. Reservations recommended. Outdoor seating. $$

★PITTYPAT'S PORCH

25 International Blvd., Atlanta, 404-525-8228; www.pittypatsrestaurant.com

Southern menu. Dinner. Bar. Children's menu. Casual attire. Reservations recommended. $$$

★★★PRICCI

500 Pharr Road, Atlanta, 404-237-2941; www.buckheadrestaurants.com

This ultra-modern upscale Italian restaurant is the place to see and be seen. Among the menu highlights are pastas like beef shortrib ravioli and ossobucco. The wine list has an extensive selection of regional Italian labels. Italian menu. Lunch, dinner. Bar. Business casual attire. Reservations recommended. Valet parking. $$$

★★★PRIME

3393 Peachtree Road N.E., Atlanta, 404-812-0555; www.heretoserverestaurants.com

Prime redefines the term "surf and turf" by including sushi. Floor-to-ceiling windows, an open kitchen that displays chef Tom Catherall in action and a location in the upscale Lenox Square Mall make this an exciting alternative to the traditional steakhouse. Seafood, steak, sushi menu. Lunch, dinner. Bar. Children's menu. Business casual attire. Reservations recommended. Valet parking. $$

★★★★QUINONES AT BACCHANALIA

1198 Howell Mill Road, Atlanta, 404-365-0410; www.starprovisions.com

Quinones at Bacchanalia has an intimate dining area—11 tables, with room for only 38 guests—and a subdued atmosphere with pressed Irish linens and oil lamps on the tables. A 10-course prix-fixe Contemporary American menu features new creations daily. Sample inspired Southern-influenced creations such as squab with turnips, turnip greens and butter beans, or flounder with local pecans, apples and butternut squash. Desserts are elegant takes on Southern classics, like pecan tart with vanilla bean ice cream. Contemporary American menu. Dinner. Closed Sunday-Tuesday. Business casual attire. Reservations recommended. $$$$

★★★RATHBUN

112 Krog St., Atlanta, 404-524-8280; www.rathbunsrestaurant.com

This polished restaurant serves American cuisine in Inman Park on Atlanta's east side. The building, which was a potbelly stove factory, is nestled among rehabbed buildings and condos. Nationally acclaimed chef Kevin Rathbun is a fixture on Atlanta's restaurant scene. American menu. Dinner. Closed Sunday. Bar. Business casual attire. Reservations recommended. Valet parking. Outdoor seating. $$$

★★RAY'S ON THE RIVER

6700 Powers Ferry Road, Atlanta, 770-955-1187; www.raysrestaurants.com

Seafood menu, oyster bar. Lunch, dinner, Sunday brunch. Bar. Live music. Children's menu. Business casual attire. Outdoor seating. $$

★★★RESTAURANT EUGENE

2277 Peachtree Road, Atlanta, 404-355-0321; www.restauranteugene.com

Restaurant Eugene co-owner Gina Hopkins and chef/co-owner Linton Hopkins aim for a friendly, exceptional dining experience. The menu features dishes like beef rib eye with beer-battered onion rings, and Berkshire black pork belly with cabbage, granny smith apples, spiced pecans and whole grain mustard. Dessert includes cornmeal pound cake with warm spiced peaches, and an ice-cream sundae with fried plantain chips, dark chocolate sauce, homemade strawberry preserves and pineapple chunks. American menu. Dinner. Bar. Business casual attire. Reservations recommended. Valet parking. Outdoor seating. $$$

★★★THE RIVER ROOM

4403 Northside Parkway, Atlanta, 404-233-5455; www.riverroom.com

Come on a Friday night to the tavern lounge and listen to some of the city's best musicians. The menu here is extensive, with dishes such as feta-stuffed free-range chicken served with couscous and chili-fried onion rings, and baked lobster with a cornbread stuffing. American menu. Lunch, dinner, Sunday brunch. Bar. Business casual attire. Reservations recommended. Valet parking. Outdoor seating. $$

★ROCK BOTTOM

3242 Peachtree Road, Atlanta, 404-264-0253; www.rockbottomsouth.com

American menu/pizza. Lunch, dinner. Bar. Children's menu. Casual attire. Reservations recommended. Outdoor seating. **$$**

★★★RUTH'S CHRIS STEAK HOUSE

5788 Roswell Road, Atlanta, 404-255-0035; www.ruthschris.com

This Atlanta outpost of the steakhouse chain is located on a busy road between Buckhead and the Perimeter area of Atlanta. The U.S. prime-aged, hand-cut, Midwestern, corn-fed beef is the main attraction. Steak menu. Dinner. Bar. Business casual attire. Reservations recommended. Valet parking. **$$$**

★★SOHO CAFÉ

4300 Paces Ferry Road, Atlanta, 770-801-0069; www.sohoatlanta.com

Modern American menu. Lunch, dinner. Bar. Children's menu. Business casual attire. Reservations recommended. Outdoor seating. **$$**

★★★SOTTO SOTTO

313 N. Highland Ave., Atlanta, 404-523-6678; www.sottosottorestaurant.com

Located right next door to its sister restaurant Fritti, this spot serves dishes that prove simplicity is the best way to highlight the best ingredients. Diners can see and smell the magic happening in the open kitchen, which is also visible from the street. Italian menu. Dinner. Bar. Business casual attire. Reservations recommended. Valet parking. Outdoor seating. **$$**

★★SOUTH CITY KITCHEN

1144 Crescent Ave., Atlanta, 404-873-7358; www.southcitykitchen.com

Southern American menu. Lunch, dinner, Sunday brunch. Bar. Children's menu. Business casual attire. Reservations recommended. Outdoor seating. **$$$**

★TAQUERIA SUNDOWN CAFÉ

2165 Cheshire Bridge Road, Atlanta, 404-321-1118;
www.sundowncafe.com

Southwestern menu. Lunch, dinner. Closed Sunday. Bar. Casual attire. Outdoor seating. **$$**

★★THAI CHILI

2169 Briarcliff Road Northeast, Atlanta, 404-315-6750; www.thaichilicuisine.com

Thai menu. Lunch, dinner. Children's menu. Casual attire. Reservations recommended. **$$**

★★TOULOUSE

2293 Peachtree Road N.E., Atlanta, 404-351-9533; www.toulouserestaurant.com

French menu. Rich wine-by-the-glass offerings. Dinner. Bar. Business casual attire. Reservations recommended. Outdoor seating. **$$**

★
★
★
★

★★TWO URBAN LICKS

820 Ralph McGill Blvd., Atlanta, 404-522-4622; www.twourbanlicks.com

American menu. Dinner. Bar. Live music. Business casual attire. Reservations recommended. Valet parking. Outdoor seating. $$

★THE VARSITY

61 North Ave., Atlanta, 404-881-1706; www.thevarsity.com

American menu. Lunch, dinner, late-night. Children's menu. Casual attire. Outdoor seating. No credit cards accepted. $

★★★VENI VIDI VICI

41 14th St., Atlanta, 404-875-8424; www.buckheadrestaurants.com

This upscale Midtown trattoria serves some of the best Italian food in town. The lunch and dinner menus are organized into small antipasti, perfect for tasting a variety of dishes. Italian menu. Lunch, dinner. Bar. Business casual attire. Reservations recommended. Valet parking. Outdoor seating. $$$

★★★VILLA CHRISTINA

4000 Summit Blvd., Atlanta, 404-303-0133; www.villachristina.com

An unpretentiousness air is one of the reasons why this spot is one of the most popular Italian restaurants in Atlanta, welcoming families as well as those looking for a fine dining experience. The menu of creative Italian dishes includes an assortment of pastas, such as spaghetti with spicy pancetta, Parmesan, garlic, eggs and herbs. Italian menu. Lunch, dinner. Closed Sunday. Bar. Business casual attire. Reservations recommended. Valet parking. Outdoor seating. $$$

★★THE VININGS INN

3011 Paces Mill Road, Atlanta, 770-438-2282; www.viningsinn.com

American menu. Lunch, dinner. Bar. Children's menu. Business casual attire. Reservations recommended. Outdoor seating. $$

★★★WISTERIA

471 Highland Ave., Atlanta, 404-525-3363; www.wisteria-atlanta.com

Soft colors and fresh flowers make for a pleasant setting at this casual, comfortable restaurant located just two and a half blocks west of downtown Decatur. Popular dishes include fried catfish with hush puppies and Country Captain stew. American menu. Dinner. Bar. Children's menu. Reservations recommended. Valet parking. $$

★ZOCALO

187 10th St., Atlanta, 404-249-7576; www.zocalocreativemex.com

Mexican menu. Lunch, dinner, Sunday brunch. Bar. Children's menu. Casual attire. Valet parking. Outdoor seating. $$

SPA

★★★★29 SPA

Mansion on Peachtree, 3376 Peachtree Road N.E., Atlanta, 404-995-7529;
www.rwmansiononpeachtree.com

Atlanta native Lydia Mondavi (whose name you may have seen on a bottle of cabernet or pinot noir) brings the anti-aging body benefits of wine to 29 Spa. The Mansion on

Peachtree is home to the 15,000-square-foot spa where all of the most fabulous Georgia peaches get pampered in the 14 rooms, each complimented with heated waterbed tables, bathed in linen and silk and serving the signature wine. Quench your thirst head to toe with wine and grape seed-infused treatments for the scalp and body, massages and facials, or get primped to the (twenty)nines at home if you grab some goodies from Mondavi's line 29 Cosmetics.

GREATER ATLANTA AREA

★★CLARION HOTEL ATLANTA AIRPORT
5010 Old National Highway, College Park,
404-768-9199, 877-424-6423; www.choicehotels.com
Restaurant, bar. Complimentary breakfast. Wireless Internet access. Business center. Fitness center. Outdoor pool. Pets not accepted. **$$**

★COMFORT INN AND SUITES
5985 Oakbrook Parkway, Norcross, 770-662-8175,
877-424-6423; www.comfortinn.com
115 rooms. Complimentary continental breakfast. High-speed Internet access. Pets accepted. **$**

★★COURTYARD BY MARRIOTT
2050 Sullivan Road, College Park, 770-997-2220, 800-321-2221;
www.marriott.com
144 rooms. Restaurant, bar. High-speed Internet access. Airport transportation available.

★★DOUBLETREE HOTEL
1075 Holcomb Bridge Road, Roswell,
770-992-9600; www.atlantaroswell.doubletree.com
172 rooms. Restaurant, bar. Wireless Internet access. Pets accepted. **$**

★★★HILTON ATLANTA NORTHEAST
5993 Peachtree Industrial Blvd., Norcross,
770-447-4747, 800-445-8667; www.hilton.com
This hotel has spacious and recently redesigned guest rooms, as well as a warm and friendly staff. 272 rooms. Restaurant, bar. Wireless Internet access. Airport transportation available. Whirlpool. Pets accepted. **$**

★★HOLIDAY INN
6050 Peachtree Industrial Blvd. N.W., Norcross,
770-448-4400; www.holidayinn.com
244 rooms. Restaurant, bar. Wireless Internet access. Pets not accepted. **$**

★HOMEWOOD SUITES
10775 Davis Drive, Alpharetta, 770-998-1622, 800-225-5466;
www.homewoodsuites.com
112 rooms, all suites. Complimentary full breakfast. Wireless Internet access. Pets accepted. **$$**

★★★MARRIOTT ALPHARETTA

5750 Windward Parkway, Alpharetta, 770-754-9600, 800-228-9290;
www.marriott.com

Chandeliers, Oriental rugs and luxurious furnishings accent the lobby of this elegant hotel located in Windward Office Park. Its corporate surroundings, business center services and upscale décor and amenities make this hotel perfect for business travelers. 318 rooms. Restaurant, bar. Wireless Internet access. Airport transportation available. $$

★★★MARRIOTT ATLANTA GWINNETT PLACE

1775 Pleasant Hill Road, Duluth, 770-923-1775, 800-228-9290; www.marriott.com

Located on 11 landscaped acres in Gwinnett County in a northeastern suburb of Atlanta, this hotel offers spacious guest rooms, an indoor and outdoor pool, whirlpool and health club. 426 rooms. Two restaurants, two bars. Wireless Internet access. Business center. Fitness room. Indoor pool, outdoor pool, whirlpool. $$

★★★MARRIOTT ATLANTA NORCROSS-PEACHTREE CORNERS

475 Technology Parkway, Norcross, 770-263-8558, 800-228-9290;
www.marriott.com

Located in Technology Park, this well-appointed 218-room hotel is great for business travelers. The hotel has a well-equipped business center and 4,000 square feet of meeting space. 218 rooms. Restaurant, bar. Wireless Internet access. $

RESTAURANTS

★★★BISTRO VG

70 W. Crossville Road, Roswell, 770-993-1156; www.knowwheretogogh.com

This out-of-the-way restaurant offers a surprisingly lovely dining experience. The food is eclectic American, while the setting is old-Southern charm. The dining room, dotted with Van Gogh reproductions, serves New American creations by chef-owners Christopher and Michele Sedgwick. The wine cellar has more than 500 selections from around the world. American menu. Lunch, dinner. Bar. Children's menu. Business casual attire. Reservations recommended. Valet parking. $$$

★★DOMINICK'S

95 S. Peachtree St., Norcross, 770-449-1611; www.dominicksitalian.com

Italian menu. Lunch Monday-Friday. Dinner Saturday-Sunday. Bar. Children's menu. $$

★★★HI LIFE

3380 Holcomb Bridge Road, Roswell, 770-409-0101; www.hiliferestaurant.com

This American restaurant has a sleek, modern design. The creative food is fresh and flavorful. Of particular note is a four-course lobster tasting menu. American menu. Lunch Monday-Friday, dinner. Closed Sunday. Bar. Children's menu. Business casual attire. Reservations recommended. Outdoor seating. $$

★★RAY'S KILLER CREEK

1700 Mansell Road, Alpharetta, 770-649-0064; www.raysrestaurants.com

Steakhouse menu. Lunch, dinner, bar. Children's menu. Casual attire. Reservations recommended. Valet parking. Outdoor seating. $$$

★★SIA'S

10305 Medlock Bridge Road, Duluth, 770-497-9727;
www.siasrestaurant.com

American, Asian, Southwestern menu. Lunch, dinner. Closed Sunday. Bar. Children's menu. Business casual attire. Reservations recommended. Outdoor seating. **$$$**

★★VINNY'S ON WINDWARD

5355 Windward Parkway, Alpharetta, 770-772-4644;
www.knowwheretogogh.com

This restaurant serves upscale Italian fare (sausage, goat cheese and fennel pizza or black truffle seafood risotto) cooked in an open-kitchen so diners can observe the chef's every move. The wine list includes both Italian and Californian offerings and by-the-glass options. Lunch Monday-Saturday. Dinner. Bar. Children's menu. Casual attire. Reservations recommended. Valet parking. Outdoor seating. **$$$**

★ZAPATA

5975 Peachtree Parkway, Norcross, 770-248-0052; www.zapata-atl.com

Mexican menu. Lunch, dinner. Bar. Casual attire. **$**

AUGUSTA

Best known for its revered National Golf Course and the prestigious Masters tournament held here each April, Augusta lures Northerners every winter for its warmth, fairways and culture. The town of 195,000 supports a symphony and an opera as well as several museums devoted to the role Augusta played in the historical South.

Founded in 1736 at the head of the Savannah River, Augusta has served as a military outpost and upriver trading town, a leading 18th-century tobacco center, a river shipping point for cotton, the powder works for the Confederacy, an industrial center for the New South and a winter resort. During the Revolution, the town changed hands several times, but Fort Augusta, renamed Fort Cornwallis by its British captors, was finally surrendered to "Lighthorse Harry" Lee's Continentals on June 5, 1781.

The Civil War ruined many of the wealthy families who had contributed to the Confederate cause. To help revive their depleted bank accounts, some locals opened their houses to paying guests. Northerners wishing to escape chilly winters took notice and began an annual migration, first as renters and eventually as owners of winter residences. Golf courses and country clubs popped up, adding to the lure. Today the Masters Tournament is one of the world's top golf tournaments. At least 10 area clubs offer nonmembers opportunities to play. For other sports attractions, check out the appropriately-named minor league baseball team, the Augusta GreenJackets or the more obscure Augusta Lynx minor league hockey team.

For those who don't play sports, Augusta has numerous boutiques and an array of sites honoring its eclectic collection of famous citizens. Where else can one day of sightseeing bring you President Woodrow Wilson's boyhood home, the only museum in the country dedicated to film comedians Laurel & Hardy and a statue honoring the Godfather of Soul, native Augustan James Brown?

Information: Augusta Convention and Visitors Bureau, 1450 Greene St., Augusta,
706-823-6600, 800-726-0243; www.augustaga.org

GEORGIA

AUGUSTA SYMPHONY ORCHESTRA

Sacred Heart Cultural Center, 1301 Greene St., Augusta,
706-826-4705; www.augustasymphony.org

The Augusta Symphony's season is packed with concerts and events designed to please all types of audiences. Choose from traditional orchestra concerts, pops performances featuring world famous guest artists and smaller and more intimate chamber concerts. Mid-September-mid-May.

THE BOYHOOD HOME OF PRESIDENT WOODROW WILSON

419 Seventh St., Augusta, 706-722-9828; www.wilsonboyhoodhome.org

Recently restored with authentic 1860s décor and artifacts, the era the Wilsons lived here, this home-turned-museum celebrates the 28th president. Tuesday-Saturday 10 a.m.-4 p.m.

LAUREL AND HARDY MUSEUM

250 N. Louisville St., Harlem, 706-556-0401,
888-288-9108; www.laurelandhardymuseum.org

Oliver Hardy was born in nearby Harlem, Georgia, and this museum of memorabilia and movies from the comedy team he formed with Stan Laurel is the only one of its kind in the country. Daily 10 a.m.-4 p.m.

NATIONAL SCIENCE CENTER'S FORT DISCOVERY

One Seventh St., Augusta, 706-821-0211,
800-325-5445; www.nationalsciencecenter.org

An innovative hands-on science, communications and technology center with 250 interactive exhibits. Also here are a Teacher Resource Center, traveling exhibits and a science store. Monday-Saturday 10 a.m.-5 p.m., Sunday noon-5 p.m.

ST. PAUL'S EPISCOPAL CHURCH

605 Reynolds St., Augusta, 706-724-2485; www.saintpauls.org

A granite Celtic cross in the churchyard marks the site of a fort and the spot where Augusta began, established by James Oglethorpe in 1736 in honor of Princess Augusta. Oglethorpe Park, a recreational area on the Savannah River, is located behind the church, which was established in 1750.

SPECIAL EVENT

MASTERS GOLF TOURNAMENT

Augusta National Golf Course, 2604 Washington Road, Augusta,
706-667-6000; www.masters.org

The Masters is one of four major golfing tournaments held each year. In addition to a cash award, the winner is presented with the famous green sport coat. First full week in April.

HOTELS

AUGUSTA MARRIOTT HOTEL & SUITES

2 10th St., Augusta, 706-722-8900, 800-228-9290; www.marriott.com

372 rooms. Restaurant, bar. High-speed Internet access. Fitness center, spa. Pets accepted. **$**

40

GEORGIA

★
★
★
★
☆

★★COURTYARD AUGUSTA

1045 Stevens Creek Road, Augusta, 706-737-3737,
800-321-2211; www.courtyard.com
130 rooms. High-speed Internet access. **$**

SPECIALTY LODGINGS

1810 WEST INN

254 N. Seymour Drive, Thomson, 706-595-3156,
800-515-1810; www.1810westinn.com
11 rooms. Children over 12 years only. Complimentary continental breakfast. Restored farmhouse; antiques. **$**

ROSEMARY HALL & LOOKAWAY HALL

804 Carolina Ave., North Augusta, 803-278-6222,
877-208-6222; www.lookawayrosemaryhalls.com
This historic inn combines two restored Greek Revival houses, one that dates from 1898 and the other from 1902. 223 rooms. Complimentary full breakfast. Children over 12 years only. Pets not accepted. **$**

RESTAURANTS

★★★CALVERTS

475 Highland Ave., Augusta, 706-738-4514;
www.calvertsrestaurant.com
Established in 1977, this restaurant in the Surrey Center maintains its position as one of the top local favorites. American menu. Dinner. Closed Sunday. Bar. Children's menu. Business casual attire. Reservations recommended. **$$$**

★★★LA MAISON RESTAURANT & VERITAS WINE & TAPAS

404 Telfair St., Augusta, 706-722-4805; www.lamaisontelfair.com
This fine restaurant in a Southern Revival house epitomizes Southern hospitality. The menu features wild game specialties, such as lamb, buffalo, pheasant and quail. International menu. Dinner. Closed Sunday. Bar. Business casual attire. Reservations recommended. Outdoor seating. **$$**

BAINBRIDGE

On the banks of the Flint River that runs into Lake Seminole, Bainbridge is Georgia's first inland port (founded in 1829) and today a recreational resource for locals and tourists.
Information: Bainbridge-Decatur County Chamber of Commerce,
229-246-4774, 800-243-4774; www.bainbridgegachamber.com

WHAT TO SEE AND DO

SEMINOLE STATE PARK

7870 State Park Drive, Donalsonville, 229-861-3137; www.gastateparks.org
Shallow by Georgia standards, the lake here holds a greater number of fish species than any other lake in the state. Swimming beach, boating, waterskiing, fishing. Daily 7 a.m.-10 p.m.

HOTELS

★★CHARTER HOUSE INN

1401 Tallahassee Highway, Bainbridge, 229-246-8550,
888-984-3466; www.thecharterhouseinn.com

84 rooms. Restaurant, bar. Wireless Internet access. **$**

★SUPER 8

751 W. Shotwell St., Bainbridge, 229-246-0015, 800-800-8000; www.super8.com

53 rooms. Complimentary continental breakfast. High-speed Internet access. Pets accepted. **$**

BLAKELY

Named for U.S. Navy Captain Johnston Blakeley, a hero of the War of 1812, this is an important peanut producing area.

Information: Chamber of Commerce, 52 Court Square,
229-723-3741; www.blakelyearlychamber.com

WHAT TO SEE AND DO

COHEELEE CREEK COVERED BRIDGE

Old River Road, Blakely

This 96-foot-long bridge, built in 1891, is the southernmost standing covered bridge in the U.S.

KOLOMOKI MOUNDS STATE HISTORIC PARK

205 Indian Mounds Road, Blakely, 229-724-2150; www.gastateparks.org

Native American mounds, temple mound and some excavation indicate a settlement here between A.D. 800 and A.D. 1200. Swimming pool, fishing, boating (ramps, dock) on Kolomoki Lake; miniature golf, hiking trails, picnicking, camping. Daily 7 a.m.-10 p.m.

HOTEL

★★★TARRER INN

155 S. Cuthbert St., Colquitt, 229-758-2888, 888-282-7737; www.tarrerinn.com

Recently restored, this charming bed and breakfast has guest rooms exquisitely decorated with beautiful antiques, and three fine dining rooms. 17 rooms. Restaurant. Complimentary full breakfast. **$**

BRASELTON

This town north of Atlanta is home to the Chateau Elan Winery and Resort, which has a luxurious inn and full winery onsite as well as an acclaimed equestrian center.

Information: www.braselton.net

HOTEL

★★★CHATEAU ELAN WINERY AND RESORT

100 Rue Charlemagne, Braselton, 678-425-0900, 800-233-9463;
www.chateauelanatlanta.com

Just 40 minutes north of Atlanta, this delightful resort feels like a continent away from big-city bustle with its charming manor house and lush vineyards. Winemaking is a

GEORGIA

★
★
★
★
★

source of great pride, and the eight restaurants complement the property's excellent product. European influences are found throughout the resort, from the classic styling of the elegant accommodations to the tranquil spa. 275 rooms. Eight restaurants, bar. Children's activity center. Golf, 63 holes. Tennis. Airport transportation available. $$

RESTAURANT

★★★CHATEAU ELAN'S LE CLOS

100 Rue Charlemagne Drive, Braselton, 678-425-0900,
800-233-9463; www.chateauelan.com

One of the many elegant restaurants found in the luxurious Chateau Elan Winery & Resort, Le Clos features contemporary French cuisine. The intimate space seats just 28 diners. Fine, estate-bottled wines from Chateau Elan's vineyards, along with choices from other regions of the world, are expertly paired with the five-course prix fixe menu of haute cuisine. Dishes include Truffled squab with chanterelle grit cakes, braised greens and blood orange glaze, and roasted beef tenderloin with celeriac and russet potato Dauphinoise and cabernet glace. French menu. Dinner. Closed Monday-Wednesday. Business casual attire. Reservations recommended. $$$

BRUNSWICK

Brunswick, on the southern third of Georgia's seacoast, separated from the Golden Isles by the Marshes of Glynn and the Intracoastal Waterway, is the gateway to St. Simons Island, Jekyll Island and Sea Island. It's also a manufacturing and seafood processing town, known as one of the shrimp capitals of the world. Its harbor is a full oceangoing seaport, as well as a home port to coastal fishing and shrimping fleets. Its natural beauty is enhanced by plantings of palms and flowering shrubs along main avenues, contrasting with moss-covered ancient oaks in spacious parks.

Information: Brunswick-Golden Isles Visitors Bureau, 4 Glynn Ave.,
912-265-0620, 800-933-2627; www.brunswick-georgia.com

WHAT TO SEE AND DO

MARSHES OF GLYNN

Traversed by causeways connecting with Highway 17, the vast saltwater marshes are bisected by several rivers and the Intracoastal Waterway. Marshes of Glynn Overlook Park has picnic facilities, view of marshes.

HOTELS

★★BEST WESTERN BRUNSWICK INN

5323 New Jesup Highway, Brunswick, 912-264-0144;
www.bestwestern.com

145 rooms. Restaurant, Complimentary continental breakfast. High-speed Internet access. $

★EMBASSY SUITES

500 Mall Blvd., Brunswick, 912-264-6100, 800-362-2779;
www.embassysuites.com

130 rooms, all suites. Complimentary continental breakfast. Airport transportation available. High-speed Internet access. Pets not accepted. $$

★
★
★
★
★

★JAMESON INN

661 Scranton Road, Brunswick, 912-267-0800, 800-526-3766;
www.jamesoninns.com
62 rooms. Complimentary continental breakfast. **$**

★QUALITY INN

125 Venture Drive, Brunswick, 912-265-4600, 877-424-6423; www.qualityinn.com
83 rooms. Complimentary continental breakfast. Pets not accepted. **$**

RESTAURANTS
★CAPTAIN JOE'S

I-95 & Highway 341, Brunswick, 912-264-8771
Seafood, steak menu. Lunch, dinner. Children's menu. Casual attire. **$$**

★★MATTEO'S ITALIAN RESTAURANT

5448 New Jesup Highway, Brunswick, 912-267-0248
Italian, pizza menu. Lunch, dinner. Closed Sunday. Children's menu. Casual attire. **$**

BUFORD

This city near Atlanta is home to Lake Lanier, a popular warm weather weekend destination for city dwellers.
Information: Gwinnett County Convention and Visitors Bureau,
6500 Sugarloaf Parkway, Duluth, 770-623-3600; www.gcvb.org

WHAT TO SEE AND DO
LAKE LANIER ISLANDS

7000 Holiday Road, Buford, 770-932-7200; www.lakelanierislands.com
A 1,200-acre, year-round resort. Swimming, waterskiing, beach and water park with wave pool, 10 water slides and other attractions, fishing, boating (ramps, rentals); horseback riding, two 18-hole golf courses, tennis, picnicking, two hotels, resort, cottages, tent and trailer camping. Special events are held May-October.

HOTELS
★★★EMERALD POINTE RESORT

7000 Holiday Road, Buford, 770-945-8787, 800-840-5253;
www.lakelanierislands.com
Best known for its championship golf course, Emerald Pointe is set on a hillside surrounded by hardwood trees and Lake Sidney Lanier. The island-like setting has swimming, boating and more. This is a favorite Southern retreat. 224 rooms. Restaurant, bar. Children's activity center. Beach. Golf. **$**

★★★WHITWORTH INN

6593 McEver Road, Flowery Branch, 770-967-2386;
www.whitworthinn.com
Bask in the tranquility of this beautifully landscaped bed and breakfast located 40 miles north of Atlanta. 10 rooms. Complimentary full breakfast.

CALHOUN

Once called Oothcaloga, "place of the beaver dams," the name was changed in 1850 to honor John Caldwell Calhoun, Secretary of State to President John Tyler. Although the town was directly in the path of General Sherman's 1864 "March to the Sea," Calhoun was not destroyed. Now, Calhoun is the seat of Gordon County and center of a dairy, beef cattle and poultry raising area. The town has a major carpet industry and several manufacturing companies that provide a wide range of products.

Information: Gordon County Chamber of Commerce, 300 S. Wall St., Calhoun, 706-625-3200, 800-887-3811; www.cityofcalhoun-ga.com

WHAT TO SEE AND DO

NEW ECHOTA STATE HISTORIC SITE

1211 Chatsworth Highway N.E., Calhoun, 706-624-1321; www.gastateparks.org-info-echota

The Cherokee Nation had a legislative hall, a supreme court house, a mission and several other buildings at New Echota. In the 1950s, the citizens of Calhoun bought the 200-acre site and donated it to the state for restoration and preservation.

After establishing a government in 1817, the legislature of the Cherokee Indian Nation established a capital surrounding the site of their Council House. The written form of the Cherokee language, created by the brilliant Sequoyah, had been developed by 1821, and the print shop was built in 1827. The first issue of the Cherokee newspaper, the *Cherokee Phoenix*, was printed in this shop in 1828 in both Cherokee and English. The paper continued publication until 1834.

Missionary Samuel A. Worcester arrived from Boston in 1827 and built a house, which is the only original building still standing. At the height of Cherokee prosperity, gold was found in the Cherokee territory, which then included parts of Georgia, North Carolina, Alabama and Tennessee. In 1835, after a long legal battle, the Cherokees were forced to sell their territory and move to Oklahoma. In the winter of 1838-1839, the Cherokees were driven to their new location over the "Trail of Tears," one-fourth of them dying on the way. Many hid out in the Great Smoky Mountains. Their descendants now form the Eastern Cherokee tribe. Tuesday-Saturday 9 a.m.-5 p.m., Sunday 2-5:30 p.m.

RESACA CONFEDERATE CEMETERY

300 S. Wall St., Calhoun, 800-887-3811; www.gordonchamber.org

Site of the Civil War battle that opened the way to Atlanta for General Sherman. Civil War markers and cemetery on the Civil War Discovery Trail. Daily 8:30 a.m.-5 p.m., Friday 8:30 a.m.-4 p.m.

HOTELS

★★★BARNSLEY GARDENS RESORT

597 Barnsley Gardens Road, Adairsville, 877-773-2447; www.barnsleyresort.com

This full-service luxury resort gets national accolades for its accommodations, grounds and top-ranking golf course. A full spa, three restaurants and a variety of suites and cottages make up the elegant resort. 70 rooms. Restaurant, bar. High-speed Internet access. Airport transportation available. $$

★
★
★
★
★

189 Jameson St. S.E., Calhoun, 706-629-8133, 800-526-3766;
www.jamesoninns.com
59 rooms. Complimentary continental breakfast. Wireless Internet access. **$**

RESTAURANT
★PENGS PAVILLION
1120 S. Wall St., Calhoun, 706-629-1453
Chinese menu. Lunch, dinner. Closed Sunday. **$**

CARROLLTON

Carrollton was named in honor of Charles Carroll, one of the signers of the Declaration of Independence. The town serves as a regional retail, service, manufacturing and health care center for several counties in western Georgia and eastern Alabama. John Tanner State Park, which has two lakes and the longest beach in the Georgia State Park system, is one good reason to visit.

Information: Carroll County Chamber of Commerce, 200 Northside Drive,
Carrollton, 770-832-2446; www.carroll-ga.org

WHAT TO SEE AND DO
THE BONNER HOUSE
1600 Maple St., Carrollton
Circa 1840. Restored plantation house, campus information center. Monday-Friday.

HOTEL
★COMFORT INN
132 Highway, 61 Connector, Villa Rica,
678-941-3401; www.comfortinnandsuites.com
64 rooms. Complimentary continental breakfast. **$**

CARTERSVILLE

Cartersville today is known as a mining center in Georgia (ocher, barite and manganese) but its ancient past is what attracts tourists. Archeologists have identified ruins from Native Americans dating back to 1000 A.D. The local state park is also a draw.

Information: Cartersville-Bartow County Convention and
Visitors Bureau, Cartersville, 770-387-1357, 800-733-2280;
www.notatlanta.org

WHAT TO SEE AND DO
ETOWAH INDIAN MOUNDS HISTORIC SITE AND
ARCHAEOLOGICAL AREA
813 Indian Mounds Road S.W., Cartersville,
770-387-3747; www.gastateparks.org
The most impressive of more than 100 settlements in the Etowah Valley, this village was occupied from A.D. 1000-1500. It was the home of several thousand people of a relatively advanced culture. Six earthen mounds grouped around two public squares, the largest of which occupies several acres, served as funeral mounds, bases

for temples and the residences of the chiefs. Museum displays artifacts from the excavations; crafts, foods, way of life of the Etowah; painted white marble mortuary. Tuesday-Saturday 9 a.m.-5 p.m., Sunday 2-5:30 p.m.

HOTELS
★COMFORT INN
28 SR 20 Spur S.E., Cartersville,
770-387-1800, 877-424-6423; www.comfortinn.com
60 rooms. Complimentary continental breakfast. Wireless Internet access. Outdoor pool. Pets accepted. **$**

★DAYS INN
5618 Highway 20 S.E., Cartersville,
770-382-1824, 800-329-7466; www.daysinn.com
52 rooms. Complimentary continental breakfast. High-speed Internet access. Outdoor pool. Pets accepted. **$**

★★HOLIDAY INN
2336 Highway 411 N.E., Cartersville,
770-386-0830, 800-315-2621; www.holidayinn.com
144 rooms. Restaurant, bar. High-speed Internet access. Whirlpool. **$**

CHATSWORTH
Almost a third of the land in Murray County is forest and mountains. Opportunities for fishing, hunting, camping, backpacking and mountain biking abound in the surrounding Cohutta Wilderness and woodlands.
Information: Chatsworth-Murray County Chamber of Commerce,
126 N. Third Ave., Chatsworth, 706-695-6060; www.northga.net-murray

WHAT TO SEE AND DO
CHIEF VANN HOUSE STATE HISTORIC SITE
82 Highway 225 N., Chatsworth, 706-695-2598; www.gastateparks.org-info-chiefvann
This brick house was the showplace of the Cherokee Nation. James Vann was half Scottish, half Cherokee. His chief contribution to the tribe was his help in establishing the nearby Moravian Mission for the education of the young Cherokees. The three-story house, with foot-thick brick walls, is modified Georgian in style; partly furnished. Tuesday-Sunday.

HOTEL
★★COHUTTA LODGE & CONFERENCE CENTER
500 Cochise Trail, Chatsworth, 706-695-9601, 800-394-9790;
www.cohuttalodge.com
61 rooms. Restaurant. **$**

RESTAURANT
★COHUTTA DINING ROOM
500 Cochise Trail, Chatsworth, 706-695-9601; www.cohuttalodge.com/restaurant
American menu. Breakfast, lunch, dinner. **$$**

COLUMBUS

Power from the falls of the Chattahoochee River feeds the industries of this dynamic city. Originally a settlement of the Creek Indians, the city reached a peak of manufacturing and commerce between 1861 and 1864, when it supplied the Confederate Army with shoes, caps, swords and pistols. Reconstruction created havoc for a time, but by 1874 Columbus's industries were more numerous and varied than before the war. From 1880-1920, a commercial ice-making machine was produced in the town, and by the beginning of World War II, Columbus was a great iron-working center and the second-largest producer of cotton in the South.

Much of the original city plan of 1827 is still evident, with streets 99-164 feet wide flanked by magnificent trees. Dogwood and wisteria add color in the spring. The atmosphere is exemplified by the brick-lined streets and gaslights in the 28-block historic district and by the Victorian gardens, gazebos and open-air amphitheaters on the Chattahoochee Promenade along the banks of the river.

Information: Tourist Division, Convention & Visitors Bureau, 900 Front Ave., Columbus, 706-322-1613, 800-999-1613; or the Georgia Welcome Center, 1751 Williams Road, 706-649-7455; www.visitcolumbusga.com

WHAT TO SEE AND DO

THE COLUMBUS MUSEUM
1251 Wynnton Road, Columbus, 706-748-2562; www.columbusmuseum.com
Features Chattahoochee Legacy, a regional history gallery with recreated period settings, fine and decorative arts galleries and Transformations, a youth-oriented participatory gallery. Tuesday-Wednesday, Friday-Saturday 10 a.m.-5p.m., Thursday until 9 p.m., Sunday 1-5 p.m.

FORT BENNING
I-185, Columbus, 706-545-2011; www.benningmwr.com
Largest infantry post in the U.S. established during World War I, the fort was named for Confederate General Henry L. Benning of Columbus. Infantry school; demonstrations of Airborne 5000 at jump tower. Monday mornings.

HOTELS

★BEST WESTERN COLUMBUS
3443 Macon Road, Columbus, 706-568-3300, 800-780-7234; www.bestwestern.com
66 rooms. Complimentary continental breakfast. $

★★FOUR POINTS BY SHERATON
5351 Sidney Simons Blvd., Columbus, 706-327-6868; www.fourpointscolumbus.com
178 rooms. Restaurant, bar. Airport transportation available. $

★LA QUINTA INN
3201 Macon Road, Columbus, 706-568-1740, 800-642-4271; www.laquinta.com
122 rooms. Complimentary continental breakfast. High-speed Internet access. Pets accepted. $

GEORGIA

★★★MARRIOTT

800 Front Ave., Columbus, 706-324-1800; www.marriott.com

Situated among the scenic downtown historic business district, this hotel caters to corporate travelers and families alike. 177 rooms. Restaurant, bar. High-speed Internet access. Airport transportation available. Pets not accepted. $

RESTAURANTS

★★★BLUDAU'S GOETCHIUS HOUSE

405 Broadway, Columbus, 706-324-4863; www.goetchiushouse.com

This classic Southern restaurant is situated in a restored antebellum mansion overlooking the river. A special Chateaubriand is the favorite entrée. Mint juleps are served in the speakeasy downstairs. American menu. Dinner. Closed Sunday, holidays. Bar. Outdoor seating. $$

★COUNTRY'S NORTH

6298 Veterans Parkway, Columbus, 706-660-1415;
www.countrysbarbecue.com

American menu. Lunch, dinner. Children's menu. Outdoor seating. $

CUMBERLAND ISLAND NATIONAL SEASHORE

Cumberland Island National Seashore, off the coast of Georgia, is accessible only by a passenger tour boat, which operates year-round. Mainland departures are from Saint Marys. A visit to the island is a walking experience, and there are no restaurants or shops. Salt marshes fringe the island's western side, while white-sand beaches decorate the Atlantic-facing east side. The interior is forested primarily by live oak. Interspersed are freshwater marshes and sloughs. Native Americans, Spanish and English have all lived on the island—most structures date from the pre-Civil War plantation era, though there are turn-of-the-century buildings built by the Thomas Carnegie family, who used the island as their 19th-century retreat. Camping; reservations by necessary. Ferry: Mid-March-September, daily; Winter Monday, Thursday-Sunday.
Information: 912-882-4336; www.nps.gov/cuis

HOTEL

★★★GREYFIELD INN

4 N. Second St., Fernandina Beach, Cumberland Island,
904-261-6408, 866-401-8581; www.greyfieldinn.com

Accessible by private ferry from Fernandina Beach, Fla., this inn is a tranquil place to enjoy Cumberland Island's natural beauty and abundant wildlife, including wild horses and many species of birds. Furnished with family heirlooms and antiques, the guest rooms and suites vary widely. Room rates include breakfast, picnic lunch, gourmet dinner (jacket required) and snacks throughout the day, as well as unlimited use of the inn's sporting, fishing and beach equipment. A two-night minimum stay is required. Not all rooms have private baths. 17 rooms. Restaurant, bar. Fitness room. Children 6 years and older only. $$$$

DAHLONEGA

Gold fever struck this area in 1828, 20 years before the Sutter's Mill discovery in California. Dahlonega, derived from the Cherokee word for the color yellow, yielded so much ore that the federal government established a local mint which produced $6,115,569 in gold coins from 1838-1861. Dahlonega is the seat of Lumpkin County, where tourism, manufacturing, higher education and agribusiness are the major sources of employment.

Information: Dahlonega-Lumpkin County Chamber of Commerce,

13 S. Park St., Dahlonega, 706-864-3711; www.dahlonega.org

WHAT TO SEE AND DO

ANNA RUBY FALLS

Off Highway 356, 6 miles north of Helen, 706-878-3574

Approximately 1,600 acres surrounding a double waterfall, with drops of 50 and 153 feet. This scenic area is enhanced by laurel, wild azaleas, dogwood and rhododendron. Daily 9 a.m.-dusk. Visitor center.

APPALACHIAN NATIONAL SCENIC TRAIL

304-535-6278; www.nps.gov/appa

Thirteen lean-tos are maintained along the 76 miles along the southern portion of the trail. Following the crest of the Blue Ridge divide, the trail begins outside Dahlonega and continues for more than 2,000 miles to Mount Katahdin, Maine.

CHATTAHOOCHEE NATIONAL FOREST

1755 Cleveland Highway, Dahlonega, 770-297-3000; www.fs.fed.us/conf

This vast forest (748,608 acres) includes Georgia's Blue Ridge Mountains toward the north, which have elevations ranging from 1,000 to nearly 5,000 feet. Because the forest ranges from the Piedmont to mountainous areas, the Chattahoochee has a diversity of trees and wildlife. There are 25 developed camping areas, 24 picnicking areas, 10 wilderness areas and six swimming beaches.

CONSOLIDATED GOLD MINES

185 Consolidated Gold Mine Road, Dahlonega,

706-864-8473; www.consolidatedgoldmine.com

Underground mine tour (40-45 minutes) through tunnel network; displays of original equipment used. Instructors available for gold panning. Daily 10 a.m.-5 p.m.

DAHLONEGA COURTHOUSE GOLD MUSEUM STATE HISTORIC SITE

1 Public Square, Dahlonega, 706-864-2257; www.gastateparks.org

In the old Lumpkin County Courthouse. Exhibits on first major gold rush; display of gold coins minted in Dahlonega. Film shown every half hour. Monday-Saturday 9 a.m.-5 p.m., Sunday 10 a.m.-5 p.m.

GEORGIA

★
★★
★★
★★
★

HOTELS

★★FORREST HILLS MOUNTAIN RESORT

135 Forrest Hills Drive, Dahlonega,
770-534-3244, 800-654-6313; www.foresths.com
30 rooms. Restaurant. **$**

★SUPER 8

20 Mountain Drive, Dahlonega, 706-864-4343, 800-800-8000; www.super8.com
60 rooms. Continental breakfast. High-speed Internet access. Pool. **$**

SPECIALTY LODGING

THE SMITH HOUSE

84 S. Chestatee St., Dahlonega, 706-867-7000, 800-852-9577;
www.smithhouse.com
16 rooms. Restaurant. Complimentary continental breakfast. **$**

RESTAURANT

★★SMITH HOUSE

84 S. Chestatee St., Dahlonega, 706-867-7000, 800-852-9577;
www.smithhouse.com
American menu. Lunch, dinner. Closed Monday. **$**

DALTON

Once a part of the Cherokee Nation, Dalton was involved in fierce battles and skirmishes in the Civil War as Union forces advanced on Atlanta. Today, Dalton has more than 100-carpet outlets and manufactures a large portion of the world's carpets. Dalton also produces other tufted textiles, chemicals, latex, thread and yarn.

Information: Convention and Visitors Bureau, 2211 Dug Gap Battle Road, Dalton,
706-270-9960, 800-331-3258; www.daltoncvb.com

WHAT TO SEE AND DO

CROWN GARDEN & ARCHIVES

715 Chattanooga Ave., Dalton, 706-278-0217
Headquarters of the Whitfield-Murray Historical Society. Genealogical library; changing exhibits include Civil War items. Tuesday-Friday 10 a.m.-5 p.m., Saturday 9 a.m.-1 p.m.

HOTEL

★★BEST WESTERN INN OF DALTON

2106 Chattanooga Road, Dalton, 706-226-5022, 800-780-7234; www.bestwestern.com
99 rooms. Restaurant, bar. High-speed Internet access. Pool. Pets accepted. **$**

RESTAURANT

★★DALTON DEPOT

450 Housatonic St., Dalton, 413-684-1730
American menu. Lunch, dinner. Closed Sunday. Bar. Children's menu. **$$**

DARIEN

James Oglethorpe recruited Scottish Highlanders to protect Georgia's frontier on the Altamaha River in 1736. Calling their town Darien, they guarded Savannah from Spanish and native attack and carved out large plantations from the South Georgia wilderness. After 1800, Darien thrived as a great timber port until the early 20th century. Today, shrimp boats dock in the river over which Darien Scots once kept watch.

Information: McIntosh Chamber of Commerce, 105 Fort King Georgia Drive, Darien, 912-437-6684; www.mcintoshcounty.com

WHAT TO SEE AND DO
FORT KING GEORGE STATE HISTORIC SITE
1600 Wayne St., Darien, 912-437-4770; www.gastateparks.org

South Carolina scouts built this fort in 1721 near an abandoned Native American village and Spanish mission to block Spanish and French expansion into Georgia, thereby establishing the foundation for the later English Colony of Georgia. The fort and its blockhouse have been reconstructed to original form. The museum interprets the periods of Native American, Spanish and British occupations, the settlement of Darien and Georgia's timber industry. Tuesday-Saturday 9 a.m.-5 p.m., Sunday 2-5:30 p.m.

HOFWYL-BROADFIELD PLANTATION STATE HISTORIC SITE
5556 Highway 17 N., Brunswick, 912-264-7333; www.gastateparks.org

The evolution of this working rice plantation (1807-1973) is depicted through tours of the plantation house, museum and trails. Tours. Tuesday-Saturday 9 a.m.-5 p.m., Sunday 2-5:30 p.m.

★
★★
★★★
★★★★
★★★★★

DUBLIN

The seat of Laurens County, Dublin sits on land once occupied by Creek Indians. Area industries manufacture a wide range of goods, including textiles, carpeting, missile control systems and computer components. Agricultural products include soybeans, wheat, grain, peanuts, corn, cotton and tobacco.

Information: Dublin-Laurens County Chamber of Commerce, 1200 Bellevue Ave., 478-272-5546; www.dublin-georgia.com

WHAT TO SEE AND DO
DUBLIN-LAURENS MUSEUM
311 Academy Ave., Dublin, 478-272-9242

Local history museum featuring Native American artifacts, art, textiles and relics from early settlers. Tuesday-Friday 1-4:30 p.m.

HOTEL
★HOLIDAY INN EXPRESS
2192 Highway 441 S., Dublin, 478-272-7862, 800-315-2621; www.holidayinn.com

124 rooms. Restaurant, bar. Complimentary full breakfast. Airport transportation available. Pets not accepted. **$**

FORSYTH

Forsyth is a small town near Macon in the center of the state. The nearby town of Juliette was the setting for the 1991 film *Fried Green Tomatoes*.

Information: Forsyth-Monroe County Chamber of Commerce,
267 Tift College Drive, Forsyth, 478-994-9239; www.forsyth-monroechamber.com

WHAT TO SEE AND DO
JARRELL PLANTATION STATE HISTORIC SITE
711 Jarrell Plantation Rd., Forsyth, 478-986-5172; www.gastateparks.org
This authentic plantation has 20 historic buildings dating from 1847-1940, including a plain-style plantation house, sawmill, gristmill and blacksmith shop. Tuesday-Saturday 9 a.m.-5 p.m., Sunday 2-5:30 p.m.

HOTELS
★BEST WESTERN HILLTOP INN
951 Highway 42 N., Forsyth, 478-994-9260, 800-780-7234; www.bestwestern.com
120 rooms. Complimentary breakfast. High-speed Internet access. Pool. Pets accepted. $

★★HOLIDAY INN
Juliette Road & I-75, Forsyth, 478-994-5691, 800-315-2621; www.holidayinn.com
120 rooms. Restaurant, bar. Complimentary breakfast. High-speed Internet access. Pets accepted. $

RESTAURANT
★WHISTLE STOP CAFÉ
443 McCrackin St., Juliette, 478-992-8886; www.thewhistlestopcafe.com
American menu. Breakfast Monday-Saturday, lunch. Film site of *Fried Green Tomatoes*. $

GAINESVILLE

On the shore of 38,000-acre Lake Sidney Lanier, Gainesville is the headquarters for the Chattahoochee National Forest.

Information: Gainesville-Hall County Convention and Visitors Bureau,
830 Green St., Gainesville, 770-536-5209; www.gainesville.org

WHAT TO SEE AND DO
BRENAU UNIVERSITY
500 Washington St., Southeast, Gainesville,
770-534-6299, 800-252-5119; www.brenau.edu
Liberal arts residential college for 2,000 women with coed evening and weekend programs; off-campus, graduate and undergraduate divisions. On campus is Brenau Academy, a four-year preparatory high school for girls. Pearce Auditorium has fine acoustics, stained-glass windows and ceiling freoes. Trustee Library has displays of American art.

GREEN STREET HISTORICAL DISTRICT
Gainesville
A broad street with Victorian and Classical Revival houses dating from the late 19th and early 20th centuries.

HOTELS

★★HOLIDAY INN LANIER CENTRE

400 E. Butler Parkway, Gainesville, 770-531-0907, 800-780-7234;
www.laniercentrehotel.com
122 rooms. Restaurant, bar. $

★★QUALITY INN & SUITES

726 Jesse Jewell Parkway, Gainesville,
770-536-4451, 877-4242-6423; www.choicehotels.com
96 rooms. Restaurant, bar. Wireless Internet access. Pets accepted. $

RESTAURANTS

★POOR RICHARD'S

1702 Park Hill Drive, Gainesville,
770-532-0499; www.prgainesville.com
Steak menu. Dinner. Closed Sunday. Bar. Children's menu. Casual attire. $$

★★RUDOLPH'S

700 Green St., Gainesville, 770-534-2226; www.rudolphsdining.com
American, Continental menu. Lunch, dinner, Sunday brunch. Bar. Children's menu. Business casual attire. Reservations recommended. $$

GREENSBORO

This central Georgia town is located near Lake Oconee and set amidst rolling hills and pine trees. The new Ritz-Carlton complex at Reynolds Plantation has made the area a center for golf.

Information: www.greeneccoc.org

HOTEL

★★★★THE RITZ-CARLTON LODGE, REYNOLDS PLANTATION

1 Lake Oconee Trail, Greensboro,
706-467-0600, 800-542-8680; www.ritzcarlton.com
Located an hour from Atlanta, this resort on the 8,000-acre Reynolds Plantation overlooks Lake Oconee, Georgia's second-largest lake. Fill your days with fishing, boating or waterskiing on the lake. Golf is a major attraction, with 99 holes designed by legends like Jack Nicklaus, Rees Jones, Tom Fazio and Bob Cupp. Then retire to one of the comfortable guest rooms, designed with a rich blend of American and European fabrics and furniture. 251 rooms. Three restaurants, three bars. High-speed Internet access. Business center. Children's activity center. Fitness room, fitness classes available, spa. Beach. Indoor pool, outdoor pool, children's pool, whirlpool. Golf, 99 holes. Tennis. Airport transportation available. Pets accepted, some restrictions; fee. $$$

RESTAURANT

★★★GEORGIA'S

1 Lake Oconee Trail, Greensboro, 706-467-0600; www.ritzcarlton.com
Located on the lower level of The Ritz-Carlton Lodge Reynolds Plantation, Georgia's offers countryside charm with a fireplace, antler chandeliers and views of Lake

Oconee. A menu of inventive regional Southern cuisine makes any occasion special. Splurge on a bottle from the Captain's Wine List, which features hard-to-find varietals that range from $200-$600 per bottle. Southern menu. Breakfast, lunch, dinner, brunch. Closed for lunch from mid-March to late October. Children's menu. Casual attire. Reservations recommended. Valet parking. Outdoor seating. $$$

SPA

★★★★THE SPA AT THE RITZ-CARLTON LODGE, REYNOLDS PLANTATION

1 Lake Oconee Trail, Greensboro,
706-467-0600, 800-241-3333; www.ritzcarlton.com

This 26,000-square-foot spa offers an array of massages, body treatments, facials and other therapies. Massage techniques include Swedish, deep tissue and reflexology. The resort's wellness center features advanced cardiovascular equipment, an indoor lap pool, health screenings and consultations with counselors who will design an individual exercise program.

HELEN

The natural setting of the mountains and the Chattahoochee River helped create the atmosphere for this logging town. Helen was reborn in 1969 when the citizens, with the help of a local artist, decided to transform it into an Alpine, Bavarian-inspired town. Here you'll find quaint cobblestone streets, gift shops with an international flavor, crafts, restaurants and festivals—a bit of the Old World in the heart of the mountains of northeast Georgia.

Information: Helen-White County Convention and Visitors Bureau,
726 Brucken St., Helen, 706-878-2181, 800-858-8027; www.helenga.org

SPECIAL EVENTS

HELEN TO THE ATLANTIC BALLOON RACE & FESTIVAL

Highway 75, Helen, 706-878-2271; www.helenballoon.com

The weekend begins with a Friday morning liftoff for about 25 balloons participating in the Helen to the Atlantic race, which ends anywhere along Interstate 95 (I-95). After those balloons take off, several more stay in Helen for local flights and special activities. First weekend in June.

OKTOBERFEST

726 Brucken Strasse, Helen, 706-878-1908;
www.helencvb.com/oktoberfest

German music and beer festival; one of the longest-running Oktoberfests in the country. September-October.

HOTELS

★★CASTLE INN

8287 Main St., Helen, 706-878-0022, 800-395-3644;
www.castleinn-helen.com

12 rooms. Restaurant. $

★ECONO LODGE

101 Edelweiss Strasse, Helen, 706-878-8000, 877-424-6423;
www.econolodge.com

56 rooms. Complimentary continental breakfast. Pets accepted. **$**

★★UNICOI LODGE AND CONFERENCE CENTER

1788 Highway 356, Helen, 706-878-2201, 800-573-9659;
www.unicoilodge.com

100 rooms. Restaurant. Access to all facilities of state park. **$**

RESTAURANT

★★HOFBRAUHAUS

9001 Main St., Helen, 706-878-2184;
www.riverfronthotel.com

German menu. Dinner. Bar. Children's menu. Internet access. Pool. **$$**

HIAWASSEE

A picturesque mountain town, Hiawassee is on Lake Chatuge, surrounded by the Chattahoochee National Forest. Its backdrop is a range of the Blue Ridge Mountains topped by Brasstown Bald Mountain, Georgia's highest peak. Rock hunting, including hunting for the highly prized amethyst crystal, is a favorite activity in surrounding Towns County.

Information: www.mountaintopga.com

GEORGIA

★
★
★
★
★

WHAT TO SEE AND DO

BRASSTOWN BALD MOUNTAIN-VISITOR INFORMATION CENTER

2941 St., Highway 180, Hiawassee, 706-896-2556; www.fs.fed.us/conf

At 4,784 feet, this is Georgia's highest peak. Observation deck affords a view of four states. Visitor center has interpretive programs presented in mountain-top theater and exhibit hall. June-October, daily; late April-May, weekends only, weather permitting.

SPECIAL EVENT

GEORGIA MOUNTAIN FAIR

1311 Music Hall Road, Hiawassee, 706-896-4191;
www.georgia-mountain-fair.com

Individual accomplishment is the theme of this gathering. Displays of arts and crafts, farm produce, flowers, minerals, Native American relics, board splitting, soap and hominy making, quilting. Camping, beach and tennis courts at Georgia Mountain Fairgrounds and Towns County Recreation Park. Twelve days in late July.

HOTEL

★★★BRASSTOWN VALLEY RESORT

6321 Highway 76, Young Harris, 706-379-9900, 800-201-3205;
www.brasstownvalley.com

Guests get lost in the views from this mountain lodge as they take in the beautiful Blue Ridge Mountain countryside. This resort offers a rustic feel with many modern touches. Don't miss the vast stables and opportunities for riding trails on horseback. 102 rooms. Restaurant, bar. Children's activity center. Spa. Golf. Pool. **$**

JEFFERSON

This small Northeast Georgia community is situated between Gainesville and Athens and an hour's drive from Atlanta. In 1842, Dr. Crawford W. Long pioneered the use of ether in surgery in Jefferson.

Information: www.cityofjeffersonga.com

RESTAURANT

★★★THE CARRIAGE HOUSE RESTAURANT

1235 Athens St., Jefferson, 706-367-1989; www.chateauelanatlanta.com

This elegant and classic restaurant is nestled in a country location amid rolling hills. Housed in a restored 1886 Victorian, it features six-stone fireplaces with cherry wood mantles, hardwood floors, etched and stained glass and a large porch where guests can enjoy a cocktail before dinner. The décor is charming, the service is warm and skillful and the food—international, with Southern influences—is memorable. International menu. Lunch, dinner. Brunch children's menu. Casual attire. Reservations recommended. Outdoor seating. $$

JEKYLL ISLAND

Connected to the mainland by a causeway, Jekyll Island, the smallest of Georgia's coastal islands with 5,600 acres of highlands and 10,000 acres of marshland, was favored by Native Americans for hunting and fishing. Spanish missionaries arrived in the late 16th and early 17th centuries and established a mission. In 1734, during an expedition southward, General James Oglethorpe passed by the island and named it for his friend and financial supporter, Sir Joseph Jekyll. Later, William Horton, one of Oglethorpe's officers, established a plantation on the island.

Horton's land grant passed to several owners before the island was sold to Christophe du Bignon, a Frenchman who was escaping the French Revolution. It remained in the du Bignon family as a plantation for almost a century. In 1858, the slave ship *Wanderer* arrived at the island and unloaded the last major cargo of slaves ever to land in the U.S. In 1886, John Eugene du Bignon sold the island to a group of wealthy businessmen from the northeast, who formed the Jekyll Island Club.

Club members who wintered at Jekyll in exclusive privacy from early January-early April included J. P. Morgan, William Rockefeller, Edwin Gould, Joseph Pulitzer and R. T. Crane Jr. Some built fabulous houses they called cottages, many of which are still standing. By World War II, the club had been abandoned for economic and social reasons, and in 1947, the island was sold to the state. The Jekyll Island Authority was created to conserve beaches and manage the island while maintaining it as a year-round resort.

Information: Jekyll Island Convention and Visitors Bureau, Jekyll Island,
912-635-3636, 800-841-6586; www.jekyllisland.com

WHAT TO SEE AND DO

HORTON HOUSE

375 Riverview Drive, Jekyll Island, 912-635-2119

Ruins of former house of William Horton, sent from St. Simons as captain by General James Oglethorpe. On Jekyll, he established an outpost and plantation. Horton became the major of all British forces at Fort Frederica after Oglethorpe's return to England.

★
★
★
★
★

JEKYLL ISLAND CLUB NATIONAL HISTORIC LANDMARK DISTRICT

901 Jekyll Island Causeway, Jekyll Island, 912-635-3636; www.jekyllisland.com

Once one of the nation's most exclusive resorts, this restored district is a memorable example of turn-of-the-century wealth. Exhibition buildings and shops are open daily. Tours are available.

HOTELS

★★★JEKYLL ISLAND CLUB HOTEL

371 Riverview Drive, Jekyll Island, 912-635-2600, 800-535-9547; www.jekyllclub.com

Once a popular and exclusive retreat for the nation's wealthy elite, this gorgeous hotel on Georgia's historic Jekyll Island pampers guests and entertains with golf, fishing, water sports, shopping and more. 157 rooms. Restaurant, bar. Internet access. Children's activity center. Beach. Airport transportation available. $$

★★VILLAS BY THE SEA

1175 N. Beachview Drive Jekyll Island, 866-920-1263; www.jekyllislandga.com

150 rooms. Pool. Beach. Internet access. $$

RESTAURANTS

★★BLACKBEARD'S

200 N. Beachview Drive., Jekyll Island, 912-635-3522

American menu. Lunch, dinner. Bar. Children's menu. Casual attire. Outdoor seating. $$

★★★GRAND DINING ROOM

371 Riverview Drive, Jekyll Island, 912-635-2400; www.jekyllclub.com

The formal dining room of this historic resort is as grand as its name suggests. A dramatic colonnade leads to a large fireplace, lined by plushly upholstered chairs. The Low Country cooking features local seafood. American menu. Breakfast, lunch, dinner, Sunday brunch. Children's menu. Jacket required (dinner). Reservations recommended. Valet parking. $$$

★LATITUDE 31

1 Pier Road, Jekyll Island, 912-635-3800; www.crossoverjekyll.com

American menu. Lunch Tuesday-Saturday, dinner. Closed Monday. Bar. Children's menu. Casual attire. Outdoor seating. $$

★★THE SURF STEAKHOUSE

1175 N. Beachview Drive, Jekyll Island, 912-635-3588

Steak menu. Dinner. $

★ZACHRY'S SEAFOOD

44 Beachview Drive, Jekyll Island, 912-635-3128

Seafood menu. Lunch, dinner. Children's menu. Casual attire. $$

MACON

One of the larger cities in Georgia, Macon stands out for its musical heritage, its cherry trees and its African-American heritage. Sure, the kazoo was invented here in the 1840s, but more notable is the number of musicians who were born here or

KENNESAW MOUNTAIN NATIONAL BATTLEFIELD PARK

In June of 1864, General William Tecumseh Sherman executed the Battle of Kennesaw Mountain, which stalled but did not halt his invasion of Georgia. Kennesaw Mountain National Battlefield Park commemorates the 1864 Atlanta campaign.

The visitor center on Highway 41 and Stilesboro Road, north of Kennesaw Mountain, has exhibits, an audiovisual program and information, daily. A road leads to the top of Kennesaw Mountain. Daily: Monday-Friday, drive or walk; Saturday-Sunday, bus leaves every half hour, February-November, or walk; no driving. The Cheatham Hill area, in the south-central section of the park, has the same hours as the Kennesaw Mountain road.

Information: Approximately 3 miles northwest of Marietta off Highway 41 or I-75, exit 116; 770-427-4686; www.nps.gov-kemo

called Macon home over the past century: Lena Horne, The Allman Brothers Band, Otis Redding and Little Richard, to name just a few. Macon is also the birthplace of poet Sidney Lanier.

Macon began as a trading post. It served as a fort and rallying point for troops in the War of 1812. Later it became a major rail center. During the Civil War, Macon manufacturers produced quartermaster supplies, ordnance, harnesses, small weapons and cannons, and the city harbored $1.5 million in Confederate gold.

Information: Macon-Bibb County Convention and Visitors Bureau,

450 Martin Luther King Jr. Blvd., 478-743-3401, 800-768-3401; www.maconga.org

59

GEORGIA

WHAT TO SEE AND DO

CITY HALL

700 Poplar St., Macon, 478-751-7170; www.cityofmacon.net

Main entrance of Classical Revival building is flanked by panels depicting history of the Macon area. Monday-Friday 8:30 a.m.-5:30 p.m.

GEORGIA MUSIC HALL OF FAME

200 Martin Luther King Jr. Blvd., Macon, 478-751-3334, 888-427-6257;
www.gamusichall.com

Exhibits such as the Soda Fountain playing songs of the 1950s, the Jazz Club, Gospel Chapel and Rhythm & Blues Revue, explore Georgia's musical heritage. Monday-Saturday 9 a.m.-5 p.m., Sunday from 1-5 p.m.

MACON HISTORIC DISTRICT

450 Martin Luther King Jr. Blvd., Macon,
800-768-3401; www.visitmacon.org

The area makes up nearly all of old Macon—48 buildings and houses have been cited for architectural excellence and listed on the National Register of Historic Places. An additional 575 structures have been noted for architectural significance. Walking and driving tours noted on Heritage Tour Markers.

OLD CANNONBALL HOUSE & MACON-CONFEDERATE MUSEUM

856 Mulberry St., Macon, 478-745-5982; www.cannonballhouse.org

Greek Revival house struck by Union cannonball in 1864. Museum contains Civil War relics and Macon historical items. March-December, Monday-Saturday 10 a.m.-5 p.m. January and February, Monday-Friday 11 a.m.-5 p.m., Saturday,10 a.m.-5 p.m.

TUBMAN AFRICAN-AMERICAN MUSEUM

340 Walnut St., Macon, 478-743-8544; www.tubmanmuseum.com

Features African-American art, African artifacts and traveling exhibits on the history and culture of African-American people. Resource center, workshops and tours by appointment. Monday-Friday 9 a.m.-5 p.m., Saturday 12-4 p.m.; closed Sunday.

SPECIAL EVENTS
CHERRY BLOSSOM FESTIVAL

794 Cherry St., Macon, 478-751-7429; www.cherryblossom.com

Historic tours, concerts, fireworks, hot air balloons, sporting events and a parade are just part of the 10-day long festival, ranked among the top 100 in the country. Mid-March.

HOTELS
★★BEST WESTERN RIVERSIDE INN

2400 Riverside Drive, Macon, 478-743-6311, 888-454-4565; www.bestwestern.com

122 rooms. Restaurant, bar. Internet access, Business center. Pets accepted. **$**

★HOLIDAY INN EXPRESS

2720 Riverside Drive, Macon, 478-743-1482, 800-315-2621;
www.holidayinn.com

94 rooms. Complimentary continental breakfast. Internet access. Pets not accepted. **$**

MARIETTA

Located just outside of Atlanta, Marietta boasts business parks, hotels for travelers and an amusement park and water park for the kids.

Information: Cobb County Convention and Visitors Bureau,
1 Galleria Parkway, Atlanta, 800-451-3480;
www.cobbcvb.com

HOTELS
★HAMPTON INN ATLANTA-MARIETTA

455 Franklin Road S.E., Marietta, 770-425-9977, 800-426-7866;
www.hamptoninnmarietta.com

139 rooms. Complimentary full breakfast. Wireless Internet access. Outdoor pool and kiddie pool. **$**

★★★HYATT REGENCY SUITES PERIMETER NORTHWEST ATLANTA

2999 Windy Hill Road, Marietta, 770-956-1234, 800-233-1234;
www.atlantasuites.hyatt.com

Located just 15 minutes from downtown Atlanta, this suburban all-suite property offers an array of amenities for business and leisure travelers alike. 202 rooms, all suites. Restaurant, bar. Airport transportation available. Business center. **$$**

★LA QUINTA INN ATLANTA MARIETTA

2170 Delk Road, Marietta, 770-951-0026, 800-642-4271;
www.lq.com

130 rooms. Complimentary continental breakfast. Wireless Internet access. Airport transportation available. Pets accepted. **$**

★★★MARIETTA CONFERENCE CENTER AND RESORT

500 Powder Springs St., Marietta, 770-427-2500, 888-685-2500;
www.mariettaresort.com

Located just a short walk from Marietta Square and overlooking a championship golf course, this resort (former site of the Georgia Military Institute) works well for business and family vacations, offering luxury suits, fine dining and first-class amenities. Along with outdoor pool, whirlpool, tennis and golf, the resort also hosts croquet games on the lawn in the summer. 199 rooms. Two restaurants, bar. Internet access. Airport transportation available. Outdoor pool, whirlpool. **$**

SPECIALTY LODGING

THE WHITLOCK

57 Whitlock Ave., Marietta, 770-428-1495; www.whitlockinn.com

Located just one block west of Marietta Square on a stately tree-lined street, this fully restored Victorian mansion with distinctively different guest rooms provides all the charm one would expect in the South. Five rooms. Children over 12 years only. Complimentary full breakfast. Wireless Internet access. Airport transportation available. **$**

RESTAURANTS

★LA STRADA

2930 Johnson Ferry Road N.E., Marietta, 770-640-7008; www.lastradainc.com
Italian menu. Dinner. Bar. Children's menu. Casual attire. **$$**

★SHILLING'S ON THE SQUARE

19 N. Park Square N.E., Marietta, 770-428-9520; www.shillingsonthesquare.com
American menu. Lunch, dinner, Sunday brunch. Bar. Casual attire. **$**

PERRY

Perry is known as the crossroads of Georgia because of its location near the geographic center of the state. The town is full of stately houses and historic churches.
Information: Perry Area Convention and Visitors Bureau,
101 General Courtney Hodges Blvd., Perry, 478-988-800; www.perryga.com

WHAT TO SEE AND DO

THE ANDERSONVILLE TRAIL

Perry, 478-988-8000; www.perryga.com

Along the drive are American Camellia Society gardens, two state parks, antebellum houses and the Andersonville National Historic Site.

OKEFENOKEE SWAMP

One of the largest preserved freshwater wetlands in the U.S., the Okefenokee Swamp encompasses more than 700 square miles, stretching an average of 25 miles in width and 35 miles in length. The swamp's southern border is beyond the Florida line. Called "land of trembling earth" by Native Americans, its lakes of dark brown water, lush with moss-draped cypress, are headwaters for the Suwannee and St. Marys rivers. Visitors can take hikes, guided canoe tours and camp in various parts of the area.

The wildlife refuge occupies more than 90 percent of the swamp region and harbors bears, deer, bobcats, alligators and aquatic birds. Naturalists have discovered many rare plants on the swamp floor. The bay, one of the swamp's most distinctive trees, blooms from May through October, producing a white flower, which contrasts its rich evergreen foliage. Aquatic flowers, such as yellow spatterdock and white water lily, blend with pickerelweed, golden club and swamp iris in the spring. The swamp is also the home of the Sandhill crane and round-tailed muskrat. For those who want to try canoeing through the swamp, there are seven overnight stops and trips available from two to five days (three-day limit, available March-April). March-May and October-early November are the most popular times to visit. Buy advance reservations (up to two months) and a special permit from the refuge manager.
Information: 5700 Okefenokee Swamp Park Road, Folkston; www.okefenokee.com

★
★
★
★

MASSEE LANE GARDENS

100 Massee Lane, Fort Valley, 478-967-2358; www.camellias-acs.com
The beautiful 10-acre Camellia garden reaches its peak blooming season between November and March. The gardens also include a large greenhouse, Japanese garden and rose garden. The Colonial-style headquarters include the Annabelle Lundy Fetterman Educational Museum, exhibition hall (rare books, porcelain). Tuesday-Saturday 10 a.m.-4:30 p.m., Sunday 1-4.30 p.m. Closed Monday.

HOTELS

★COMFORT INN

1602 Sam Nunn Blvd., Perry, 478-987-7710, 800-424-6423; www.comfortinn.com
102 rooms. Complimentary continental breakfast. Internet access. Pool. Pets accepted. **$**

★★HOLIDAY INN

200 Valley Drive, Perry, 478-987-3313, 800-315-2621; www.holidayinn.com
203 rooms. Restaurant. Bar. Internet access. Pets accepted, some restrictions. Pool. **$**

★★NEW PERRY HOTEL

800 Main St., Perry, 478-987-1000, 800-877-3779; www.newperryhotel.com
43 rooms. Restaurant. **$**

PINE MOUNTAIN

This lush area of West Central Georgia is home to Callaway Gardens, a well-preserved vacation destination. It's less than an hour from Atlanta.
www.pinemountain.org

WHAT TO SEE AND DO

FRANKLIN D. ROOSEVELT STATE PARK

2970 Highway 190, Pine Mountain, 706-663-4858; www.gastateparks.org

One of the largest parks in the state system, it has many historic buildings and King's Gap Indian trail. Swimming pool, fishing, hiking, bridle and nature trails, picnicking, camping, cottages. Parking hours: 7 a.m.-10 p.m.

THE GARDENS AT CALLAWAY

17800 U.S. Highway 27, Pine Mountain, 706-663-2281,
800-225-5292; www.callawaygardens.com

This distinctive public garden and resort, consisting of 14,000 acres of gardens, woodlands, lakes, recreation areas and wildlife, was conceived by textile industrialist Cason J. Callaway to be "the finest garden on earth since Adam was a boy." Originally the family's weekend vacation spot in the 1930s, Callaway and his wife, Virginia, expanded the area and opened it to the public in 1952. Callaway is now home to more than 100 varieties of butterflies, 230 varieties of birds, 400 varieties of fruits and vegetables and thousands of species of plant life, including the rare planifolia azalea, which is indigenous to the area. The complex offers swimming, boating and other water recreation on its 13 lakes, including 175-acre Mountain Creek Lake and the white sand beach of Robin Lake; 23 miles of roads and paths for hiking or jogging, 63 holes of golf (a 9-hole and three 18-hole courses), 10 lighted tennis courts, two indoor racquetball courts, 10 miles of bike trails, skeet and trapshooting ranges, fishing, fly-fishing, picnicking, a country store, cottages, villas, an inn and restaurants.

HOTEL

★★★MOUNTAIN CREEK INN AT CALLAWAY GARDENS

17800 Highway 27, Pine Mountain, 706-663-2281,
800-225-5292; www.callawaygardens.com

Offering plenty of outdoor pursuits, including tennis and a championship golf course, this 14,000-acre property provides a relaxing venue to enjoy the entire Callaway Gardens area. 323 rooms. Restaurant, bar. Children's activity center. Beach. Multiple pools. Airport transportation available. $

ROME

According to legend, five men, seven hills, three rivers and a hat were the equation that led to the founding of Rome, Ga. The seven hills spurred the five founders to suggest that "Rome" be one of the names for the town, discovered at the junction of three rivers, to be drawn from a hat.

Nobles' Foundry Lathe, one of the few that produced Confederate cannons, is on display on Civic Center Hill and is a reminder of Sherman's occupation. Rome fell despite the frantic ride of Georgia's Paul Revere, a mail carrier named John E. Wisdom, who rode 67 miles by horse from Gadsden, Alabama, in 11 hours to warn that the Yankees were coming.

★
★
★
★
★

Information: Greater Rome Convention and Visitors Bureau,
402 Civic Center Hill, Rome, 706-295-5576, 800-444-1834; www.romegeorgia.org

WHAT TO SEE AND DO

BERRY COLLEGE

2277 Martha Berry Highway, Mt. Berry, 706-232-5374; www.berry.edu

Just 1,800 students enjoy the more than 26,000 acres of buildings and forest preserves that make this one of the largest campuses in the world.

OAK HILL AND THE MARTHA BERRY MUSEUM

24 Veterans Memorial Highway, Rome, 706-368-6789; www.berry.edu

Antebellum plantation house of Martha Berry, founder of Berry College. Manicured lawns, formal gardens and nature trails. Museum is located on grounds of Oak Hill and serves as reception center for visitors. Monday-Saturday 10 a.m.-5 p.m.

CHIEFTAINS MUSEUM

501 Riverside Parkway, Rome, 706-291-9494;
www.chieftainsmuseum.org

Eighteenth-century house of prominent Cherokee leader Major Ridge; artifacts with emphasis on Cherokee history. Tuesday-Friday 9 a.m.-3 p.m., Saturday 10 a.m.-4 p.m.

HOTELS

★DAYS INN

840 Turner McCall Blvd., Rome, 706-295-0400, 800-329-7466; www.daysinn.com

107 rooms. Complimentary continental breakfast. Internet access. Pool. Business center. $

★★HOLIDAY INN

20 Highway 411 E., Rome, 706-295-1100, 800-315-2621; www.ramada.com

200 rooms. Restaurant, bar. $

★
★
★
★
★

ST. MARYS

St. Marys sits on the Georgia coast in the northeast corner near Florida and the Okefenokee Swamp and is the main access point for Cumberland Island Wilderness area.

Information: www.stmaryswelcome.com

WHAT TO SEE AND DO

CROOKED RIVER STATE PARK

6222 Charlie Smith Sr. Highway, St. Marys, 912-882-5256;
www.gastateparks.org

Swimming pool, water sports, fishing in coastal tidewaters, boating; hiking, picnicking, camping, cottages. Daily 7 a.m.-10 p.m.

SPECIALTY LODGINGS

GOODBREAD HOUSE BED & BREAKFAST

209 Osborne St., St. Marys, 912-882-7490, 877-205-1453;
www.goodbreadhouse.com

Five rooms. Complimentary full breakfast. Pets accepted. $

SPENCER HOUSE INN BED & BREAKFAST

200 Osborne St., St. Marys, 912-882-1872, 888-840-1872;
www.spencerhouseinn.com

Built in 1872 as a hotel. 14 rooms. Complimentary full breakfast. **$$**

ST. SIMONS ISLAND

One of Georgia's Golden Isles, St. Simons Island has been under five flags: Spain, France, Britain, the U.S. and Confederate States of America. Fragments of each culture remain, including Fort Frederica national monument, the fort defending the Georgia colony from the Spaniards. Cotton plantations ruled the island for a time, but today it's a thriving resort community with sandy beaches, golf courses, dolphin watches, shopping and restaurants.

Information: St. Simons Visitors Center, 530 Beachview Drive, Neptune Park,
800-933-2627; www.gacoast.com

WHAT TO SEE AND DO
GASCOIGNE BLUFF

Arthur J. Moore Drive (where the bridge crosses the Frederica
River on the southwest side of island), St. Simons Island

This is a low-wooded, shell-covered bank named for Captain James Gascoigne, commander of HMS *Hawk*, which convoyed the two ships bringing the original settlers to the area in 1736. Great live oaks cut here were used to build the first U.S. Navy vessels, including the *Constitution* ("Old Ironsides") in 1794. St. Simons Marina is open to the public.

ST. SIMONS LIGHTHOUSE

101 12th St., St. Simons Island, 912-638-4666;
www.saintsimonslighthouse.org

The original lighthouse, which stood 75 feet high, was destroyed by Confederate troops in 1861 to prevent it from guiding Union invaders onto the island. The present lighthouse, 104 feet high, has been in continuous operation, except during wartime, since 1872. Visitors may climb to the top.

HOTELS
★BEST WESTERN ISLAND INN

301 Main St., St. Simons Island, 912-638-7805, 800-780-7234;
www.bestwestern.com

61 rooms. Complimentary continental breakfast. Wireless Internet access. Pets not accepted. **$**

★★★KING AND PRINCE RESORT

201 Arnold Road, St. Simons Island, 912-638-3631,
800-342-0212; www.kingandprince.com

Located on the ocean's edge directly on the beach, the resort is within minutes of a quaint shopping village and restaurants. The property offers ocean-front rooms, a one-bedroom house and a five-bedroom house. Outdoor amenities are abundant, including biking, kayaking and sailboat rentals, pools, a beach and tennis. 186 rooms. Two restaurants, two bars. Wireless Internet access. Beach. Whirlpool. Airport transportation available. **$$**

GEORGIA

★
★
★
★
★

★★★★★THE LODGE AT SEA ISLAND GOLF CLUB

100 Retreat Ave., St. Simons Island,
912-638-3611, 888-732-4752; www.seaisland.com

Generations of privileged travelers have made Sea Island their top vacation destination. Created in the spirit of European sporting estates, this resort features first-rate tennis and equestrian facilities, three championship golf courses and tastefully decorated accommodations with private balconies. 40 rooms. Complimentary continental breakfast. Wireless Internet access. Three restaurants, two bars. Fitness room, fitness classes available, spa. Beach. Whirlpool. Golf, 36 holes. Tennis. Business center.

★★★THE LODGE ON LITTLE ST. SIMONS ISLAND

1000 Hampton Point Drive, St. Simons Island, 912-638-7472, 888-733-5774;
www.littlestsimonsisland.com

This small inn is a collection of five cottages and 15 rooms vested in preserving the natural wilderness. The inn offers comfortable lodging and fine restaurants, plus a great view of the surrounding flora and fauna. 15 rooms. Restaurant. $$$$

★★SEA PALMS GOLF & TENNIS RESORT

5445 Frederica Road, St. Simons Island, 912-638-3351, 800-841-6268;
www.seapalms.com

140 rooms. Two restaurants, bar. Fitness center. Swimming pool. Tennis court. Airport transportation available. $$

RESTAURANTS

★BENNIE'S RED BARN

5514 Frederica Road, St. Simons Island, 912-638-2844; www.benniesredbarn.com

Seafood and American menu. Dinner. Bar. Children's menu. $$

FORT FREDERICA NATIONAL MONUMENT

Fort Frederica marked the southern boundary of British Colonial North America. Georgia founder General James Oglethorpe placed the site of the fort on a bluff commanding the Frederica River, then returned to England and helped select families to build and settle it. Forty-four men and 72 women and children landed at St. Simons Island on March 16, 1736. Two years later 650 British soldiers arrived to strengthen the settlement and build the fort, which surrounded the entire town. Oglethorpe used Fort Frederica as a command post for his invasion of Florida against the Spanish and in July 1742 held off the Spanish in the ambush at Bloody marsh and ending Spanish attempts to gain control of Georgia.

Frederica flourished as a military town until after the peace of 1748. With the withdrawal of the regiment the following year, the shopkeepers and tradesmen at Frederica had to move elsewhere. Archaeological excavations have exposed some of the original town, and stabilization work has been done by the National Park Service. Outdoor exhibits make it easy to visualize the town as it was, and the visitor center has exhibits, touch computers and a film dealing with its life and history. Daily. Information: St. Simons Island; www.nps.gov/fofr

★BROGEN'S SOUTH

504 Beachview Drive, Simons Island, 912-638-1109; www.brogens.com
American menu. Lunch, dinner. Closed Sunday, October-April. Bar. Outdoor seating. **$$**

★★CHELSEA

1226 Ocean Blvd., St. Simons Island, 912-638-2047; www.chelsea-stsimons.com
Seafood and American menu. Dinner. Bar. Children's menu. **$$**

★★J. MAC'S

407 Mallory St., St. Simons Island, 912-634-0403;
www.jmacsislandrestaurant.com
Seafood menu. Dinner. Closed Sunday. Bar. **$**

SAVANNAH

Savannah has a wealth of history and architecture that few American cities can match. Savannah natives pride themselves on their Southern charm and hospitality. Famous Southern chef Paula Deen hails from Savannah, and author John Berendt gave the rest of the country a taste of the city's allure in his 1990s novel (and later movie) *Midnight in the Garden of Good and Evil.*

The city's many rich, green parks—it has 16 in the historic district alone—are blooming legacies of the brilliance of its founder, General James E. Oglethorpe, who landed at Yamacraw Bluff with 120 settlers on February 12, 1733. His plan for the colony was to make the "inner city" spacious, beautiful and all that a city should be. Savannah quickly took its place as a leading city first in the settling of America and later in the wealth and grandeur of the Old South as the leading market and shipping point for tobacco and cotton.

Reconstruction was painful, but 20 years after the Civil War, Cotton was king again. Surrounding pine forests produced lumber and resins. The Cotton and Naval Stores Exchange was launched in 1882 when financiers and brokers strode the streets with confidence. By the 20th century, Savannah turned to manufacturing. With more than 200 industries by World War II, the city's prosperity has been measured by the activity of its port, which included shipbuilding booms during both world wars. Today more than 1,400 historically and architecturally significant buildings have been restored in Savannah's historic district, making it one of the largest urban historic landmark districts in the country. Fountains, small gardens, intricate ironwork and other amazing architectural details decorate this town and add to its beauty. Another area, the Victorian district south of the historic district, offers some of the best examples of post-Civil War Victorian architecture in the country.

Information: Savannah Area Convention and Visitors Bureau,
101 E. Bay St., 912-944-0455; www.savcvb.com

WHAT TO SEE AND DO
ANDREW LOW HOUSE

329 Abercorn St., Savannah, 912-233-6854; www.andrewlowhouse.com
Built for Andrew Low (circa 1848), this was later the residence of Juliette Gordon Low, founder of Girl Scouts of America. Period furnishings. Monday-Wednesday, Friday-Saturday 10 a.m.-4:30 p.m., Sunday 12-4:30 p.m. Closed Thursday and major holidays.

67

GEORGIA

CHRIST EPISCOPAL CHURCH

28 Bull St., Savannah, 912-234-4131; www.christchurchsavannah.org

The mother church of Georgia, the congregation dates from 1733. Among early rectors were John Wesley and George Whitfield. The present church is the third building erected on this site. Tuesday and Friday, limited hours.

CITY HALL

Bull and Bay streets, Savannah, 912-651-6410; www.ci.savannah.ga.us

A gold dome tops the four-story neoclassic façade of this 1905 building, which replaced the original 1799 structure. A tablet outside commemorates the sailing of the *SS Savannah*. A model is displayed in the Council Chamber. Another tablet is dedicated to the *John Randolph*, the first iron-sided vessel launched in American waters Monday-Friday.

COLONIAL PARK CEMETERY

E. Oglethorpe Ave. and Abercorn St., Savannah, 912-651-6843; www.savannahga.gov

This was the colony's first and only burial ground for many years. Button Gwinnett, a signer of the Declaration of Independence, is buried in cemetery, as are other distinguished Georgians. Closed since 1853, it has been a city park since 1896.

DAVENPORT HOUSE

324 E. State St., Savannah, 912-236-8097;
www.davenporthousemuseum.org

Constructed by master builder Isaiah Davenport, this is one of the finest examples of Federal architecture in Savannah (1815-1820). Saved from demolition in 1955 by the Historic Savannah Foundation, it is now restored and furnished with period antiques. Gardens. Monday-Saturday 10 a.m.-4 p.m., Sunday 1-4.p.m.

GREEN-MELDRIM HOUSE

1 W. Macon St., Savannah, 912-233-3845;
www.stjohnssav.org

Antebellum house used by General Sherman during occupation of Savannah (1864-1865) is now Parish House of St. John's Church. Tours. Tuesday and Thursday-Saturday, 10 a.m.-3:30 p.m.

HISTORIC SAVANNAH WATERFRONT AREA

John P. Rousakis Riverfront Plaza, Savannah

Restoration of the riverfront bluff to preserve and stabilize the historic waterfront, including a nine-block brick concourse of parks, studios, museums, shops, restaurants and pubs.

JULIETTE GORDON LOW BIRTHPLACE

10 E. Ogelthorpe Ave., Savannah, 912-233-4501;
www.girlscouts.org-who/we_are/birthplace

This restored Regency town house was the birthplace of the founder of Girl Scouts of the USA in 1860. Many original Gordon family pieces. Garden restored to Victorian period. Monday-Tuesday, Thursday-Saturday 10 a.m.-4 p.m., Sunday 11 a.m.-4 p.m.

★
★
★
★
★

LAUREL GROVE CEMETERY (SOUTH)

37th St., Ogeechee Road, Savannah, www.savannahga.gov

Possibly the oldest black cemetery currently in use; graves of both antebellum slave and free blacks. Andrew Bryan (1716-1812), a pioneer Baptist preacher, is buried here. Daily 8 a.m.-5 p.m.

OWENS-THOMAS HOUSE

124 Abercorn St., Savannah, 912-233-9743; www.telfair.org

Authentically furnished Regency-style house designed between 1816 and 1819 by William Jay. Walled garden is designed and planted in 1820s style. Tuesday-Saturday 10 a.m.-5 p.m., Sunday 1-5 p.m.; Monday 12-5 p.m. Closed January.

SAVANNAH HISTORY MUSEUM

303 Martin Luther King Jr. Blvd., Savannah,
912-651-6825; www.chsgeorgia.org/shm

This 19th-century railroad shed was renovated to house historical orientation center. Mural in the lobby chronicles major events in Savannah's 250-year history. Monday-Friday 8:30 a.m.-5 p.m., Saturday-Sunday 9 a.m.-5 p.m.

TRUSTEES' GARDEN SITE

10 E. Broad St., Savannah, 912-443-3277; www.trusteesgarden.com

Original site of 10-acre experimental garden modeled in 1733 after the Chelsea Gardens in London. Peach trees planted in the garden launched Georgia's peach industry. The Pirates' House, a former inn for visiting seamen, has been restored and is now a restaurant. Robert Louis Stevenson referred to the inn in *Treasure Island*.

U.S. CUSTOMS HOUSE

1-5 E. Bay St., Savannah

Erected in 1850 on the site of the colony's first public building. The granite columns' carved capitals were modeled from tobacco leaves. Tablet on Bull Street marks the site where John Wesley preached his first Savannah sermon; tablet on Bay Street marks the site of Oglethorpe's headquarters.

GEORGIA

★
★
★
★
★

SPECIAL EVENTS

SAVANNAH SCOTTISH GAMES AND HIGHLAND GATHERING

J.F. Gregory Park, Highway 144, Richmond Hill;
www.savannahscottishgames.com

Clans gather for a weekend of Highland games, piping, drumming, dancing and the traditional "Kirkin' o' the Tartans." Early May.

SAVANNAH SEAFOOD FESTIVAL

404 E. Bay St., Savannah, 912-234-0295; www.riverstreetsavannah.com

Restaurants sell samples, entertainment, arts and crafts. October 31-November 2.

SAVANNAH TOUR OF HOMES AND GARDENS

18 Abercorn St., Savannah, 912-234-8054; www.savannahtourofhomes.org

Sponsored by Christ Episcopal Church with Historic Savannah Foundation. Day and candlelight tours of more than 30 private houses and gardens. March.

ST. PATRICK'S DAY PARADE

912-233-4804; www.savannahsaintpatricksday.com

This parade rivals the one in New York City in size. Route runs north of Jones Street to the river, west of East Broad Street, east of Boundary Street and the Talmadge Bridge. March.

HOTELS

★★★17 HUNDRED 90 INN AND RESTAURANT

307 E. President St., Savannah, 912-236-7122, 800-487-1790;
www.17hundred90.com

Savannah's oldest inn features 14 rooms furnished with antiques and fireplaces. The inn also has an excellent restaurant. Restaurant, bar. Complimentary continental breakfast. **$$**

★★COURTYARD SAVANNAH MIDTOWN

6703 Abercorn St., Savannah, 912-354-7878,
888-832-0327; www.courtyard.com

144 rooms. Restaurant, bar. Pets not accepted. Internet access. **$**

★★DAYS INN

201 W. Bay St., Savannah, 912-236-4440, 800-329-7466; www.daysinn.com

257 rooms. Restaurant. Business center. Internet access. Pool. **$**

★★★EAST BAY INN

225 E. Bay St., Savannah, 912-238-1225, 800-500-1225; www.eastbayinn.com

Just steps away from the historic waterfront, this romantic inn has many beautiful rooms filled with period furnishings and antiques. Cheese and wine reception every evening. 28 rooms. Restaurant. Complimentary continental breakfast. Internet access. **$$**

★★★HILTON SAVANNAH DE SOTO

15 E. Liberty St., Savannah, 912-232-9000, 800-774-1500; www.hilton.com

This fully equipped hotel is close to shops, sightseeing and restaurants. The hotel, built in the 1890s, has a rooftop pool and fine-dining restaurant. 246 rooms. Restaurant, bar. Internet access. Business center. Airport transportation available. Pets accepted. **$$**

★★★HYATT REGENCY SAVANNAH

2 W. Bay St., Savannah, 912-238-1234; www.hyatt.com

Perched on the scenic waterfront of the Savannah River, this hotel offers superb accommodations, first-class amenities and an attentive staff. 351 rooms, Restaurant, bar. Internet access. Business center. **$**

★★★MARRIOTT SAVANNAH RIVERFRONT

100 General McIntosh Blvd., Savannah,
912-233-7722, 800-228-9200; www.marriott.com

Adjacent to the world-renowned River Street and the historic riverfront, this hotel makes for a truly delightful stay. Inside are handsomely appointed accommodations. A stroll along the hotel's riverwalk leads to taverns, quaint shops and great restaurants. 341 rooms. Restaurant, bar. Internet access. Pets not accepted. **$$**

★★★THE PRESIDENT'S QUARTERS INN

225 E. President St., Savannah,
912-233-1600, 800-233-1776; www.presidentsquarters.com

Once a place where diplomats and generals rested their heads, The President's Quarters now opens its doors to guests of all stripes. Feel like royalty relaxing in the elegantly appointed parlors or strolling through the renowned gardens. 16 rooms. Restaurant. Complimentary full breakfast. Internet access. **$$**

★★★RIVER STREET INN

124 E. Bay St., Savannah, 912-234-6400, 800-253-4229; www.riverstreetinn.com

Rooms have four-poster beds and French balconies and offer views of the Savannah River. Wine and appetizers are served in the afternoon, homemade chocolates are delivered to rooms in the evening. 86 rooms. Restaurant, bar. **$$**

★★★THE WESTIN SAVANNAH HARBOR GOLF RESORT AND SPA

1 Resort Drive, Savannah, 912-201-2000, 800-937-8461; www.westin.com

Just a water taxi ride away from the historic district, resort features include a PGA-tour quality golf course, full-service spa, waterfront pools, four tennis courts and access to fishing charter boats. 403 rooms. Restaurant, bar. Internet access. Business center. Children's activity center. Spa. Children's pool, whirlpool. Airport transportation available. **$$**

SPECIALTY LODGINGS
BALLASTONE INN & TOWNHOUSE

14 E. Oglethorpe Ave., Savannah, 912-236-1484, 800-822-4553;
www.ballastone.com

One of Savannah's first bed and breakfasts, the Inn is set in a 160-year-old mansion. Voted annually by locals as the best romantic getaway in Savannah. 16 rooms. Complimentary full breakfast. Children over 16 years only. **$$**

BED & BREAKFAST INN

117 W. Gordon St., Savannah,
912-238-0518, 888-238-0518; www.savannahbnb.com

Restored 1853 Federal town house in the Historic District. 15 rooms. Complimentary full breakfast. Internet access. **$**

ELIZA THOMPSON HOUSE

5 W. Jones St., Savannah, 912-236-3620,
800-348-9378; www.elizathompsonhouse.com

Elegantly restored and recently refurbished, rooms offer quiet and comfortable surroundings. 25 rooms. Complimentary full breakfast. Internet access. **$$**

FOLEY HOUSE INN

14 W. Hull St., Savannah, 912-232-6622, 800-647-3708; www.foleyinn.com

Located in the heart of historic Savannah, this inn has been serving guests since the Civil War. Made up of two restored mansions facing Chippewa Square. 19 rooms. Complimentary full breakfast. Spa. **$$**

★
★
★
★
★

THE GASTONIAN

220 E. Gaston St., Savannah, 912-232-2869, 800-322-6603; www.gastonian.com

17 rooms. Children over 12 years only. Complimentary full breakfast. Whirlpool. **$$$**

OLDE HARBOUR INN

508 E. Factors Walk, Savannah, 912-234-4100, 800-553-6533;
www.oldeharbourinn.com

24 rooms. Complimentary continental breakfast. Pets accepted, fee. **$$**

RESTAURANTS

★★17 HUNDRED 90 INN & RESTAURANT

307 E. President St., Savannah, 912-236-7122; www.17hundred90.com

International menu. Lunch, dinner. Bar. Casual attire. **$$$**

★★BELFORD'S

313 W. St. Julian St., Savannah, 912-233-2626; www.belfordssavannah.com

American menu. Breakfast, lunch, dinner, Sunday brunch. Bar. Children's menu. Casual attire. Reservations recommended. Outdoor seating. **$$**

★★BISTRO SAVANNAH

309 W. Congress St., Savannah, 912-233-6266

American menu, Seafood menu. Dinner. Bar. Casual attire. **$$$**

★★CHART HOUSE

202 W. Bay St., Savannah, 912-234-6686; www.chart-house.com

Seafood, steak menu. Dinner. Bar. Children's menu. Casual attire. Outdoor seating. **$$**

★★★ELIZABETH ON 37TH

105 E. 37th St., Savannah, 912-236-5547; www.elizabethon37th.net

Opened in 1981 by chef Elizabeth Terry and her husband, Michael, this charming restaurant is the birthplace of New Southern cuisine. The interior of the 1900 Greek Revival-style mansion has a homey feel with brightly painted walls, antique chairs and warm service. Fresh and authentic cuisine (Terry extensively researched 18th- and 19th-century Savannah cooking) draws admiration from across the country. American menu. Dinner. Closed last two weeks of August. Casual attire. **$$$**

★★GARIBALDI'S CAFÉ

315 W. Congress St., Savannah, 912-232-7118; www.garibaldisavannah.com

Seafood menu. Dinner. Bar. Casual attire. Former Germania firehouse in historic district. **$$$**

★JOHNNY HARRIS

1651 E. Victory Drive, Savannah, 912-354-7810,
888-547-2823; www.johnnyharris.com

American menu. Lunch, dinner. Closed Sunday. Bar. Children's menu. Casual attire. **$$**

★MOON RIVER BREWING CO.

21 W. Bay St., Savannah, 912-447-0943; www.moonriverbrewing.com
American menu. Lunch, dinner. Bar. Children's menu. Casual attire. **$$**

★★MRS. WILKES' DINING ROOM

107 W. Jones St., Savannah, 912-232-5997; www.mrswilkes.com
American menu. Lunch. Closed Saturday-Sunday. Casual attire. **$**

★★OLDE PINK HOUSE

23 Abercorn St., Savannah, 912-232-4286
American menu. Dinner. Bar. Children's menu. Casual attire. **$$**

★★RIVER HOUSE

125 W. River St., Savannah, 912-234-1900, 800-317-1912;
www.riverhouseseafood.com
Seafood menu. Lunch, dinner. Bar. Children's menu. Casual attire. **$$**

SEA ISLAND

This exclusive island retreat was created in the 1920s by Hudson Motor Company magnate Howard Coffin. The first hotel to open on the island was the Cloisters, which underwent an extensive and impressive multimillion dollar renovation in 2006. The outstanding golf courses have also been renovated. The small and luxurious Lodge at Sea Island offers an intimate 40-room retreat.
Information: www.seaisland.com

HOTEL
★★★★★THE CLOISTER

100 First St., Sea Island, 912-634-3964; www.cloister.com
This 80-year-old resort recently underwent an impressive $350 million renovation, including the addition of a magnificent spa. Wood-beamed rooms are now decorated with rich, jewel-toned Turkish rugs and plush, pillow-topped beds. Restaurants include a casual raw bar and grill, where after-beach oysters and cocktails are the specialty. 212 rooms. Restaurants, bar. Complimentary continental breakfast. Wireless Internet access. Children's activity center. Spa and fitness center. Whirlpool. Golf, 54 holes. Airport transportation available. **$$$$**

RESTAURANT
★★★COLT & ALISON

The Lodge at Sea Island, 100 First St., Sea Island, 800-732-4752;
www.seaisland.com
After working up an appetite on Sea Island Resort's renowned 18 holes, take a seat at the steakhouse named after the golf course's creators: Colt & Allison. Nestled in the Lodge, the restaurant is a cozy backdrop for a scrumptious meal, enjoyed at the fireside tables and leather chairs. Foodies will fill their bellies with classic Caesar salads, filet mignon au poivre and Bananas Foster all prepared tableside. Colt & Allison stays true to its Southern roots with family style comfort food, decadent desserts and wine from the resort's extensive cellar. American, steakhouse menu. Dinner, Sunday brunch. **$$$$**

GEORGIA

★
★
★
★
★

★★★★★THE GEORGIAN ROOM
100 First St., Sea Island, 800-732-4752; www.seaisland.com

The magnificent Georgian Room is tucked inside the Cloister. The décor is stunningly grand, with bas-relief details, gilded chandeliers and a carved stone fireplace. Tables are set with crisp white linens, hand-painted china and silver flatware. Dishes highlight seasonal, fresh ingredients and might include butter-poached sea bass with frog's leg confit and herb dumplings, or succulent kobe beef filet with smoked morel mushrooms. Vegetarian dishes are available. Staff is polished and attentive. A gorgeous private dining room for up to 10 guests makes special events even more memorable. Continental cuisine. Dinner. Jacket and tie required. Reservations required. **$$$$**

SPA

★★★★★THE CLOISTER SPA
100 First St., Sea Island, 912-638-3611, 888-732-4752; www.seaisland.com

Recently renovated, the Spa at Sea Island focuses on customization, with 26 treatment rooms dedicated to an extensive menu of offerings. Spa guides design an experience for guests that may include anything from nutritional consultations to body work, baths, wraps and energy treatments. Turkish and Japanese baths personify the spa's simple approach, with the signature bathing ritual with a seven-step infusion of ginger grass and cherry blossom rice body polishes. A special KidSpa program for spagoers ages 8-15 promotes healthy skin care and includes kid-friendly massages, sports and nature hikes.

STATESBORO

This quaint town is home to Georgia Southern University, as well as a huge water park, which is popular with families.

Information: Convention and Visitors Bureau, 322 S. Main St.,
912-489-1869; www.visit-statesboro.com

WHAT TO SEE AND DO

GEORGIA SOUTHERN UNIVERSITY
Highway 301 S., Statesboro, 912-681-5611; www.georgiasouthern.edu

The campus has 14,000 students. For visitors there is an art department gallery. Museum: Monday-Friday; closed holidays; Planetarium: by appointment; Botanical garden: daily.

HOTEL

★★★HISTORIC STATESBORO INN
106 S. Main St., Statesboro, 912-489-8628, 800-846-9466;
www.statesboroinn.com

This country inn has a comfortable and stylish atmosphere and surroundings. Rich in local history, it offers elegant dining featuring a menu of seasonal favorites with Southern flavors. 17 rooms. Restaurant. Complimentary full breakfast. Pets accepted. **$**

THOMASVILLE

This small town near the Florida border has been a resort destination for those wishing to escape winter weather since the 1800s.

Information: Welcome Center, 135 N. Broad St., 229-227-7099;
www.thomasvillega.com

WHAT TO SEE AND DO

PEBBLE HILL PLANTATION

1251 Highway, 319 S., Thomasville, 229-226-2344; www.pebblehill.com

This historic plantation dates from the 1820s. Elaborate Greek Revival house furnished with art, antiques, porcelains, crystal, silver and Native American relics belonging to the Hanna family of Ohio, who rebuilt the house, guest houses, stables and garages after a fire in the 1930s. Gardens; livestock. Wagon rides; tours Tuesday-Saturday 10 a.m.-5 p.m., Sunday 1-5 p.m. Must be over 6 years of age.

THOMAS COUNTY MUSEUM OF HISTORY

725 N. Dawson St., Thomasville, 229-226-7664; www.thomascountyhistory.org

Five buildings on the property include a log house with period furnishings; an 1877 frame house furnished in middle-class fashion of that period; an 1893 Victorian bowling alley; a garage housing historic vehicles; and a 1920s mansion, which houses the main museum. Photographs, period costumes, artifacts. Closed last two weeks in August. Monday-Saturday 10 a.m.-12 p.m. and 2-4 p.m. Closed Sunday.

THOMASVILLE CULTURAL CENTER

600 E. Washington St., Thomasville, 229-226-0588;
www.thomasvilleculturalcenter.com

A center for visual and performing arts. Facilities include art galleries with permanent and changing exhibits, children's room and 550-seat auditorium. Concerts, musicals, children's programs, art classes and other programs are offered. Galleries, building tours Monday-Friday 9 a.m.-5 p.m., Saturday 1-5 p.m.

HOTEL

★★★MELHANA THE GRAND PLANTATION

301 Showboat Lane, Thomasville, 229-226-2290, 888-920-3030; www.melhana.com

Built on the grounds of an historic plantation, this resort has an indoor pool, tennis courts, horseback riding and a wide assortment of leisure activities. 33 rooms. Restaurant, bar. Complimentary full breakfast. Children's activity center. Airport transportation available. $$

SPECIALTY LODGINGS

1884 PAXTON HOUSE INN

445 Remington Ave., Thomasville, 229-226-5197;
www.1884paxtonhouseinn.com

This Victorian mansion is a great base for exploring the history and beauty of Thomasville. Nine rooms. Complimentary full breakfast. Children over 12 years only. $$

GEORGIA

★
★
★
★
★

SERENDIPITY COTTAGE

339 E. Jefferson St., Thomasville, 229-225-8394, 800-383-7377;
www.serendipitycottage.com

Four rooms. Complimentary full breakfast. Children over 12 years only. **$**

RESTAURANT

★★PLAZA RESTAURANT

217 S. Broad St., Thomasville, 229-226-5153; www.thomasvilleplaza.com

Greek, American menu. Breakfast, lunch, dinner Monday-Saturday and Sunday Brunch.
Bar. Children's menu. **$$**

TYBEE ISLAND

This popular year-round Georgia resort is essentially a V-shaped sandbar front-
ing the Atlantic for nearly four miles and the Savannah River for more than two
miles. The beach runs the entire length of the island. Its north end is marked by old
coastal defenses, a museum and a lighthouse at the tip. Reached by a causeway from
Savannah and Highway 80, the beach has a boardwalk, fishing pier, amusements,
hotels, motels and vacation cottages.

Information: Savannah Area Convention and Visitors Bureau,
101 E. Bay St., 877-728-2662; www.tybeeisland.com

WHAT TO SEE AND DO

TYBEE MUSEUM AND LIGHTHOUSE

30 Meddin Drive, Tybee Island, 912-786-5801; www.tybeelighthouse.org

The lighthouse is one of the oldest active lighthouses in the U.S. Visitors may climb
to the top for a scenic view of Tybee and historic Fort Reven. A museum tracing the
history of Tybee from colonial times to 1845 is housed in a coastal artillery battery
built in 1898. Exhibits and gift shop in 1880s lighthouse keeper's cottage. Open every
day, except Tuesday, 9 a.m.-5:30 p.m.

VALDOSTA

When local citizens discovered that surveyors had left the town off the railroad right-
of-way, they lost no time moving the town four miles east of the original community
(then called Troupville), and the town developed into a rail center with seven branch
lines. Such industrious enterprise still defines the area—Valdosta is one of Georgia's
most prosperous small cities. Today products include timber, tobacco and cattle. Tour-
ism is also a big industry given the large wooded area and numerous lakes nearby.
Moody Air Force Base is 12 miles to the north.

Information: Chamber of Commerce, 416 N. Ashley St., Valdosta,
229-247-8100; www.valdostachamber.com

WHAT TO SEE AND DO

BARBER HOUSE

416 N. Ashley St., Valdosta, 229-247-8100;
www.valdostachamber.com

Restored 1915 neo-Classical house serves as offices for Valdosta-Lowndes County
Chamber of Commerce; elaborate woodwork, original light fixtures and furniture.
Self-guided tours. Monday-Friday 8:30 a.m.-5 p.m.

★
★
★
★
★

CONVERSE DALTON FERRELL HOUSE

305 N Patterson St., Valdosta, 229-244-8575; www.vjsl.org/house.asp

This 1902 neo-Classical house has a wide two-story porch that wraps around the front and two sides. The interior has 20-foot ceilings, 14-foot high-pocket doors, golden-oak woodwork and some original light fixtures. By appointment only, contact the Convention and Visitors Center.

LOWNDES COUNTY HISTORICAL SOCIETY MUSEUM

305 W. Central Ave., Valdosta, 229-247-4780; www.valdostamuseum.org

Originally a Carnegie library, now contains collection of artifacts from Civil War to present; genealogical library. Monday-Friday 10 a.m.-5 p.m. Saturday 10 a.m.-2 p.m.

HOTELS

★★BEST WESTERN KING OF THE ROAD

1403 N. St. Augustine Road, Valdosta, 229-244-7600, 800-780-7234;
www.bestwestern.com

137 rooms. Restaurant, bar. Complimentary continental breakfast. High-speed Internet access. Pool. Airport transportation available. Free parking. **$**

★COMFORT INN

2101 W. Hill Ave., Valdosta, 229-242-1212, 877-424-6423;
www.comfortinnvaldosta.com

137 rooms. Bar. Complimentary continental breakfast. Free Wireless Internet access. Airport transportation available. **$**

★HAMPTON INN

1705 Gornto Road, Valdosta, 229-244-8800, 800-426-7866;
www.hamptoninn.com

102 rooms. Complimentary continental breakfast. High-speed Internet access. Business center. Pool. Pets not accepted. **$**

★LA QUINTA INN AND SUITES

1800 Club House Drive, Valdosta, 229-247-7755,
800-642-4271; www.laquinta.com

121 rooms. Complimentary continental breakfast. Fitness center. Spa. Pool. Pets accepted. Free parking. **$**

RESTAURANTS

★★CHARLIE TRIPPER'S

4479 N. Valdosta Road, Valdosta, 229-247-0366; www.charlie-trippers.com

American menu. Dinner. Closed Sunday-Monday. Bar. **$$$**

★★MOM & DAD'S

4143 N. Valdosta Road, Valdosta, 229-333-0848

Italian menu. Dinner. Closed Sunday-Monday. Bar. Children's menu. **$$**

GEORGIA

WARM SPRINGS

President Franklin D. Roosevelt visited this quaint town in the 1920s after he was stricken by polio because the area's natural mineral springs were said to heal ailments. He built a house here and is thought to have crafted his plan for the New Deal while staying in Warm Springs. The pools Roosevelt visited are now part of the Roosevelt Warm Springs Institute for Rehabilitation.

Information: www.warmspringsga.com

LITTLE WHITE HOUSE HISTORIC SITE

401 Little White House Road, Warm Springs, 706-655-5870;
www.gastateparks.org

President Franklin D. Roosevelt died here on April 12, 1945. Original furniture, memorabilia and the portrait on which Elizabeth Shoumatoff was working on when the president was stricken with a massive cerebral hemorrhage are on display. A film about Roosevelt's life at Warm Springs and in Georgia is shown at the F. D. Roosevelt Museum and Theater. Daily 9 a.m.-4:45 p.m.

RESTAURANT
★★BULLOCH HOUSE

47 Bulloch St., Warm Springs, 706-655-9068;
www.thebullochhouse.com

American menu. Lunch, dinner Friday-Saturday. Children's menu. Outdoor seating. House built in 1892; original floors and fireplaces. **$**

WAYCROSS

The name Waycross reflects the town's strategic location at the intersection of nine railroads and five highways. Situated at the edge of the Okefenokee Swamp, the town's early settlers put up blockhouses to protect themselves from local Native Americans. The production of naval stores and the fur sales were the main industry before Okefenokee became a national wildlife refuge. Today the economy of Waycross is based on a timber, railroad and tourism.

Information: Tourism and Conference Bureau, 317 Plant Ave., Waycross,
912-283-3742; www.swampgeorgia.com

WHAT TO SEE AND DO
OKEFENOKEE HERITAGE CENTER

1460 N. Augusta Ave., Waycross, 912-285-4260;
www.okefenokeeheritagecenter.org

Exhibits on Okefenokee area history. Native Americans of Southern Georgia; 1912 train depot and railroad cars; turn-of-the-century print shop; nature trails; Power House building; 1840s pioneer house. Tuesday-Saturday 10 a.m.-5 p.m., Sunday 1 p.m.

SOUTHERN FOREST WORLD

1440 N. Augusta Ave., Waycross, 912-285-4056;
www.brantleycountychamber.org/sfworld.htm

Exhibits, with audiovisual displays, detail the development and history of forestry in the South; logging locomotive, 38-foot model of a loblolly pine, giant cypress tree. Nature trails. Tuesday-Saturday.

HOTEL

★★HOLIDAY INN

1725 Memorial Drive, Waycross, 912-283-4490, 800-315-2621; www.holidayinn.com

142 rooms. Restaurant, bar. Complimentary full breakfast. High-speed Internet access. Fitness center. Pool. Airport transportation available. **$**

★
★
★
★
★

NORTH CAROLINA

NORTH CAROLINA HAS THREE DISTINCTIVE REGIONS: THE COAST, THE HEARTLAND AND the mountains, each with its own regional capital and featured attractions. From bluegrass music and mountain hiking in Asheville to Atlantic beaches a quick drive from Wilmington and the cultural and business centers surrounding the capital city, Raleigh, the state is diverse.

In 1585, the first English settlement was unsuccessfully started on Roanoke Island. Another attempt at settlement was made in 1587, but the colony disappeared, leaving only the crudely ratched word "CROATOAN" on a tree—perhaps referring to the Croatan Indians living in the area. To this day historians and archaeologists are still trying to solve the mystery of "The Lost Colony." Eventually English settlers moving south from Virginia founded farms in the North Carolina territory, and even today, the state produces two-thirds of the nation's flue-cured tobacco, as well as cotton, peanuts and vegetables. Pine tar and turpentine were other early commodities produced in North Carolina and thus responsible for the "Tar Heels" moniker given to the people of North Carolina and was adopted as the mascot for the University of North Carolina. Tales of the exact origins of the nickname are varied (and not always complimentary) but North Carolinians like to say it refers to their ability to persevere. It's said North Carolina troops fighting in the Civil War would stand their ground in battle as though stuck with "tar on their heels."

Individualist and democratic from the beginning, this state refused to ratify the Constitution until the Bill of Rights had been added. In 1860, its Western citizens strongly supported the Union, and the North Carolina did not join the Confederate States of America until after Fort Sumter was attacked. Tobacco helped the state recover during Reconstruction and remains a major crop, but mountain communities are also famous for their furniture-making centers. For sports fans, North Carolina delivers with two perennial basketball powerhouses, Duke University and the University of North Carolina at Chapel Hill (Michael Jordan's alma mater). Top-ranking golf courses crisscross the state, and 70 miles of the Appalachian Trail extends along North Carolina's border. For vacationers, this realism translates into a wealth of things to do.

Information: www.visitnc.com

★ **FUN FACTS**

The Wright brothers made the first flight of an airplane at Kitty Hawk in 1903.

"To be rather than to seem" is the North Carolina state motto.

ASHEVILLE

Asheville has gained a reputation as a charming vacation destination in the Blue Ridge Mountains. George W. Vanderbilt built his mansion here in the 1890s, and the house and winery attract scores of visitors each year. Asheville is the North Carolina city closest to the Great Smoky Mountains National Park and is also the headquarters for the Uwharrie National Forest, Pisgah National Forest, Nantahala National Forest and Croatan National Forest.

Information: Convention and Visitors Bureau, 151 Haywood St., 828-258-6101, 800-257-1300; www.exploreasheville.com

WHAT TO SEE AND DO

ASHEVILLE ART MUSEUM

Two South Pack Square, Asheville, 828-253-3227; www.ashevilleart.org

Permanent collection and changing exhibits. Tuesday-Saturday 10 a.m.-5 p.m., Friday until 8 p.m., Sunday 15 p.m.

BILTMORE ESTATE

1 Approach Road, Asheville, 828-255-1333, 800-411-3812; www.biltmore.com

The 8,000-acre country estate includes 75 acres of formal gardens, numerous varieties of azaleas and roses and the 250-room chateau, which is the largest house ever built in the New World. Eighty-five rooms are open for viewing. In the 1890s, George W. Vanderbilt commissioned Richard Morris Hunt to design the house, which took five years to build. Vanderbilt also employed Gifford Pinchot, later governor of Pennsylvania and famous for forestry and conservation achievements, to manage his forests. Biltmore was the site of the first U.S. forestry school. Tours of the estate include gardens, conservatory and winery facilities. Four restaurants on grounds; wine tasting. Guidebook is recommended. Daily.

BOTANICAL GARDENS AT ASHEVILLE

151 WT Weaver Blvd., Asheville, 828-252-5190; www.ashevillebotanicalgardens.org

A 10-acre tract with thousands of flowers, trees and shrubs native to southern Appalachia; 125-year-old "dog trot" log cabin, on the campus of the Asheville branch of the University of North Carolina. Daily dawn-dusk. Visitor center, gift shop. March-mid-November daily 9:30 a.m.-4 p.m.

CHIMNEY ROCK PARK

Highway 64-74A, Asheville, 828-625-9611, 800-277-9611; www.chimneyrockpark.com

The towering granite monolith Chimney Rock affords a 75-mile view. Four hiking trails lead to the 404-foot Hickory Nut Falls, Moonshiner's Cave, Devil's Head balancing rock and Nature's Showerbath. Trails, stairs and catwalks, picnic areas, playground, nature center, observation lounge with snack bar, gift shop. 26-story elevator shaft through granite. Daily 8:30 a.m.-6 p.m., weather permitting.

FOLK ART CENTER

382 Blue Ridge Parkway, Asheville, 828-298-7928; www.southernhighlandguild.org

Home of the Southern Highland Craft Guild. Stone and timber structure, and the Blue Ridge Parkway info center; craft exhibits, demonstrations, workshops, related programs. Daily.

THOMAS WOLFE MEMORIAL

52 N. Market, Asheville, 828-253-8304; www.wolfememorial.com

The state maintains the Wolfe boardinghouse as a literary shrine, restored and furnished to appear as it did in 1916. Visitor center with exhibit. Tuesday-Saturday 9 a.m.-5 p.m., Sunday 1-5 p.m.

81

NORTH CAROLINA

WALKING IN ASHEVILLE

Asheville is best known for the glamorous Biltmore Estate south of town. By comparison, downtown Asheville seems rather homespun. In fact, its most notorious landmark, the house where the novelist Thomas Wolfe grew up, is positively down at the heels, preserved that way to remain true to its description in Wolfe's famous novel, *Look Homeward, Angel*, a thinly disguised portrait of Asheville. Yet that appeal makes Asheville a prominent retirement destination as well as a worthy weekend retreat. Look for live music and theater and gallery shopping from the thriving arts community.

The heart of downtown Asheville is Pack Square at the intersection of Broadway and Patton Avenue. City Hall, a library and Pack Place, which contains a variety of museums, performing arts venues, galleries and shops, can all be found there. Nearby is the mineral and gem museum. The YMI Cultural Center highlights African-American history.

The southwest corner of the square holds the statue of an angel, looking homeward, marking the spot where the angel appears in Wolfe's famous story. This was also the site of the stonecutting shop once run by Wolfe's father. Head two blocks north to Walnut Street, turn east on Walnut, then north again on Spruce to find the Thomas Wolfe National Historic Site, where Wolfe lived from 1900 to 1920, known locally as the Old Kentucky Home.

★
★
★
★
★

ZEBULON B. VANCE BIRTHPLACE STATE HISTORIC SITE

911 Reems Creek Road, Weaverville, 828-645-6706; www.nchistoricsites.org

Log house (reconstructed in 1961) and outbuildings on site where Civil War governor of North Carolina lived during childhood. It honors the Vance family, which was deeply involved with the early history of the state. Visitor center, exhibits. Picnic area. April-October, Monday-Friday; rest of year, Tuesday-Friday.

SPECIAL EVENTS

MOUNTAIN DANCE AND FOLK FESTIVAL

2 S. Pack Square, Asheville, 828-257-4530; www.folkheritage.org

Diana Wortham Theater. Folk songs and ballads. The nation's longest running such festival; finest of its kind for devotees of the five-string banjo, gut-string fiddle, clogging and smooth dancing. Early August.

SHAKESPEARE IN THE PARK

246 Cumberland Ave., Asheville, 828-254-5146; www.montfordparkplayers.org

Weekends early June-late August.

HOTELS

★COMFORT SUITES BILTMORE SQUARE MALL

890 Brevard Road, Asheville, 828-665-4000, 877-424-6423; www.comfortsuites.com

125 rooms, all suites. Breakfast. Wireless Internet access. Fitness center. Pool. **$**

★★★CUMBERLAND FALLS BED & BREAKFAST

254 Cumberland Ave., Asheville, 828-253-4085, 888-743-2557;
www.cumberlandfalls.com

When driving up to the tree- and flower-lined house, you'll think you're returning home…if your home had freshly baked treats, a three-course breakfast and a two person whirlpool tub always waiting for you. So basically, the Cumberland Falls Bed and Breakfast is like the home sweet home you always dreamed about, with different themed rooms and an attentive staff to help plan your day and ensure you feel comfortable when you return. Besides included amenities, the innkeeper can help you set up a special surprise, like chocolate covered strawberries and champagne to accompany that Jacuzzi. Six rooms. Wireless Internet access. Children over 10 years only. Complimentary full breakfast. **$$**

★DAYS INN

1435 Tunnel Road, Asheville, 828-298-4000; www.daysinn.com

84 rooms. Complimentary continental breakfast. Wireless Internet access. Heated outdoor pool. Pets accepted. **$**

★★DOUBLETREE HOTEL BILTMORE-ASHEVILLE

115 Hendersonville Road, Asheville, 828-274-1800, 800-222-8733;
www.biltmoreasheville.doubletree.com

160 rooms. Wireless Internet access. Restaurant, bar. Business center. Children's menu. **$$**

★★★THE GROVE PARK INN RESORT & SPA

290 Macon Ave., Asheville, 828-252-2711, 800-438-5800; www.groveparkinn.com

Set in Asheville's Blue Ridge Mountains, guest rooms are decorated in Arts and Crafts style. Choose from the 18-hole Donald Ross-designed golf course, a superb tennis facility or a 40,000-square-foot spa crafted from natural rock which offers a range of special services from hydro bath treatments to flotation body masques. 510 rooms. Six restaurants, two bars. Children's activity center. **$$$**

★★★HAYWOOD PARK HOTEL & PROMENADE

1 Battery Park Ave., Asheville, 828-252-2522, 800-228-2522;
www.haywoodpark.com

This all-suite hotel is decorated with polished brass, warm oak and Spanish marble. Rooms have fine furnishings, a wet bar and a bathroom that features either a garden tub or a Jacuzzi. 33 suites. Restaurants, bar. Wirless Internet access. **$$**

★★★★INN ON BILTMORE ESTATE

1 Anter Hill Road, Asheville, 828-225-1660,
866-336-1240; www.biltmore.com

The Inn on Biltmore Estate provides world-class accommodations on the grounds of an American landmark—the historic Vanderbilt Biltmore Estate. Carriage rides, horseback rides and river float trips are just a few of the unique recreational activities. The hotel's distinguished character extends to its dining establishments—Bistro, Deerpark, the dining room and stable café. 213 rooms. Restaurant, bar. Wireless Internet access. Spa. Airport transportation available. **$$$**

★
★
★
★
★

★★★RENAISSANCE ASHEVILLE HOTEL

31 Woodfin St., Asheville, 828-252-8211, 800-359-7951; www.marriott.com

Centrally located around Asheville's main plaza, this comfortable hotel offers visitors shopping in the nearby mall, a farmers' market and other complexes in the area. Also nearby are art galleries, a civic center and more. 277 rooms. Restaurant, bar. High-speed Internet access. Pets not accepted. **$$**

★★★★RICHMOND HILL INN

87 Richmond Hill Drive, Asheville, 828-252-7313, 800-549-9238;
www.richmondhillinn.com

Once the private home of an influential politician, this Queen Anne-style mansion and croquet cottages are set among nine acres of formal gardens. Rooms and suites are decorated with antiques and have either canopy or four-poster beds. The restaurant, Gabrielle's, is heralded for its Continental menu. 37 rooms. Two restaurants, two bars. Complimentary full breakfast. Wireless Internet access. **$$$**

SPECIALTY LODGINGS

ALBEMARLE INN

86 Edgemont Road, Asheville, 828-255-0027, 800-621-7435;
www.albemarleinn.com

This dramatic, majestic home, with enormous white pillars and manicured gardens, offers guests luxurious rooms, a complimentary breakfast, plus afternoon wine and hors d'oeuvres. 11 rooms. Complimentary full breakfast. Children over 12 years only. **$$**

APPLEWOOD MANOR INN

62 Cumberland Circle, Asheville, 828-254-2244, 800-442-2197;
www.applewoodmanor.com

Colonial turn-of-the-century home built in 1910; antiques. Four rooms. Complimentary full breakfast. Children over 12 years only. **$**

THE BEAUFORT HOUSE VICTORIAN INN

61 N. Liberty St., Asheville, 828-254-8334, 800-261-2221; www.beauforthouse.com

Experience Victorian afternoon tea, gourmet breakfasts and elegant guest rooms in the former home of Charleton Heston. The mansion is surrounded by two acres of landscaped grounds complete with 5,000 flowers. 11 rooms. Complimentary full breakfast. Children over 10 years only. **$**

CEDAR CREST VICTORIAN INN

674 Biltmore Ave., Asheville, 828-252-1389, 877-251-1389; www.cedarcrestinn.com

Dating from 1891, this luxurious mansion has been transformed into a romantic inn that is listed on the National Register of Historic Places. Of particular note is the ornate woodwork on the first floor and the Victorian gardens filled with dogwood and rhodo-dendrons. 12 rooms. Complimentary full breakfast. Children over 10 years only. **$$**

LION AND THE ROSE

276 Montford Ave., Asheville, 828-255-7673, 800-546-6988; www.lion-rose.com

This elegantly restored Georgian mansion is nestled in beautifully landscaped gardens in one of Asheville's historic districts and within walking distance of downtown.

★
★
★
★
★

Decadent complimentary breakfasts are a draw. Five rooms. Wireless Internet access. Children over 12 years only. **$$**

THE OLD REYNOLDS MANSION

100 Reynolds Heights, Asheville, 828-254-0496, 800-709-0496;
www.oldreynoldsmansion.com
Antebellum mansion on a hill overlooking mountains, verandas. 10 rooms. Complimentary full breakfast. Closed November-June, Sunday-Thursday. **$**

OWL'S NEST

2630 Smokey Park Highway, Candler, 828-665-8325, 800-665-8868;
www.engadineinn.com
Located just outside of Asheville, this inn was built in 1885 and has been restored to its original Victorian grandeur. The mountain views from the wraparound porches are exquisite. Enjoy a cozy, romantic dinner by the fireplace. Five rooms. Complimentary full breakfast. Children over 12 years only. **$**

RESTAURANTS

★★★FLYING FROG CAFÉ

1 Battery Park Ave., Asheville, 828-254-9411; www.flyingfrogcafe.com
Located in the first floor of the Haywood Park Hotel, the Flying Frog Restaurant is in the center of downtown Asheville, surrounded by shopping, lodging and entertainment venues. Decorated in a modern Indian theme, the restaurant has booths draped with sheer curtains, a display kitchen and private wine room. The variety of menu options changes seasonally. Continental, Indian, International menu. Dinner. Closed Monday-Tuesday. Bar. Business casual attire. Valet parking. **$$$**

★★★GABRIELLE'S

87 Richmond Hill Drive, Asheville, 828-252-7313, 800-545-9238;
www.richmondhillinn.com
Victorian ambiance and contemporary Southern Cuisine come together at the Richmond Hill Inn. Chef Duane Fernandes offers a choice between a seasonal three-course prix fixe and five-course menu. American menu. Dinner. Closed Tuesday. Bar. Coat recommended. Reservations required. Not suitable for children under 8 years. Valet parking. **$$$$**

★★★HORIZONS

290 Macon Ave., Asheville, 828-252-2711, 800-438-5800; www.groveparkinn.com
Located in the Grove Park Inn, this restaurant has elegant décor and innovative classic cuisine. Enjoy views of the mountains and the groomed golf course through large windows while listening to live piano music. House specialties include wild-striped bass and an extensive wine list. A special nine-course meal at the chef's table in the kitchen and wine dinners organized around specific tastes and interests are available. International menu. Dinner. Closed Sunday-Monday. Bar. Jacket required. Reservations recommended. Valet parking. **$$$$**

★★LA PAZ

10 Biltmore Plaza, Asheville, 828-277-8779; www.lapaz.com
Mexican menu. Lunch, dinner. Bar. Children's menu. Casual attire. Outdoor seating. **$$**

NORTH CAROLINA

★
★
★
★
★

★★★THE MARKET PLACE RESTAURANT & WINE BAR

20 Wall St., Asheville, 828-252-4162; www.marketplace-restaurant.com

Located in the center of downtown on a side street with quaint shops, this restaurant offers organic cheeses and salads, free-range chickens and local trout. Meat is smoked over hickory and oak. American, French menu. Dinner. Closed Sunday. Bar. Casual attire. Outdoor seating. $$$

★MOOSE CAFÉ AT WESTERN NORTH CAROLINA FARMER'S MARKET

570 Brevard Road, Asheville, 828-255-0920; www.moosecafe.samsbiz.com

Southern, American menu. Breakfast, lunch, dinner. $

★★★REZAZ

28 Hendersonville Road, Asheville, 828-277-1510; www.rezaz.com

Rezaz is two restaurants in one: the main dining room has sleek, modern décor and an upscale Mediterranean menu; Enoteca, a wine bar, is the informal side of the restaurant and has display cases of meat, cheeses and decadent desserts. The restaurant is located in the historic Biltmore Village, opposite the entrance to the Biltmore Estate. Mediterranean menu. Breakfast, lunch, dinner. Closed Sunday. Bar. Casual attire. Reservations recommended. $$

★★★SAVOY

641 Merrimon Ave., Asheville, 828-253-1077; www.savoyasheville.com

A must for those traveling to Asheville, and a favorite of the North Carolina locals, Savoy features a Mediterranean-spiced menu that puts a tasty spin on American favorites. The fresh food—the only freezer on the premises is for their *homemade* ice cream, so we'll let that slide—is 80 percent organic with a "farm to table" lunch and dinner menu that ranges from Carolina bison short ribs to local line-caught trout. Get intimate at the bar with small plates and their diverse wine selection and signature martini list. Yellow cake martini? Make it a double. American menu. Lunch (Monday-Friday), dinner. $$$

★★TUPELO HONEY CAFÉ

12 College St., Asheville, 828-255-4404; www.tupelohoneycafe.com

American, Southern menu. Breakfast, lunch, dinner, late-night. Closed Monday. Children's menu. Casual attire. Outdoor seating. $$

★★ZAMBRA

85 W. Walnut St., Asheville, 828-232-1060; www.zambratapas.com

Spanish-tapas menu. Dinner. Bar. Casual attire. Reservations recommended. Outdoor seating.

BEAUFORT

Beaufort, dating from the colonial era, is a seaport with more than 125 historic houses and sites.

Information: Crystal Coast Visitors Center, 3409 Arendell St., Morehead City,
252-726-8148, 800-786-6962; www.historicbeaufort.com

WHAT TO SEE AND DO
BEAUFORT HISTORIC SITE
138 Turner St., Beaufort, 252-728-5225; www.historicbeaufort.com
Old burying ground, 1829 restored old jail, restored houses (1767-1830), courthouse (circa 1796), apothecary shop, art gallery and gift shop. Get a self-guided walking tour map from the historical center, 138 Turner Street, Monday-Saturday.

CAPE LOOKOUT NATIONAL SEASHORE
131 Charles St., Harkers Island, 252-728-2250; www.nps.gov/calo
Part of the National Park System on the outer banks of North Carolina, the Cape Seashore extends 55 miles south from Ocracoke Inlet and includes unspoiled barrier islands. There are no roads or bridges; accessible by boat only. Catch a ferry from Beaufort, Harkers Island, Davis, Atlantic, or Ocracoke (April-November). Excellent fishing and shell collecting; primitive camping; interpretive programs (seasonal). The lighthouse at Cape Lookout is still operational. Visitor center daily 8:30 a.m.-4:30 p.m.

SPECIAL EVENT
OLD HOMES TOUR AND ANTIQUES SHOW
138 Turner St., Beaufort, 252-728-5225; www.beauforthistoricsite.org
Private homes and historic public buildings; Carteret County Militia; bus tours and tours of old burying ground; historical crafts. Sponsored by the Beaufort Historical Association. Last weekend in June.

SPECIALTY LODGINGS

THE CEDARS INN
305 Front St., Beaufort, 252-728-7036; www.cedarsinn.com
11 rooms, children over 10 years only. Complimentary full breakfast. Restaurant. Beach. $

PECAN TREE INN
116 Queen St., Beaufort, 252-728-6733; www.pecantree.com
Seven rooms. Restaurant. Complimentary continental breakfast. Children over 10 years only. $

BELHAVEN
Along the banks of the Pungo River and Pantego Creek, Belhaven is one of several towns along the Pamlico Sound, the Sailing Capital of North Carolina.

SPECIALTY LODGING
RIVER FOREST MANOR
738 E. Main St., Belhaven, 252-943-2151, 800-346-2151; www.riverforestmanor.com
Nine rooms. Restaurant. Complimentary continental breakfast. Airport transportation available. View of river. Golf carts available for touring town. $

RESTAURANT
★★RIVER FOREST MANOR
738 E. Main St., Belhaven, 252-943-2151; www.riverforestmanor.com
American menu. Dinner, Sunday brunch. Bar. $$

NORTH CAROLINA

★
★
★
★
★

BLOWING ROCK

On the Blue Ridge Parkway, Blowing Rock was named, based on Native American folklore, for the cliff near town where lightweight objects thrown outward are swept back to their origin by the wind. It has been a mountain resort area for more than 100 years. A wide variety of recreational facilities and shops can be found nearby.

Information: Chamber of Commerce, Blowing Rock,
828-295-4636, 800-750-4636; www.blowingrock.com

WHAT TO SEE AND DO

APPALACHIAN SKI MOUNTAIN

940 Ski Mountain Road, Blowing Rock,
828-295-7828, 800-322-2373; www.appskimtn.com

Two quad, double chair lift, rope tow, handle-pull tow; patrol; French-Swiss Ski College, Ski-Wee children's program; equipment rentals; snowmaking; restaurant; eight runs, longest run 2,700 feet, vertical drop 400 feet. December-mid-March. Night skiing (all slopes lighted); half-day and twilight rates.

BLOWING ROCK

432 Rock Road, Blowing Rock, 828-295-7111; www.blowingrock.com

Cliff hangs over Johns River Gorge 2,000-3,000 feet below. Scenic views of Grandfather, Grandmother, Table Rock and Hawksbill mountains. Daily.

MOSES H. CONE MEMORIAL PARK

Blue Ridge Parkway, Blowing Rock, 828-295-7938; www.nps.gov

Former summer estate of textile magnate. Bridle paths, two lakes, 25 miles of hiking and cross-country skiing trails. May-October, daily.

PARKWAY CRAFT CENTER

Blue Ridge Parkway, Blowing Rock, 828-295-7938; www.nps.gov

Demonstrations of weaving, wood carving, pottery, jewelry making, other crafts. May-October, daily. Handcrafted items for sale.

TWEETSIE RAILROAD

300 Tweetsie Railroad Lane, Blowing Rock, 828-264-9061,
800-526-5740; www.tweetsierailroad.com

A 3-mile excursion, with mock holdup and raid, on an old narrow-gauge railroad; Western town with variety show at Tweetsie Palace; country fair, petting zoo; amusement park rides, craft village; chair lift to Mouse Mountain Picnic Area. May-October, limited hours.

HOTELS

★ALPINE VILLAGE INN

297 Sunset Drive, Blowing Rock, 828-295-7206; www.alpine-village-inn.com

17 rooms. Pets accepted; fee. **$**

★BLOWING ROCK INN

788 N. Main St., Blowing Rock, 828-295-7921; www.blowingrockinn.com

24 rooms. Closed mid-December-March. **$**

★CLIFF DWELLERS INN

116 Lakeview Terrace, Blowing Rock, 828-295-3121, 800-322-7380;
www.cliffdwellers.com

21 rooms. Complimentary Continental breakfast. **$**

★★★CHETOLA RESORT AT BLOWING ROCK

North Main St., Blowing Rock, 828-295-5500, 800-243-8652; www.chetola.com

This Blue Ridge Mountains retreat, bordered on one side by a national forest, houses the Highlands Sports and recreation center. A conference center, professional tennis courts and other amenities are within the resort's 78-acre property. 104 rooms. Three restaurants, bar. Wireless Internet access. Children's activity center. Fitness classes available. **$$**

★★★CRIPPEN'S COUNTRY INN

239 Sunset Drive, Blowing Rock, 828-295-3487, 877-295-3487;
www.crippens.com

This mountain inn offers a lively atmosphere and well-rated restaurant. Eight rooms. Restaurant. Bar. Complimentary continental breakfast. Wireless Internet access. Children over 12 years permitted. **$**

★★★GLENDALE SPRINGS INN

7414 Highway 16, Glendale Springs, 336-982-2103, 800-287-1206;
www.glendalespringsinn.com

Located in a quaint community on the top of the Blue Ridge Mountains, this historic is well-known for its dining room and its accommodations. Nine rooms. Complimentary full breakfast. Restaurant. **$**

★★★HOUND EARS CLUB

328 Shulls Mills Road, Blowing Rock, 828-963-4321;
www.houndears.com

Set atop the Blue Ridge Mountains, this small, secluded resort is a relaxing respite. The 18-hole golf course was designed by George Cobb, and the views are gorgeous. 28 rooms, two restaurants, three bars. Children's activity center. Fitness classes available. **$$**

SPECIALTY LODGINGS

INN AT RAGGED GARDENS

203 Sunset Drive, Blowing Rock, 877-972-4433; www.ragged-gardens.com

The 19th-century inn has original stone pillars and floors, period furnishings, individually decorated rooms and a full acre of beautifully landscaped property. 11 rooms. Complimentary full breakfast. Children over 12 years only. **$$**

MAPLE LODGE

152 Sunset Drive, Blowing Rock, 828-295-3331, 866-795-3331; www.maplelodge.net

11 rooms. Complimentary full breakfast. Children over 12 years only. Closed January-February. **$$**

NORTH CAROLINA

RESTAURANTS

★★BEST CELLAR

203 Sunset Drive, Blowing Rock, 877-972-4433

International-Fusion menu. Dinner. Bar. Casual attire. Reservations recommended. Valet parking. Outdoor seating. **$$$**

★★★CRIPPEN'S

239 Sunset Drive, Blowing Rock, 828-295-3487, 877-295-3487;
www.crippens.com

This spacious, cozy dining room is located in Crippen's Country Inn. Chef James Welch's award-winning seasonal menu features many organic meats, seafood and homemade breads and desserts. American menu. Dinner. Bar. Children's menu. Business casual attire. Reservations recommended. Outdoor seating. **$$$**

BOONE

Boone was named for Daniel Boone, who had a cabin and hunted here in the 1760s. This area sprawls over a long valley, which provides a natural pass through the hills. Watauga County is the location of Appalachian State University. Mountain crafts are featured in a variety of craft fairs, festivals and shops.

Information: Convention and Visitors Bureau, 208 Howard St., Boone,
828-262-3516, 800-852-9506; www.visitboonenc.com

WHAT TO SEE AND DO

APPALACHIAN CULTURAL MUSEUM

University Hall Drive, Blowing Rock, 828-262-3117; www.museum.appstate.edu

This regional museum presents an overview of the Blue Ridge area. Exhibits include Native American artifacts, plus exhibit on Daniel Boone, mountain music, and the environment. Tuesday-Saturday 10 a.m.-5 p.m., Sunday 1-5 p.m.

HOTEL

★HOLIDAY INN EXPRESS

1943 Blowing Rock Road, Boone, 828-264-2451, 800-315-2621;
www.holiday-inn.com

138 rooms, complimentary continental breakfast. Outdoor pool. High-speed Internet access. **$**

SPECIALTY LODGING

LOVILL HOUSE INN

404 Old Bristol Road, Boone, 828-264-4204, 800-849-9466; www.lovillhouseinn.com

Captain E. F. Lovill, a Civil War hero and state senator, built this traditional farmhouse in 1875. The 11-acre, wooded property has a charming wraparound porch with plenty of rocking chairs. Six rooms. Children over 12 years only. Complimentary full breakfast. closed March. **$$**

RESTAURANTS

★DAN'L BOONE INN

130 Hardin St., Boone, 828-264-8657; www.danlbooneinn.com

American menu. Breakfast, lunch, dinner. Casual attire. No credit cards accepted. **$**

★★MAKOTO
2124 Blowing Rock Road, Boone, 828-264-7976; www.makotos-boone.com
Japanese menu. Lunch, dinner. Bar. Children's menu. Casual attire. Outdoor seating. **$$**

CASHIERS
High in the Blue Ridge Mountains, this well-known summer resort area offers scenic drives on twisting mountain roads, hiking trails, views, waterfalls, lake sports, fishing and other recreational activities.
Information: Cashiers Area Chamber of Commerce,
828-743-5191; www.cashiersnorthcarolina.com

WHAT TO SEE AND DO
FAIRFIELD SAPPHIRE VALLEY SKI AREA
4350 Highway 64 W., Sapphire, 828-743-3441, 800-722-3956;
www.skisapphire.com
Chair lift, rope tow; patrol, school, snowmaking. Longest run 1,600 feet, vertical drop 200 feet. Mid-December-mid-March, daily. Night skiing. Evenings, half-day rates. Other seasons: swimming, fishing, boating; hiking, horseback riding; golf, tennis; recreation center. Restaurants, inn.

HOTELS
★★★THE GREYSTONE
Greystone Lane, Lake Toxaway, 828-966-4700, 800-824-5766;
www.greystoneinn.com
The main building of this historic inn was built in 1915 and welcomed the Ford and Rockefeller families. The inn offers extra fine touches including individually decorated rooms, a full-service spa and outdoor recreation. 33 rooms. Restaurant. Complimentary full breakfast. Children's activity center. Beach. **$$$**

★★★HIGH HAMPTON INN AND COUNTRY CLUB
1525 Highway 107 S., Cashiers, 828-743-2411,
800-334-2551; www.highhamptoninn.com
Located in the Blue Ridge Mountains, this 1,400-acre property boasts a private lake and a quiet, wooded landscape. Guests of the inn, private cottages or colony homes, stay busy with the scenic 18-hole golf course, six clay tennis courts and hiking trails. 120 rooms. Two restaurants, bar. Children's activity center. Beach. Airport transportation available. Closed mid-November-April. **$$**

CHAPEL HILL
The University of North Carolina is the oldest state university in the country. The town of Chapel Hill's mission from its inception has been to support the college. And residents do cheer loudly for the blue and white Tarheels. Most notorious for its basketball fandom and renowned athletic alumni such as Michael Jordan, UNC is also a leading academic institution and part of the "research triangle" with Duke University in Durham and North Carolina State University in Raleigh.
Information: Chapel Hill-Carrboro Chamber of Commerce, 104 S. Estes Drive,
Chapel Hill, 919-967-7075; www.carolinachamber.org

★
★
★
★
★

WHAT TO SEE AND DO

HORACE WILLIAMS HOUSE

610 E. Rosemary St., Chapel Hill, 919-942-7818; www.chapelhillpreservation.com

Historic house is home to the Chapel Hill Preservation Society; changing art exhibits, chamber music concerts. Guided tours. Tuesday-Friday, also Sunday afternoons; closed holidays and the first two weeks in August.

MOREHEAD-PATTERSON MEMORIAL BELL TOWER

Stadium Drive and South Road, Chapel Hill

A 172-foot Italian Renaissance campanile; concert chimes. The 12 bells range in weight from 300 pounds to almost two tons. Popular tunes ring daily.

NORTH CAROLINA BOTANICAL GARDEN

15501 Old Mason Farm Road, Chapel Hill, 919-962-0522;
www.ncbg.unc.edu

Approximately 600 acres; variety of trees and plants of the southeastern U.S.; wildflower areas, herb gardens. Nature trails. Daily.

OLD WELL

Cameron Avenue, Chapel Hill

Long the unofficial symbol of the university, this well was the only source of water here for nearly a century. The present Greek temple structure dates from 1897.

SOUTH (MAIN) BUILDING

Cameron Avenue, and Raleigh Street, Chapel Hill

Cornerstone laid in 1798, but the building was not completed until 1814, during which time students lived inside the roofless walls in little huts. Future President James K. Polk lived here from 1814 to 1818.

UNIVERSITY OF NORTH CAROLINA AT CHAPEL HILL

250 E. Franklin St., Chapel Hill, 919-962-1630; www.unc.edu

Approximately 27,000 students attend the institution, founded in 1795. The 720-acre campus has more than 200 buildings.

HOTELS

★★★THE CAROLINA INN

211 Pittsboro St., Chapel Hill, 919-933-2001, 800-962-8519;
www.carolinainn.com

A historic 1924 inn set in the middle of the University of North Carolina Campus and around the corner from the Chapel Hill Medical Center. The entrance, with a high portico and pillars, and its red-brick building echo a Georgian Revival theme. Inside, hardwood floors, Oriental rugs, mahogany tables, palms and fresh flowers add to the beautiful setting. Guest rooms continue the theme and include mahogany two-poster beds and furnishings. Art galleries, museum, charming shops and fine restaurants are all just a short distance away. 184 rooms. Restaurant, bar. Wireless Internet access. $$

★★★FRANKLIN HOTEL

311 W. Franklin St., Chapel Hill, 919-442-9000,
866-831-5999; www.franklinhotelnc.com

The Franklin Hotel combines the intimacy and charm of a bed and breakfast with the services and amenities of a larger hotel. The guestrooms, are beautifully done in chocolate brown and celadon, while the seven VIP penthouse suites are in the definition of luxury. Breakfast is an elegant affair at Windows Restaurant, while guests and locals mingle over drinks and light fare at Roberts, the lobby and patio bar. 67 rooms. Restaurant, bar. Wireless Internet access. $$$

★HAMPTON INN CHAPEL HILL

1740 Fordham Blvd., Chapel Hill, 919-968-3000,
800-426-7866; www.hamptoninn.com

120 rooms, complimentary continental breakfast. Wireless Internet access. $

★★HOLIDAY INN CHAPEL HILL

1301 N. Fordham Blvd., Chapel Hill, 919-929-2171,
888-452-5765; www.hichapelhill.com

For the truly school-spirited, this lobby is painted in UNC colors, the front desk staff dress in referee uniforms, all types of sports equipment are displayed on the outside walls leading to the rooms, and the floors have blue foot prints with tar on the heel. 134 rooms. Restaurant, bar. Wireless Internet access. $

★★★SHERATON HOTEL

1 Europa Drive, Chapel Hill, 919-968-4900,
800-325-3535; www.sheraton.com/chapelhill

This modern hotel is located on the main road and connects the UNC-Chapel Hill campus and the Duke University campus, just a short distance to Interstate 85 (I-85) and the Research Triangle. The wraparound open lobby features marble floors and floor-to-ceiling windows looking out to the pool and water fountain. Guest rooms are spacious with desks and sofas. 168 rooms. Restaurant, bar. Wireless Internet access. $$

★★★SIENA HOTEL

1505 E. Franklin St., Chapel Hill,
919-929-4000, 800-223-7379; www.sienahotel.com

Southern hospitality and grand European styling make the Siena Hotel a favorite in Chapel Hill. The guest rooms and suites are tastefully decorated with fine Italian furnishings and rich fabrics, while modern amenities ensure the highest levels of comfort. Guests receive privileges at the UNC golf course and nearby fitness center. Il Palio Ristorante charms visitors throughout the day with a delicious Northern Italian-influenced menu. 79 rooms. Restaurant, bar. Complimentary full breakfast. Wireless Internet access. $$

RESTAURANTS

★ALLEN & SON BARBEQUE

6203 Milhouse Road, Chapel Hill, 919-942-7576

Barbecue menu. Lunch, dinner. Closed Sunday-Monday. Children's menu. Casual attire. Outdoor seating. $

NORTH CAROLINA

★
★
★
★
★

★★★BONNE SOIRÉE

431 W. Franklin St., Chapel Hill, 919-928-8388

Smack dab in the middle of Chapel Hill's vibrant Franklin Street, Bonne Soirée is a hit with locals and visitors alike. This intimate restaurant is sophisticated without being stuffy. The menu is handwritten and the wines are handpicked. The chef crafts his country French cooking with precision and pride, at times, making it difficult to believe you're in North Carolina rather than the French countryside. French menu. Dinner. $$

★★★★CAROLINA CROSSROADS

211 Pittsboro St., Chapel Hill, 919-933-9277, 800-962-8519; www.carolinainn.com

Set in the historic Carolina Inn, the Carolina Crossroads dining room is elegantly classic and delivers a picture-perfect example of Southern hospitality and charm. The menu features regional dishes, from a classic North Carolina pulled pork sandwich to dishes such as salmon with grilled acorn squash in white-wine butter sauce, that incorporate local, seasonal ingredients. Southern menu. Breakfast, lunch, dinner, brunch. Bar. Children's menu. Business casual attire. Reservations recommended. Valet parking. Outdoor seating. $$$

★★★ELAINE'S ON FRANKLIN

454 W. Franklin St., Chapel Hill, 919-960-2770; www.elainesonfranklin.com

Elaine's on Franklin promises that each meal is made up of "food for the soul, prepared for the heart," which they'll win over through your stomach, of course. Among a menu of fresh greens and local meat and seafood, you'll see some truly unique dishes such as tuna ceviche and even something for the herbivores: white lasagna with housemade wheat pasta. Your palate will continue the love affair with a selection of organic wines and the definition of soul food: a dessert menu with bread pudding and warm chocolate cake. American, Southern menu. Dinner. Closed Sunday-Monday. $$$

★★★IL PALIO

1505 E. Franklin St., Chapel Hill, 919-929-4000, 800-223-7379; www.sienahotel.com

Located in the Siena Hotel, this Italian restaurant offers guests a fine-dining experience with tasteful interpretations of Italian-Mediterranean classics. A prix fixe Market Tasting Menu offers a chef's choice selection of food made from all local and seasonal ingredients. The restaurant features nightly live piano or guitar music and an impressive wine and martini list. Northern Italian menu. Breakfast, lunch, dinner, brunch. Bar. Business casual attire. Reservations recommended. Valet parking. $$$

★★★JUJUBE RESTAURANT

1201-L Raleigh Road, Glen Lennox Shopping Center, Chapel Hill,
919-960-0555; www.jujuberestaurant.com

Jujube proclaims it's "almost Asian," but that doesn't mean it's a copout or a fake. Southern stomachs will delight as they ease their way into exotic cuisine, with North Carolina shrimp lo mein and wontons made of beef short rib and goat cheese. Dates can cuddle at secluded tables along the brightly colored wall or adventurous types can sit chef-side at the open-kitchen bar. Each week the restaurant hosts special dinners and events where food and drink are the main guests. On Wednesdays, the kitchen goes Italian with its specials, and an advanced reservation will get you the Tuesday 20-course chef's table. Asian menu. Lunch, dinner. $$

★
★
★
★

★★LA RESIDENCE

202 W. Rosemary St., Chapel Hill, 919-967-2506; www.laresidencedining.com

Continental, French menu. Dinner, late-night. Bar. Business casual attire. Reservations recommended. Outdoor seating. **$$**

★★★LANTERN

423 W. Franklin St., Chapel Hill, 919-969-8846; www.lanternrestaurant.com

Lantern's head chef and owner Andrea Reusing wanted to create authentic Asian food using local, seasonal ingredients in a simply chic setting. Restaurant-goers' taste buds are treated with entrees tickled by curries and ginger, tamarind and lemongrass spices, mingling American cooking with Thai and Vietnamese flavors. Save room for spirits; Lantern's exhaustive wine selection is only to be outdone by the uber-cosmopolitan cocktail list, which features The Red Geisha (muddled fresh organic strawberries with lime, ginger and vodka) and a Saketini worth raising a pinky to. Asian menu. Dinner. Closed Sunday. **$$$**

★SPANKY'S

101 E. Franklin St., Chapel Hill, 919-967-2678; www.spankysrestaurant.com

American menu. Lunch, dinner. Bar. Children's menu. Casual attire. **$$**

★SQUID'S

1201 N. Fordham Blvd., Chapel Hill, 919-942-8757; www.squidsrestaurant.com

Seafood menu. Dinner. Bar. Children's menu. Casual attire. **$$**

CHARLOTTE

The Carolinas' largest metropolis, and one of the country's fastest growing areas, Charlotte is a top banking center. British General Cornwallis occupied the town for a short time in 1780, but met such determined resistance that he called it a "hornet's nest," a name that has been applied to the city seal and by sports teams such as the NBA's Carolina Hornets. Gold was discovered here in 1799, and the region around Charlotte was the nation's major gold producer until the California gold rush in 1848. The city had a U.S. Mint between 1837 and 1861. The last Confederate Cabinet meeting was held here in 1865.

Today there is much to see and do, whether it's history (the birthplace of the 11th president, James K. Polk), religion (the birthplace and headquarters for evangelical minister Billy Graham), sports (professional football, baseball, basketball, NASCAR) or the arts (try the free and fabulous Public art Walking Tour).

Information: Convention and Visitors Bureau, 500 S. College St., Charlotte, 704-334-2282, 800-722-1994; www.charlottecvb.org

NORTH CAROLINA

★
★
★
★
★

WHAT TO SEE AND DO

THE CHARLOTTE MUSEUM OF HISTORY AND HEZEKIAH ALEXANDER HOMESITE

3500 Shamrock Drive, Charlotte, 704-568-1774; www.charlottemuseum.org

Includes the Hezekiah Alexander House, the oldest dwelling still standing in Mecklenburg County; two-story springhouse; working log kitchen. Tours. Tuesday-Saturday 10 a.m.-5 p.m., Sunday 1-5 p.m.; open Monday in summer.

DISCOVERY PLACE

301 N. Tryon St., Charlotte, 704-372-6261, 800-935-0553;
www.discoveryplace.org

A hands-on science museum that gives kids a chance to learn about electricity, weather, rocks, minerals and other scientific wonders. Visit the aquarium, science circus, life center, rain forest, collections gallery and OMNIMAX theater, as well as major traveling exhibits. Daily.

JAMES K. POLK MEMORIAL STATE HISTORIC SITE

308 S. Polk St., Pineville, 704-889-7145; www.nchistoricsites.org/polk

Replica of log cabin and outbuildings at the birthplace of the 11th President of the United States. Visitor center with exhibits, film. Guided tour. Tuesday-Saturday 9 a.m.-5 p.m.

LEVINE MUSEUM OF THE NEW SOUTH

200 E. Seventh St., Charlotte, 704-333-1887; www.museumofthenewsouth.org

Chronicles the history of the post-Civil War South with an ever-changing series of exhibits featuring industry, ideas, people and historical eras such as the Civil rights movement. Monday-Saturday 10 a.m.-5 p.m., Sunday noon-5 p.m.

PARAMOUNT'S CAROWINDS

14523 Carowinds Blvd., Charlotte, 704-588-2600, 800-888-4386;
www.carowinds.com

This 100-acre family theme park has more than 40 rides, shows and attractions including the 12-acre water entertainment complex WaterWorks, Nickelodeon Central children's area, Drop Zone stunt tower and roller coasters. The 13,000-seat Paladium amphitheater hosts special events. June-late August, daily; March-May and September-October, weekends.

U.S. NATIONAL WHITEWATER CENTER

820 Hawfield Road, Charlotte, 704-391-3900; www.usnwc.org

An official Olympic training site and site for World Cup whitewater rafting, this 307-acre park on the Catawba River was modeled after Olympic rafting courses and opened in 2006. Four thousand linear feet of whitewater rafting as well as biking, canoeing, wall climbing, kayaking and more are offered at this playground for serious sports enthusiasts. Mountain bikes are available to rent.

HOTELS

★★★★THE BALLANTYNE RESORT, A LUXURY COLLECTION HOTEL

10000 Ballantyne Commons Parkway, Charlotte,
704-248-4000, 866-248-4824; www.ballantyneresort.com

This elegant resort within the city limits Charlotte is a paradise for golf enthusiasts, with one of the state's best 18-hole courses and the renowned Dana Rader Golf school. Rooms are crisply and classically decorated and have lavish finishes, such as marble entrances and bathrooms. The Gallery Restaurant offers creative selections and seasonal ingredients. The Gallery bar serves a tapas menu and lengthy selection of cocktails, whiskeys and after-dinner drinks. 249 rooms. Restaurant, two bars. Wireless Internet access. Fitness classes available, spa. Airport transportation available. $$

★★COURTYARD CHARLOTTE CITY CENTER

237 S. Tryon St., Charlotte, 704-926-5800, 800-321-2211; www.marriott.com

181 rooms. Bar. High-speed Internet access. Fitness center. Pets not accepted. **$$**

★★COURTYARD CHARLOTTE UNIVERSITY RESEARCH PARK

333 W. T. Harris Blvd., Charlotte, 704-549-4888, 888-270-8582;
www.marriott.com

152 rooms. High-speed Internet access. Business center. Fitness center. **$**

★★DOUBLETREE HOTEL

895 W. Trade St., Charlotte, 704-347-0070, 800-222-8733; www.doubletree.com

187 rooms. Restaurant, bar. Wireless Internet access. Business center. Fitness room. Pool. Pets accepted. **$$**

★★DOUBLETREE HOTEL CHARLOTTE AIRPORT

2600 Yorkmont Road, Charlotte, 704-357-9100, 800-222-8733;
www.charlotteairport.doubletree.com

173 rooms. Restaurant, bar. Wireless Internet access. Business center. Airport transportation available. Pool. Fitness center. Pets not accepted. **$$**

★★★THE DUKE MANSION

400 Hermitage Road, Charlotte, 704-714-4400, 888-202-1009;
www.dukemansion.com

This 1915 Southern estate is a lovely setting for a weekend getaway, and the mansion also serves as a facility for meetings and retreats. The charming Colonial Revival house was once owned by James Buchanan Duke, founder of Duke University. Acres of gardens surround the well-maintained house. Treetop rooms as well as standard guest rooms—some with sleeping porches—are decorated with traditional and antique furniture. 20 rooms. Complimentary full breakfast. Wireless Internet access. **$$**

★★★THE DUNHILL HOTEL

237 N. Tryon St., Charlotte, 704-332-4141, 800-354-4141; www.dunhillhotel.com

This was one of the city's first luxury hotels when it opened as the Mayfair Manor in 1929. Guest rooms feature 18th-century furniture, antiques and four-poster beds. The Dunhill's onsite restaurant, the Monticello, is an elegant spot for a special night out. 60 rooms. Restaurant, bar. Wireless Internet access. Business center. **$$**

★★EMBASSY SUITES

4800 S. Tryon St., Charlotte, 704-527-8400,
800-362-2779; www.embassy-charlotte.com

274 rooms, all suites. Restaurant, bar. Complimentary full breakfast. Wireless Internet access. Business center. Fitness room. Indoor pool. **$$**

★★★HILTON CHARLOTTE CENTER CITY

222 E. Third St., Charlotte, 704-377-1500, 800-445-8667; www.charlotte.hilton.com

Perfect for business or pleasure, this hotel in the financial district is near shops and restaurants. Also nearby are beaches, golf courses and the Carolina Mountains.

★
★
★
★
★

Rooms have oversized desks, 42-inch flatscreen TVs and black marble bathrooms. 400 rooms. Restaurant, bar. Wireless Internet access. Business center. Fitness center. Pool. Pets accepted. **$$**

★★★HILTON UNIVERSITY PLACE

8629 J. M. Keynes Drive, Charlotte, 704-547-7444,
800-445-8667; www.charlotteuniversity.hilton.com

A beautiful sunlit atrium lobby anchors the Hilton. Guest rooms and suites feature a contemporary, sleek style and great views of the university area. The Lakefront Restaurant offers a menu of steak and seafood-focused fare. 393 rooms. Restaurant, bar. Wireless Internet access. Business center. Fitness center. Pool. Pets accepted. **$$**

★HYATT SUMMERFIELD SUITES

4920 S. Tryon St., Charlotte, 704-525-2600; www.hyatt.com

135 rooms, all suites. Complimentary continental breakfast. Wireless Internet access. Business center. Airport transportation available. Spa. Outdoor heated pool, whirlpool. **$**

★LA QUINTA INN AND SUITES CHARLOTTE COLISEUM

4900 S. Tryon St., Charlotte, 704-523-5599, 800-687-6667;
www.laquinta.com

131 rooms. Complimentary continental breakfast. Wireless Internet access. Fitness center. Airport transportation available. Pets accepted. **$**

★★★MARRIOTT CITY CENTER

100 W. Trade St., Charlotte, 704-333-9000,
800-228-9290; www.marriottcitycenter.com

Located in the central uptown business district, this hotel is only blocks from the New Charlotte Convention Center and Bank of America Stadium. 438 rooms. Three restaurants, three bars. High-speed Internet access. Fitness center. Pets not accepted. **$$**

★★★THE MOREHEAD INN

1122 E. Morehead St., Charlotte, 704-376-3357,
888-667-3432; www.moreheadinn.com

Meticulously kept gardens can be found at this charming Southern inn, an historic building listed on the National Register of Historic Places. Hardwood floors, Oriental rugs, antiques and beautiful tapestries are placed throughout, while four-poster beds and fireplaces provide cozy touches in guest rooms. 12 rooms. Complimentary full breakfast. Wireless Internet access. **$$**

★★★OMNI HOTEL

132 E. Trade St., Charlotte, 704-377-0400, 800-843-6664; www.omnihotels.com

The ultramodern Omni Hotel is located in within walking distance of the Charlotte Convention Center and the Overstreet Mall, which offers shopping and dining. The Charlotte-Douglas Airport is 15 minutes away. Comfortable guest rooms have views of the city. 374 rooms. Restaurant, bar. Wireless Internet access. Business center. Fitness room. **$$**

★RAMADA

7900 Nations Ford Road, Charlotte, 704-522-7110, 800-272-6232; www.ramada.com

110 rooms, complimentary continental breakfast. Wireless Internet access. Pool. Pets accepted. **$**

★★RENAISSANCE CHARLOTTE SUITES

2800 Coliseum Centre Drive, Charlotte, 704-357-1414, 800-468-3571;
www.renaissancehotels.com

275 rooms, all suites. Restaurant, bar. High-speed Internet access. Business center. Airport transportation available. Fitness center. Whirlpool. **$$**

★★VAN LANDINGHAM ESTATE

2010 The Plaza, Charlotte, 704-334-8909, 888-524-2020;
www.vanlandinghamestate.com

Nine rooms. Complimentary full breakfast. Wireless Internet access. **$$**

★★★THE WESTIN CHARLOTTE

601 S. College St., Charlotte, 704-375-2600, 800-937-8461; www.westin.com/charlotte

Rooms and suites are modern and comfortable and feature countless amenities from in-room video games to the hotel's signature luxury bedding. Spa services are available. The Ember Grille serves American fare for breakfast, lunch and dinner, while Charlotte's Treats and Eats offers light fare during the day. 700 rooms. Restaurant, two bars, Wireless Internet access. Business center. Spa. **$$**

SPECIALTY LODGING

THE VICTORIAN VILLA

10925 Windy Grove Road, Charlotte, 704-394-5545; www.victorianvillainn.com

Five rooms. Breakfast, dinner. **$$**

RESTAURANTS

★AMALFI'S

8542 University City Blvd., Charlotte, 704-547-8651; www.amalfi-charlotte.com

Italian menu. Lunch, dinner. Bar. Closed Monday; week of July 4. Children's menu. Casual attire. Outdoor seating. **$$**

★★★BONTERRA

1829 Cleveland Ave., Charlotte, 704-333-9463; www.bonterradining.com

Bonterra is located close to Uptown Charlotte in the historic Southend District. Choose from an extensive wine list featuring 100 wines by the glass and 300 bottles—wine tastings can be booked for groups of 15 to 50 people. Menu selections include deep-fried lobster tails, braised veal osso bucco, fire-roasted filet mignon and Sonoma County duck breast. American, California menu. Dinner. Closed Sunday. Bar. Business casual attire. Reservations recommended. Valet parking. Outdoor seating. **$$$**

★BRIXX PIZZA

225 E. Sixth St., Charlotte, 704-347-2749; www.brixxpizza.com

Pizza menu. Lunch, dinner, late-night. Bar. Children's menu. Casual attire. Outdoor seating. **$$**

★FLYING SAUCER DRAFT EMPORIUM

9605 N. Tryon St., Charlotte, 704-568-7253; www.beerknurd.com

American menu. Lunch, dinner, late-night. Bar. Children's menu. Casual attire. Outdoor seating. $$

★FUEL PIZZA CAFÉ

1501 Central Ave., Charlotte, 704-376-3835; www.fuelpizza.com

American menu. Lunch, dinner. Children's menu. Casual attire. Outdoor seating. $

★★FUSE BOX

227 W. Trade St., Charlotte, 704-376-8885: www.fuseboxcharlotte.com

Sushi, Thai menu. Lunch, dinner. Closed Sunday. Bar. Casual attire. Reservations recommended. $$

★★★★GALLERY RESTAURANT & BAR

10000 Ballantyne Commons Parkway, Charlotte,
704-248-4000, 866-248-4824; www.gallery-restaurant.com

The setting is relaxing and welcoming at Gallery Restaurant & Bar, located on the ground level of the Ballantyne Resort. Enjoy artfully presented dishes such as cedar plank-roasted sea bass with blue crab, shallots and English pea risotto, and rosemary and citrus-roasted free-range chicken dazzle the palate. Fine service makes dining here a delight. American menu. Breakfast, lunch, dinner. Bar. Business casual attire. Reservations recommended. Valet parking. Outdoor seating. $$$

★★THE KABOB HOUSE

6432 E. Independence Blvd., Charlotte, 704-531-2500;
www.kabobhousenc.com

Persian menu. Lunch, dinner. Casual attire. Reservations recommended. Outdoor seating. $$

★★★LAVECCHIA'S SEAFOOD GRILLE

225 E. Sixth St., Charlotte, 704-370-6776; www.lavecchias.com

LaVecchia's features seafood entrées such as Chilean sea bass and seared yellowfin tuna, as well as prime steaks. To complement the menu, the restaurant is decked out in a modern, urban, marine-themed design. Live jazz band on Friday and Saturday nights. Seafood, steak menu. Dinner. Closed Sunday. Bar. Children's menu. Business casual attire. Reservations recommended. Valet parking. Outdoor seating. $$$

★LUPIE'S CAFÉ

2718 Monroe Road, Charlotte, 704-374-1232; www.lupiescafe.com

American menu. Lunch, dinner. Closed Sunday. Bar. Casual attire. $

★MAMA FU'S ASIAN HOUSE

1600 E. Woodlawn, Charlotte, 704-714-5080; www.mamafus.com

Pan-Asian menu. Lunch, dinner. Children's menu. Casual attire. Reservations recommended. Outdoor seating. $

★★★MCNINCH HOUSE

511 N. Church St., Charlotte, 704-332-6159;
www.mcninchhouserestaurant.com

This restaurant's unique setting, attention to detail and ever-changing but consistently strong French menu are well-suited for special-occasion dinners. Situated in a historic building, McNinch House is in a residential area on the west side of Church Street and within walking distance of downtown hotels and businesses. French menu. Dinner. Closed Sunday-Monday. Bar. Jacket required. Reservations recommended. Valet parking. $$$$

★MERT'S HEART & SOUL

214 N. College St., Charlotte, 704-342-4222; www.mertsuptown.com

American menu. Lunch, dinner, brunch. Children's menu. Casual attire. Outdoor seating. $$

★PRESTO BAR AND GRILL

445 W. Trade St., Charlotte, 704-334-7088; www.prestobarandgrill.com

American menu. Lunch, dinner. Closed Sunday. Bar. Casual attire. Reservations recommended. Outdoor seating. $$

★RAINBOW CAFÉ

201 S. College St., Charlotte, 704-372-2256; www.rainbowcafeuptown.com

American menu. Lunch, dinner. Closed Saturday-Sunday. Bar. Children's menu. Casual attire. $

★RANCH HOUSE

5614 Wilkinson Blvd., Charlotte, 704-399-5411;
www.ranchhouseofcharlotte.com

Seafood, steak menu. Dinner. Closed Sunday; first two weeks in July. Bar. Children's menu. Casual attire. Reservations recommended. $$

★★★TAVERNA 100

100 N. Tryon St., Charlotte, 704-344-0515; www.taverna100.com

Located in uptown Charlotte, Taverna 100 is housed in Founders Hall in the Bank of America's Corporate Center. Fresh herbs and olive oils accent the flavorful Mediterranean dishes, many of which are prepared on the wood-burning grill or the rotisserie. Mediterranean menu. Lunch, dinner. Closed Sunday. Bar. Children's menu. Business casual attire. Reservations recommended. Valet parking. Outdoor seating. $$$

★★★UPSTREAM

6902 Phillips Place, Charlotte, 704-556-7730; www.upstreamit.com

With a wide selection of fresh seafood, a sushi and oyster bar and an extensive wine list, this Charlotte dining spot (near SouthPark Mall) is a local favorite. Start with the lobster bisque or the jumbo lump crab cakes before trying a main entrée such as the mushroom-crusted mahimahi, sake-marinated South American sea bass or the pan-roasted Idaho trout. Seafood menu. Lunch, dinner, brunch. Bar. Business casual attire. Reservations recommended. Valet parking. Outdoor seating. $$$

NORTH CAROLINA

★
★
★
★

SPA

★★★★THE SPA AT BALLANTYNE RESORT

1000 Ballantyne Commons Parkway, Charlotte,
704-248-4141; www.ballantyneresort.com

Tucked inside Charlotte's luxurious Ballantyne Resort, this spa offers a classic pampering experience delivered by an amiable, well-trained staff. With 16 treatment rooms, there's ample space for sampling Swedish massages, rejuvenating facials or moisturizing body wraps. The spa also offers a full range of nail and salon services. Couples can opt for massages delivered in the privacy of a couples' suite.

CHEROKEE

This is the capital of the Eastern Band of the Cherokee, who live on the Qualla Reservation at the edge of Great Smoky Mountains National Park and the Blue Ridge Parkway. The reservation, the largest east of the Mississippi, is shared by the descendants of members of the tribe who avoided being driven to Oklahoma on the "Trail of Tears."

Information: Cherokee Travel and Promotion,
828-497-9195, 800-438-1601; www.cherokee-nc.com

WHAT TO SEE AND DO

CHEROKEE HERITAGE MUSEUM AND GALLERY

Acquoni Road, Cherokee

This is located in Saunooke Village. Interpretive center features Cherokee culture and history. Gift shop. Daily; closed three weeks late December-early January.

MUSEUM OF THE CHEROKEE INDIAN

Highway 441 N., On Cherokee Reservation, Cherokee,
828-497-3481; www.cherokeemuseum.org

Arts and crafts, audiovisual displays, portraits, prehistoric artifacts. Daily.

OCONALUFTEE INDIAN VILLAGE

Highway 441 N., Cherokee, 828-497-2111; www.cherokee-nc.com

Replica of Native American village of more than 250 years ago. Includes seven-sided council house, herb garden, craft demonstrations, lectures. Guided tours Mid-May-late October, daily.

SPECIAL EVENT

UNTO THESE HILLS

Mountainside Theater, Highway 441 N.,
Cherokee, 828-497-2111; www.cherokee-nc.com

Kermit Hunter drama re-creating the history of the Cherokee Nation from 1540 to 1838 in a natural amphitheater. Mid-June-late August, Monday-Saturday evenings.

HOTELS

★★BEST WESTERN GREAT SMOKIES INN

1636 Acquoni Road, Cherokee, 828-497-2020, 800-937-8376;
www.bestwestern.com

152 rooms. Restaurant. High-speed Internet access. Pool. Pets accepted. **$**

★COMFORT INN

44 Tsalagi Road, Cherokee, 828-497-2411, 800-424-6423; www.comfortinn.com

88 rooms. Complimentary continental breakfast. Wireless Internet access. Pets not accepted. **$**

★★HOLIDAY INN

Highway 19 S., Cherokee, 828-497-9181, 800-315-2621; www.hicherokeenc.com

154 rooms. Indoor and outdoor pools. Fitness center. **$**

CONCORD

Concord located in the heart of Carolina NASCAR country. The town boasts several NASCAR teams, Lowe's Motor Speedway and a NASCAR research and development office. For those who need a break from car racing, hit more than 200 stores at Concord Mills outlet mall.

Information: Chamber of Commerce, 23 Union St., North,
704-782-4111; www.cabarruscvb.com

WHAT TO SEE AND DO

CONCORD MILLS

8111 Concord Mills Blvd., Concord, 704-979-3000; www.concordmills.com

This outlet mall has more than 200 stores, including factory outlets for popular chains such as Banana Republic and Saks Fifth Avenue. It includes a movie theater. Daily. Closed holidays.

CONCORD MOTORSPORT PARK

7940 Highway 601 S., Concord, 704-782-4221; www.concordmotorsportpark.com

The NASCAR weekly series runs Saturday nights from April through October at this asphalt tri-oval 30 miles northeast of Charlotte in the heart of NASCAR country. The grandstands seat 8,000, and there are spots for 28 RVs at Turn 3.

DALE EARNHARDT TRIBUTE

3003 Dale Earnhardt Plaza, Kannapolis, 800-848-3740; www.visitcabarrus.com

The people of Kannapolis have preserved the memory of their favorite son, Dale Earnhardt, in 900 pounds of bronze. Nearby are murals depicting Earnhardt's race car driving career.

NASCAR SPEEDPARK, CONCORD MILLS

8461 Concord Mills Blvd., Concord, 704-979-6770; www.nascarspeedpark.com

A 7-acre race-themed amusement park with five racetracks, a state-of-the-art interactive arcade, one 18-hole miniature golf course, kiddie rides, Lazer Tag. Daily.

REED GOLD MINE STATE HISTORIC SITE

9621 Reed Mine Road, Midland, 704-721-4653; www.reedmine.com

The Reed Gold Mine State Historic Site boasts the first documented discovery of gold in the United States in 1799. Stop and check out the underground mine tours, history trail, working machinery, demonstrations, exhibits, visitor center and film, or enjoy the panning area and see what you find. Tuesday-Saturday. Panning area: April-October, daily; fee.

★
★
★
★
☆

RICHARD PETTY DRIVING EXPERIENCE

Lowe's Motor Speedway, 5555 Concord Parkway South, Concord, 800-237-3889; www.1800bepetty.com

Always wanted to rip a stock car around the curves at a NASCAR racetrack? This is the largest of the driving schools that takes fans right onto the track at Lowe's Motor Speedway. For anywhere between $99 for a ride along to almost $3,000 for an advanced racing experience, you can live your racing dream.

CORNELIUS

Like Concord, Cornelius is close to Lowe's Motor Speedway and steeped in NASCAR culture. Nearby Mooresville is the home of the North Carolina Auto Racing Hall of Fame.

Information: 704-892-1922; www.lakenorman.org

WHAT TO SEE AND DO

LAKE NORMAN

www.visitlakenorman.org

Lake Norman is the state's largest freshwater lake at 32,510 acres. It was created by the Cowans Ford Dam, a Duke Power project on the Catawba River. There are nine public access areas, with fishing areas and boating access.

MEMORY LANE MOTORSPORTS & HISTORIC AUTOMOTIVE MUSEUM

769 River Highway, Mooresville, 704-662-3673; www.memorylaneautomuseum.com

One-of-a-kind vehicles from race to vintage cars and motorcycles are on display at the museum, as well as toys, memorabilia and more. Monday-Saturday 10 a.m.-5 p.m.

NORTH CAROLINA AUTO RACING HALL OF FAME

119 Knob Hill Road, Mooresville, 704-663-5331; www.ncarhof.com

As Mooresville's official visitor's center, the museum offers a large display of more than 35 cars dedicated to all types of auto racing. The gift shop is also the official Race City, USA merchandise headquarters, and carries a wide selection of racing memorabilia. Monday-Friday 10 a.m.-5 p.m. Saturday-Sunday 10 a.m.-3 p.m.

HOTEL

★HAMPTON INN

19501 Statesville Road, Cornelius, 704-892-9900, 800-426-7866; www.hamptoninn.com

116 rooms. Complimentary continental breakfast. High-speed Internet access. $

SPECIALTY LODGING

DAVIDSON VILLAGE INN

117 Depot St., Davidson, 704-892-8044, 800-892-0796; www.davidsoninn.com

18 rooms. Complimentary continental breakfast. $

RESTAURANT

★★KOBE JAPANESE HOUSE OF STEAK & SEAFOOD

20465 Chartwell Center Drive, Cornelius, 704-896-7778; www.kobeherolkn.com

Japanese menu. Lunch, dinner. Bar. Casual attire. Reservations recommended. $$

★
★
★
★
★

DURHAM

Durham's sparkle has brought it near-top national ranking in livability studies. Known for excellence in medicine, education, research and industry, Durham is also a recreational and cultural center in the rolling Piedmont region.

In 1924, an endowment from James B. Duke, head of the American Tobacco Company, helped establish Duke University as one of the nation's top universities. North Carolina Central University is located here as well. In the 1950s, Durham County was chosen as the site of Research Triangle Park, a planned scientific research center that includes the Environmental Protection Agency, the National Institute for Environmental Health Sciences, IBM Corporation, the Glaxo Wellcome Company and others.

Information: Convention and Visitors Bureau, 101 E. Morgan St., Durham, 800-772-2855; www.durham-nc.com

WHAT TO SEE AND DO

BENNETT PLACE STATE HISTORIC SITE

4409 Bennett Memorial Road, Durham, 919-383-4345; www.nchistoricsites.org/bennett

This was the site of the signing on April 26, 1865, Confederate General Johnston's surrnder to Union General Sherman, one of the last and most significant of the Confederate surrenders. Reconstructed Bennett homestead. Picnicking. Visitor center, exhibits, audiovisual show. Tuesday-Saturday 9 a.m.-5 p.m.

DUKE HOMESTEAD STATE HISTORIC SITE

2828 Duke Homestead Road, Durham, 919-477-5498; www.nchistoricsites.org

Ancestral home of the Duke family; first Duke tobacco factory; curing barn; outbuildings; farm crops. Tobacco museum, exhibits, film; furnishings of period. Tours. Tuesday-Saturday 9 a.m.-5 p.m.

DUKE UNIVERSITY

2138 Campus Drive, Durham, 919-684-3214; www.duke.edu

Duke University is one of the nation's top private universities, situated on 8,000 acres. It includes original Trinity College. The West Campus, occupied since 1930, is the showplace of the university.

DUKE'S WALLACE WADE STADIUM

290 Frank Bassett Road, Durham, 919-681-2583; www.goduke.com

Home of the Duke Blue Devils. Also the 8,564-seat Cameron Indoor Stadium.

DURHAM BULL ATHLETIC PARK

409 Blackwell St., Durham, 919-687-6500; www.durhambulls.com

This 10,000-seat stadium is home to the Durham Bulls Triple A baseball team, affiliated with the Tampa Bay Devil Rays. Full-service stadium, kids playground. Schedule varies.

NORTH CAROLINA

★
★
★
★
★

NORTH CAROLINA MUSEUM OF LIFE AND SCIENCE
433 W. Murray Ave., Durham, 919-220-5429; www.ncmls.org

North Carolina wildlife; hands-on science exhibits; aerospace, weather and geology collections; train ride; farmyard; science park; discovery rooms; Butterfly House. Picnic area. Tuesday-Saturday 10 a.m.-5 p.m. Sunday noon-5 p.m.

SARAH P. DUKE GARDENS
426 Anderson St., Durham, 919-684-3698; www.hr.duke.edu/dukegardens

Main entrance on Anderson Street. 55 acres of landscaped gardens, pine forest. Continuous display. Monday-Saturday 9 a.m.-6 p.m., Sunday noon-5 p.m.

SPECIAL EVENTS
AMERICAN DANCE FESTIVAL
715 Broad St., Durham, 919-684-6402; www.americandancefestival.org

Page Auditorium and Reynolds Industries Theater, Duke University, West Campus. Six weeks of performances by the finest of both major and emerging modern dance companies from the United States and abroad. June-July.

BULL DURHAM BLUES FESTIVAL
804 Old Fayetteville St., Durham, 919-683-1709; www.hayti.org/blues

This acclaimed blues festival, held in early September, has been running for more than 20 years and features performances by blues legends.

HOTELS

★★ARROWHEAD INN BED & BREAKFAST
106 Mason Road, Durham, 919-477-8430, 800-528-2207;
www.arrowheadinn.com

Nine rooms. Complimentary full breakfast. Wireless Internet access. **$$**

★BEST WESTERN SKYLAND INN
5400 U.S. Highway, 70 W., Durham, 919-383-2508, 800-937-8376;
www.bestwestern.com

31 rooms, complimentary continental breakfast. Wireless Internet access. Pool. **$**

★COURTYARD BY MARRIOTT DURHAM
1815 Front St., Durham, 919-309-1500, 800-321-2211; www.courtyard.com

146 rooms. Restaurant. Wireless Internet access. Business center. **$**

★★DOUBLETREE GUEST SUITES RALEIGH-DURHAM
2515 Meridian Parkway, Durham, 919-361-4660,
800-365-9876; www.doubletree.com

203 rooms, all suites. High-speed Internet access. Restaurant, bar. Airport transportation available. **$$**

★★HILTON DURHAM
3800 Hillsborough, Durham, 919-383-8033, 800-445-8667; www.hilton.com

195 rooms. High-speed Internet access. Restaurant, bar. **$$**

★★★MARRIOTT DURHAM CIVIC CENTER

201 Foster St., Durham, 919-768-6000, 800-909-8375; www.marriott.com

This hotel is near the theater district, Durham Athletic Park, and Duke University. The elegant charm is enhanced by fountains that flow through the atrium lobby. 187 rooms. Wireless Internet access. Restaurant, bar. **$$**

★★★MARRIOTT RESEARCH TRIANGLE PARK

4700 Guardian Drive, Durham, 919-941-6200,
800-228-9290; www.marriott.com

This ultramodern hotel is only five minutes from Research Triangle Park and the Raleigh-Durham Airport. North Carolina State, University of North Carolina and Duke University campuses are all close by. 223 rooms. Restaurant, bar. High-speed Internet access. Airport transportation available. **$$**

★★★MILLENNIUM HOTEL

2800 Campus Walk Ave., Durham, 919-383-8575,
866-866-8086; www.millennium-hotels.com

Conveniently located near Duke University and Medical Center, this hotel caters to business travelers with amenities such as wireless Internet access and a business center. Relax in the lounge, where mahogany bookshelves, overstuffed sofas and wing-backed chairs provide the atmosphere of a private club. 313 rooms. Restaurant, bar. High-speed Internet access. Meeting and banquet facilities. Business center. **$**

★QUALITY INN & SUITES

3710 Hillsborough Road, Durham, 919-382-3388,
877-424-6423; www.choicehotels.com

115 rooms. Complimentary continental breakfast. Wireless Internet access. **$**

★★★WASHINGTON DUKE INN & GOLF CLUB

3001 Cameron Blvd., Durham, 919-490-0999,
800-443-3853; www.washingtondukeinn.com

Campus living never looked this elegant, yet the Washington Duke Inn & Golf Club calls Duke University campus home. Rooms and suites reflect English country influences, as does the daily afternoon tea. With four resturants, dining choices here are terrific. A leading golf course just outside the door and privileges at the university's fitness facilities means there's always plenty to do. 271 rooms. Four restaurants, bar. Wireless Internet access. Fitness room. **$$$**

RESTAURANTS

★★★FAIRVIEW

3001 Cameron Blvd., Durham, 919-490-0999,
800-443-3853; www.washingtondukeinn.com

Located in the Washington Duke Inn & Golf Club, this Southern-influenced restaurant has traditional décor and nightly piano music. Try for a seat by one of the many windows for a beautiful view of the golf course. Weather permitting, the terrace is the perfect spot for outdoor dining. American menu. Breakfast, lunch, dinner, Sunday brunch. Bar. Children's menu. Business casual attire. Reservations recommended. Valet parking. Outdoor seating. **$$$**

NORTH CAROLINA

★
★
★
★
★

★★★FOUR-SQUARE RESTAURANT

2701 Chapel Hill Road, Durham, 919-401-9877; www.foursquarerestaurant.com

The location might throw you off, but once you sidle up to the elegant converted Victorian that houses Four-Square, you'll be in the right place for a romantic meal. Past the wraparound porch await seven dining rooms—easily converted to party space if you're in need of a venue—with fireplaces, and a screened porch for warmer weather use. Dining here will never get old, as the menu changes monthly to make sure the kitchen is always cooking up the freshest tastes, using local produce, cheese and meat each season. American menu. Dinner. Closed Sunday. $$$

★★★MAGNOLIA GRILL

1002 Ninth St., Durham, 919-286-3609; www.magnoliagrill.net

At Magnolia Grill, husband-and-wife chefs and co-owners Ben and Karen Barker exhibit an independent streak in Southern cooking. He handles the savories, taking Southern ingredients beyond regional confines in dishes such as smoked trout with avocado and red pepper slaw and sea bass carpaccio with Thai crab vinaigrette; she creates the sweets that take Southern comforts upscale, including shaker pie and upside-down caramel banana cake with bourbon praline ice cream. American, Southern menu. Dinner. Closed Sunday-Monday. Bar. Casual attire. Reservations recommended. $$$

★★★NANA'S RESTAURANT

2514 University Drive, Durham, 919-493-8545; www.nanasdurham.com

Locals like to frequent the bar for a quick bite and a glass or two off the wine list, but first-timers might want to treat their taste buds to all three courses: pate or peekytoe crab chowder to start, fish or fowl next, and a local cheese plate or Nana's Crème Brulee for dessert. All of your special occasion needs are covered with space to host big parties or a tasting menu with wine pairings for a more intimate outing. You can also bring home more than the doggy bag—the restaurant offers cooking classes with the chef. American menu. Dinner. Closed Sunday. $$$

★★★PAPA'S GRILLE

1821 Hillandale Road, Durham,
919-383-8502; www.papasgrille.com

Watch the chef's work in the open display kitchen of this restaurant located in a little strip mall near Route 70 and Interstate 85 (I-85). Bistro tables surround the outside of the room, while dining room tables are set with crisp white tablecloths, dark blue glasses and candles. Executive chef Sam Papanikas is known for his cast-iron pan-seared graviera cheese flambé and lavender-glazed lamb tenderloin. Mediterranean menu. Lunch, dinner. Closed Sunday. Bar. Children's menu. Business casual attire. Reservations recommended. $$$

★★PARIZADE

2200 W. Main St., Durham, 919-286-9712; www.parizaderestaurant.com

Mediterranean menu. Lunch, dinner. Bar. Business casual attire. Reservations recommended. Outdoor seating. $$

★
★
★
★
★

★★WATT'S GROCERY

1116 Broad St., Durham, 919-416-5040; www.wattsgrocery.com

American menu. Lunch (Tuesday-Friday), dinner, late-night, Sunday brunch. Closed Monday. $$

EDENTON

This is one of the oldest communities in North Carolina and was the capital of the colony for more than 22 years. The women of Edenton staged their own Revolutionary tea party on October 25, 1774, signing a resolution protesting British injustice. A bronze teapot, at the west side of the Courthouse Green, commemorates the event. Today Edenton, the seat of Chowan County, is known as the South's prettiest small town because of the large number of original historic homes dating back to the 1700s.

Information: Chamber of Commerce, 116 E. King St., 252-482-3400 or
Historic Edenton, 108 N. Broad St., 252-482-2637; www.edenton.org

WHAT TO SEE AND DO

HISTORIC EDENTON

108 N. Broad St., Edenton, 252-482-2637; www.nchistoricsites.org/iredell/iredell.htm

Tour of historic properties, which may be seen individually or as a group; allow 2 1/2 to 3 hours for complete tour. April-October, Monday-Saturday 9 a.m.-5 p.m. Sunday 1-5 p.m. November-March, Monday-Saturday 10 a.m.-4 p.m. Sunday 1-4 p.m.

JAMES IREDELL HOUSE

108 N. Broad St., Edenton, 252-482-2637;
www.nchistoricsites.org

Home of early attorney general of North Carolina who was appointed by George Washington to first U.S. Supreme Court.

SOMERSET PLACE STATE HISTORIC SITE

2572 Lake Shore Road, Creswell, 252-797-4560; www.albemarle-nc.com/somerset

On Lake Phelps in Pettigrew State Park. Original plantation, one of the largest in North Carolina, encompassed more than 100,000 acres. First primary crop was rice, which gave way to corn and wheat. Mansion and outbuildings built in circa 1830. April-October, Monday-Saturday 9 a.m.-5 p.m.; Sunday 1-5 p.m. November-March, Tuesday-Saturday 10 a.m.-4 p.m.; Sunday 1-4 p.m.

SPECIALTY LODGINGS

CAPTAIN'S QUARTERS INN

202 W. Queen St., Edenton, 252-482-8945, 800-482-8945;
www.captainsquartersinn.com

Eight rooms. Complimentary full breakfast. Children over 8 years only.

LORDS PROPRIETORS INN

300 N. Broad St., Edenton, 252-482-3641, 888-394-6622; www.edentoninn.com

This inn is actually three separate homes set on two acres of land. All 20 rooms are decorated with period antiques and reproductions. The New American dining room is for guests only and offers an impressive seasonal menu. 20 rooms. High-speed Internet access. $$

NORTH CAROLINA

★
★
★
★
★

ELIZABETH CITY

A town with a freshwater harbor on the Pasquotank River and accessible to the ocean, Elizabeth City has been a busy port since the middle of the 17th century. The Dismal Swamp Canal, dug in 1793, provided a critical north-south transportation route and brought much prosperity to the area. Shipyards, warehouses, fisheries, tanneries, sawmills and other industries flourished alongside commission merchants, artisans and navigators.

Although captured in the Civil War, Elizabeth City sustained minor damage. Today, many antebellum houses still stand alongside the historic homes and commercial buildings of the late 19th and early 20th centuries. The town welcomes boating traffic from the Intracoastal Waterway and is a great location for sportfishing. It serves as a gateway to Nags Head and Cape Hatteras National Seashore.

Information: Elizabeth City Area Chamber of Commerce, 502 E. Ehringhaus St., 252-335-4365; www.elizabethcitychamber.org

WHAT TO SEE AND DO
HISTORIC DISTRICT
Elizabeth City; www.historicelizabethcity.com
A 30-block area in the city center that contains the largest number of antebellum commercial buildings in the state. Tour brochures are available at the Chamber of Commerce.

MUSEUM OF THE ALBEMARLE
501 S. Water St., Elizabeth City, 252-335-1453
Regional historical displays; Native American exhibits; local artifacts, including decoys, fire engines; changing exhibits. Tuesday-Saturday 9 a.m.-5 p.m., Sunday 2-5 p.m.

HOTELS
★HAMPTON INN
402 Halstead Blvd., Elizabeth City, 252-333-1800, 800-426-7866; www.hamptoninn.com
100 rooms. Complimentary continental breakfast. High-speed Internet access. **$**

★HOLIDAY INN EXPRESS
306 S. Hughes Blvd., Elizabeth City, 252-338-8900, 800-315-2621; www.hiexpress.com
80 rooms. Complimentary continental breakfast. High-speed Internet access. Health and fitness center. **$**

RESTAURANT
★MARINA
Camden Causeway, Elizabeth City, 252-335-7307; www.elizcity.com
Seafood, steak menu. Dinner. Bar. Children's menu. Casual attire. Outdoor seating. **$**

FAYETTEVILLE

In 1783, the towns of Cross Creek and Campbellton merged and were renamed Fayetteville for the Revolutionary War hero the Marquis de Lafayette. It was the site of North Carolina's Constitutional Convention in 1787 and the capital of the state from 1789 to 1793. By 1831 it had become a busy commercial city.

Fayetteville is the state's farthest inland port, at the head of navigation on the Cape Fear River, with an eight-foot-deep channel connecting it to the Intracoastal Waterway. Today, the town is a center for retail, manufacturing and conventions, and the home of Fort Bragg and Pope Air Force Base.

Information: Convention and Visitors Bureau, 245 Person St., Fayetteville, 910-483-5311, 800-255-8217; www.visitfayettevillenc.com

WHAT TO SEE AND DO

CAPE FEAR BOTANICAL GARDEN
536 N. Eastern Blvd., Fayetteville, 910-486-0221; www.capefearbg.org
This garden is on 85 acres overlooking Cross Creek and the Cape Fear River. Wildflowers, oaks, native plants. Nature trails. Mid-December-mid-February, Monday-Saturday 10 a.m.-5 p.m. March-mid-December, Monday-Saturday 10 a.m.-5 p.m., Sunday noon-5 p.m.

FIRST PRESBYTERIAN CHURCH
102 Ann St., Fayetteville, 910-483-0121; www.firstprez.com
Classic Southern colonial-style architecture and whale-oil chandeliers. Among contributors to the original building (destroyed by fire in 1831) were James Monroe and John Quincy Adams. Tours by appointment only.

FORT BRAGG AND POPE AIR FORCE BASE—82ND AIRBORNE DIVISION WAR MEMORIAL MUSEUM
Gela and Ardennes Streets, Fort Bragg, 910-432-3443; www.bragg.army.mil
Weapons, relics of World War I and II, Vietnam, Korea, Desert Storm; history of 82nd airborne division; gift shop. Tuesday-Saturday.

HOTELS

★COMFORT INN
735 South Shiloh Drive, Fayetteville, 479-695-2121,
800-621-6596; www.comfortinn.com
60 rooms. Complimentary continental breakfast. Exercise room. Seasonal outdoor pool. $

★FAIRFIELD INN
720 E. Millsap Road, Fayetteville, 479-587-8600, 800-228-2800;
www.igougo.com
135 rooms. Complimentary continental breakfast. $

★HAMPTON INN
915 Krupa Drive, Fayetteville, 479-587-8300, 800-426-7866; www.hamptoninn.com
121 rooms. Complimentary continental breakfast. Business center. Fitness room. Pool. Pets not accepted. $

★★HOLIDAY INN
1944 Cedar Creek Road, Fayetteville, 910-323-1600,
800-315-2621; www.holiday-inn.com
198 rooms. Restaurant, bar. High-speed Internet access. $

NORTH CAROLINA

★
★
★
★
★

★HOLIDAY INN EXPRESS
1706 Skibo Road, Fayetteville, 910-867-6777, 800-315-2621; www.hiexpress.com
84 rooms. Complimentary continental breakfast. High-speed Internet access. Fitness center. Outdoor pool, whirlpool. **$**

★★QUALITY INN
2035 S. Eastern Blvd., Fayetteville, 910-485-8135, 800-828-2346; www.qualityinn.com
62 rooms. Restaurant. Free local calls. Seasonal outdoor pool. **$**

FRANKLIN

Home of the Cowee Valley ruby mines, Franklin attracts rock hounds who often find interesting gems in surface mines. Franklin is surrounded by waterfalls, mountain lakes and streams that offer excellent fishing for trout and bass, as well as boating, tubing and swimming. Around the county are 420,000 acres of the Nantahala National Forest, offering hiking trails, camping and fishing. A Ranger District office is located here. The Appalachian Trail bisects the western part of the county through Standing Indian Wildlife Management area and over Wayah Bald Mountain.
Information: Chamber of Commerce, 425 Porter St., Franklin,
828-524-3161, 866-372-5546; www.franklin-chamber.com

WHAT TO SEE AND DO
FRANKLIN GEM AND MINERAL MUSEUM
25 Phillips St., Franklin, 828-369-7831; www.fgmm.org
Gems and minerals; Native American artifacts, fossils; fluoreent mineral display. May-October, Monday-Friday noon-4 p.m., Saturday 11 a.m.-3 p.m., 6-9 p.m. November-April, Saturday 11 a.m.-3 p.m.

NANTAHALA NATIONAL FOREST
90 Sloan Road, Franklin, 828-524-6441
Nantahala, a Native American name meaning Land of the Noonday Sun, refers to Nantahala Gorge, so deep and narrow that the sun reaches the bottom only at noon. In addition to the gorge, the park offers scenic drives through the southern Appalachians, sparkling waterfalls (including the Whitewater Falls a series of cascades dropping 411 feet) and the 17,013-acre Joyce Kilmer-Slickrock Wilderness, with more than 100 species of trees native to the region. Hiking, camping, swimming, boating, fishing for bass and trout, hunting for deer, wild boar, turkey and ruffed grouse.

SCOTTISH TARTANS MUSEUM
W.C. Burrell Building, 86 E. Main St., Franklin, 828-524-7472; www.scottishtartans.org
An American extension of the Scottish Tartans Society in Edinburgh, Scotland. Exhibits trace heritage of Scottish Tartan and traditional Scottish dress. Research library. Monday-Saturday 10 a.m.-5 p.m.

RESTAURANTS
★★FROG & OWL KITCHEN
46 E. Main St., Franklin, 828-349-4112
French menu. Lunch, dinner. Children's menu. Casual attire. Reservations recommended. **$$**

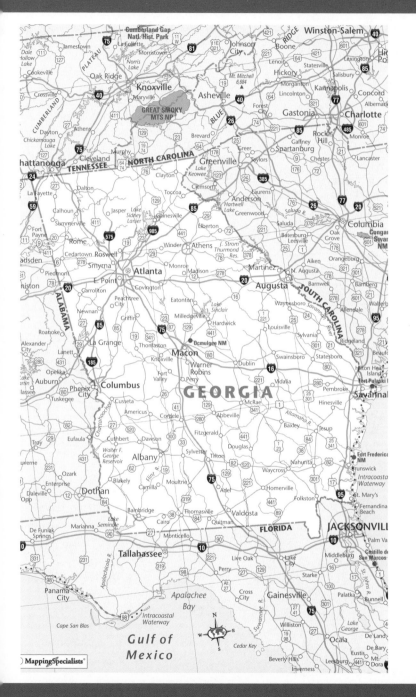

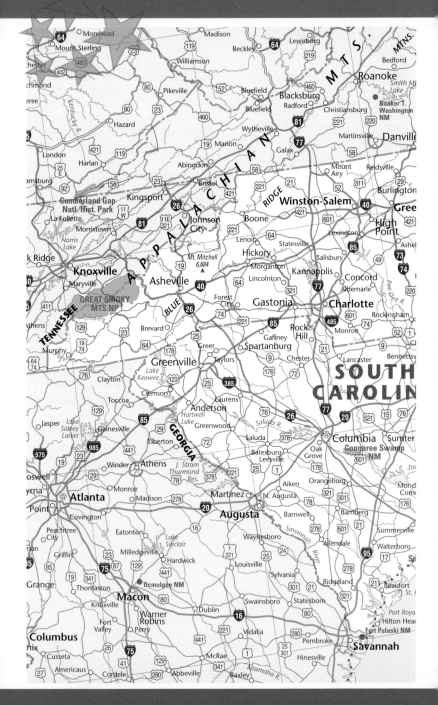

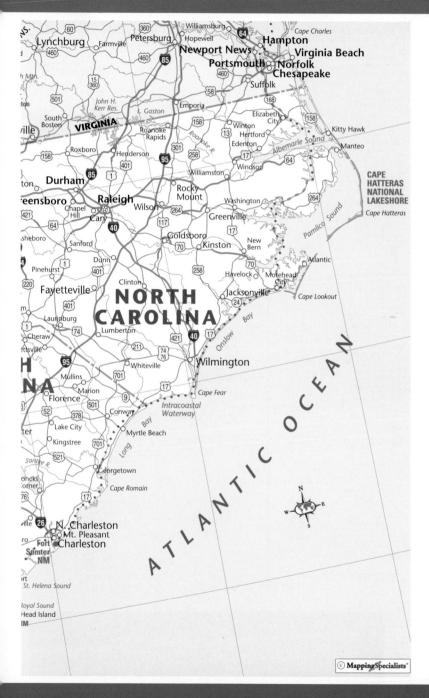

The Center for Hospitality Research
Hospitality Leadership Through Learning

The Cornell School of Hotel Administration's
world-class faculty explores new ways
to refine the practice of hospitality
management.

Our research drives better results.
Better strategy.
Better management.
Better operations.

See our work at:
www.chr.cornell.edu

537 Statler Hall • hosp_research@cornell.edu • 607.255.9780

Cornell University
School of Hotel Administration

★GAZEBO CAFÉ

44 Heritage Hollow, Franklin, 828-524-8783

American menu. Lunch. Closed mid-November-mid-April. Children's menu. Casual attire. Entire restaurant is outdoors; three different patio levels for dining. **$**

GOLDSBORO

Center of the bright-leaf tobacco belt, Goldsboro is also the seat of Wayne County and home of Seymour Johnson Air Force Base. There are also many food, wood product and textile plants here.

Information: Wayne County Chamber of Commerce, 308 N. William St.,
919-734-2241, 866-440-2245; www.greatergoldsboro.com

WHAT TO SEE AND DO

CLIFFS OF THE NEUSE STATE PARK

345 Park Entrance Road, Seven Springs, 919-778-6234; www.ncparks.gov

More than 700 acres on the Neuse River. Swimming, bathhouse, fishing, boating (rowboat rentals). Nature trails. Picnicking. Tent and trailer sites: mid-March-November; fee. Museum, interpretive center.

GREAT SMOKY MOUNTAINS NATIONAL PARK

Half in North Carolina and half in Tennessee, the 800-square-mile Great Smoky Mountains National Park is made for hiking. Seventy miles of the Appalachian Trail follow the ridge along the state line, and there are hundreds of miles of foot trails and bridle paths with formal campsites along the way. The deciduous trees and plants make every season—even winter—beautiful. In the lowlands are the cabins, barns and mills of the mountain people whose ancestors came from England and Scotland as well as the descendants of the Cherokee Nation, whose ancestors hid in the mountains from the soldiers in the winter of 1839 to avoid being driven out on the Trail of Tears to Oklahoma.

Of particular note are the spectacular views from Newfound Gap and the observation tower at Clingmans Dome (closed in winter). Cades Cove is an outdoor museum of log cabins and barns demonstrating the life of the original mountain people, about 25 miles west of Sugarlands. Park naturalists conduct campfire programs and hikes during the summer. There are also self-guided nature trails. **LeConte Lodge**, reached only by foot or horseback, is an accommodation within the park (*423-429-5704, late March-mid-November*).

Stop at one of three visitor centers: **Oconaluftee Center** in North Carolina, two miles north of Cherokee on Newfound Gap Road, designated Highway 441 outside the park (*daily; 423-436-1200*); **Sugarlands** in Tennessee, two miles southwest of Gatlinburg (*daily; 423-436-1200*) or **Cades Cove** in Tennessee, 10 miles southwest of Townsend (*daily; 423-436-1200*). All have exhibits and information about the park.

Information: 107 Park Headquarters Road, Gatlinburg, 865 436-1200;
www.nps.gov/grsm

NORTH CAROLINA

★
★
★
★

GOVERNOR CHARLES B. AYCOCK BIRTHPLACE STATE HISTORIC SITE

264 Governor Avcock Road, Fremont, 919-242-5581;
www.nchistoricsites.org
Mid-1800s farmhouse and outbuildings; audiovisual presentation in 1893 one-room school. Picnicking. Monday-Saturday.

HOTELS
★HOLIDAY INN EXPRESS

909 N. Spence Ave., Goldsboro, 919-751-1999,
800-315-2621; www.hiexpress.com-goldsboronc
122 rooms. Complimentary continental breakfast. High-speed Internet access. **$**

★★QUALITY INN

708 Corporate Drive, Goldsboro, 919-735-7901; www.qualityinn.com
125 room. Restaurant, bar. Complimentary continental breakfast. Wireless Internet access. **$**

GREENSBORO

North Carolina's third largest city, Greensboro has historically been an industrial town, manufacturing textiles, cigarettes, machinery and electronic components. Urban redevelopment and a growing population have also brought more cultural, nightlife and recreational activities—from the unique science museum, the numerous high-quality golf courses and even the biggest water park in the Carolinas.
Information: Greensboro Area Convention and Visitors Bureau, 317 S. Greene St.,
Greensboro, 336-274-2282, 800-344-2282; www.greensboronc.org

★
★
★
★
★

WHAT TO SEE AND DO
CHARLOTTE HAWKINS BROWN MEMORIAL STATE HISTORIC SITE

6136 Burlington Road, Sedalia, 336-449-4846;
www.nchistoricsites.org/chb/chb.htm
In 1902, C. H. Brown, granddaughter of a former slave, founded Palmer Memorial Institute, which became one of the finest preparatory schools for blacks in the nation. The campus later became the state's first historic site honoring education for African Americans. Guided tours of the historic campus, visitor center, audiovisual program. Picnicking. April-October, Tuesday-Saturday; rest of year, Tuesday-Sunday; closed holidays.

FIRST HORIZON PARK

408 Bellemeade St., Greensboro, 336-268-2255;
www.gsohoppers.com
The Greensboro Grasshoppers, minor league affiliates of the Florida Marlins, play in this new 8,000-seat brick stadium.

GREENSBORO HISTORICAL MUSEUM

130 Summit Ave., Greensboro, 336-373-2043; www.greensborohistory.org
Housed in an 1892 building in the downtown area, the museum features displays on the Revolutionary War, First Lady Dolley Madison and writer O. Henry, among others. Tuesday-Saturday 10 a.m.-5 p.m., Sunday 2-5 p.m.

GUILFORD COURTHOUSE NATIONAL MILITARY PARK

2332 New Garden Road, Greensboro, 336-288-1776;
www.nps.gov/guco

On March 15, 1781, Lord Cornwallis won a costly victory that was one link in a series of events that led to his surrender at Yorktown in October of the same year. After destroying a quarter of the enemy troops, General Nathanael Greene (for whom the city is named) made a successful retreat and then severely hampered the British plan of subduing the Southern colonies. The 220-acre park, established in 1917, has monuments marking important locations and honoring those who fought here. Self-guided auto tour; walking trails. The visitor center has a museum housing Revolutionary War weapons, other items; 20-minute film. Daily 8:30 a.m.-5 p.m.

NATURAL SCIENCE CENTER OF GREENSBORO

4301 Lawndale Drive, Greensboro, 336-288-3769; www.natsci.org

Natural science museum with zoo and indoor exhibits including geology, paleontology an aquarium, herpetarium and science and technology. Check out the 36-foot-tall Tyrannosaurus Rex model. Planetarium shows; inquire for schedule. Monday-Saturday 9 a.m.-5 p.m., Sunday 12:30-5 p.m.

HOTELS

★COMFORT INN GREENSBORO

2001 Veasley St., Greensboro, 336-294-6220, 877-424-6423;
www.choicehotels.com

121 rooms. Complimentary continental breakfast. Wireless Internet access. Pets accepted. $

115

★★★GRANDOVER RESORT & CONFERENCE CENTER

1000 Club Road, Greensboro, 336-294-1800, 800-472-6301;
www.grandover.com

The Grandover Resort & Conference Center features exceptional, award-winning golf, fine dining, stylish accommodations and Southern hospitality. The Ken Venturi Golf school is located here along with 36 holes. A full-service spa, four clay tennis courts, a state-of-the-art fitness center, indoor-outdoor pool, two racquetball courts and volleyball court also provide fun diversions. 247 rooms. Two restaurants, three bars. High-speed Internet access. Spa. Airport transportation available. $$

★★EMBASSY SUITES HOTEL GREENSBORO-AIRPORT

204 Centreport Drive, Greensboro, 336-668-4535,
800-362-2779; www.embassysuitesgreensboro.com

219 rooms, all suites. Restaurant, bar. Complimentary full breakfast. Wireless Internet access. Indoor pool, whirlpool. $$

★HAMPTON INN GREENSBORO-FOUR SEASONS

2004 Veasley St., Greensboro, 336-854-8600, 800-426-7866;
www.hamptoninn.com

120 rooms. Complimentary continental breakfast. Wireless Internet access. Business center. Outdoor pool. $

★★★MARRIOTT GREENSBORO AIRPORT

1 Marriott Drive, Greensboro, 336-852-6450,
800-228-9290; www.marriott.com

This hotel is located at the Piedmont Triad International Airport but offers 17 acres of its own landscaped grounds with a lake and a pavilion. The comfortable guest rooms feature the Marriott Revive bedding. Try dinner at JW's Steakhouse or a nightcap at Pitchers Bar and Grill. 299 rooms. High-speed Internet access. Restaurant, bar. Airport transportation available. **$$**

★★MARRIOTT GREENSBORO DOWNTOWN

304 N. Greene St., Greensboro, 336-379-8000, 800-228-9290; www.marriott.com

281 rooms. Restaurant, bar. High-speed Internet access. Business center. Pets not accepted. **$$**

★★★O. HENRY HOTEL

624 Green Valley Road, Greensboro, 336-854-2000;
877-854-2100; www.ohenryhotel.com

This locally-owned boutique hotel, named for the writer William Sydney Porter (O. Henry) who was born and raised in Greensboro, is decorated with North Carolina pine walls and ceilings, marble floors, Oriental carpets, leather and brocade furniture and large windows that overlook a cloistered courtyard. Spacious guest rooms include separate dressing rooms and soaking tubs. 131 rooms. Restaurant, bar. Wireless Internet access. Airport transportation available. **$$**

RESTAURANTS

★★★BISTRO SOFIA

616 Dolley Madison Road, Greensboro, 336-855-1313; www.bistrosofia.com

This restaurant, located northwest of downtown Greensboro, serves dishes created using homegrown organic vegetables, berries and herbs. The early-evening prix fixe menu is $25 for three courses, with bistro favorites such as steak frites making appearances on the ever-changing menu. Dinner. Closed Monday. Bar. Children's menu. Business casual attire. Reservations recommended. Outdoor seating. Dinner, Tuesday-Sunday 5-10 p.m. **$$$**

★★GATE CITY CHOP HOUSE

106 S. Holden St., Greensboro, 336-294-9977; www.gatecitychophouse.com

The main dining room at this steakhouse features a display kitchen and walls adorned with pictures of Greensboro. Menu selections include grilled peppered salmon, Carolina crab cakes, roasted prime rib and filet mignon. Seafood, steak menu. Lunch, dinner. Closed Sunday. Bar. Children's menu. Business casual attire. Reservations recommended. Outdoor seating. Monday-Friday 11.30 a.m.-10 p.m., Saturday 4.30-10 p.m. **$$$**

★★★RESTAURANT MUSE

3124 Kathleen Ave., Greensboro, 336-323-1428; www.restaurantmuse.net

Exquisite French cuisine prepared with fresh local ingredients draws diners back to Restaurant Muse time and time again. Chef/owner Mitchell Nicks offers creative plates that include roasted rack of lamb brushed with bergamot and mustard as well as his "untraditional Brutus salad" with pancetta, spicy chile dressing, fried artichoke hearts and a manchego cheese crisp. An à la carte menu is available, as is a chef's tasting menu. French menu. Lunch Monday-Friday 11 a.m.-3 p.m., dinner Monday-Thursday 5:30-9 p.m., brunch Saturday-Sunday 11-3 a.m. Bar. Business casual attire. Reservations recommended. Outdoor seating. $$$

GREENVILLE

An educational, cultural, commercial and medical center, Greenville is one of the towns named for General Nathanael Greene, a hero of the American Revolutionary War.
Information: Greenville-Pitt County Convention and Visitors Bureau,
525 S. Evans St., 252-752-8044, 800-537-5564; www.visitgreenvillenc.com

WHAT TO SEE AND DO
GREENVILLE MUSEUM OF ART
802 Evans St., Greenville, 252-758-1946; www.gmoa.org
Collections emphasize North Carolina contemporary fine arts and drawings, also paintings and prints of the period 1900-1945. Tuesday-Friday 10 a.m.-4.30 p.m., Saturday 1-4 p.m.

RIVER PARK NORTH SCIENCE AND NATURE CENTER
1000 Mumford Road, Greenville, 252-329-4560; www.greenvillenc.gov
A 309-acre park with four lakes and a mile of Tar River water frontage. Science center near park entrance offers hands-on exhibits. Fishing, pedal boats. Picnicking. Tuesday-Sunday.

HOTELS
★FAIRFIELD INN
821 S. Memorial Drive, Greenville, 252-758-5544,
877-424-6423; www.qualityinn.com
110 rooms. Complimentary continental breakfast. High-speed Internet access. Outdoor pool. Airport transportation available. Pets accepted. $

RESTAURANTS
★★BEEF BARN
400 St. Andrews Drive, Greenville, 252-756-1161; www.beefbarn.net
Steak, seafood menu. Lunch, dinner. Bar. Children's menu. Casual attire. Reservations recommended. Lunch 11.30 a.m.-2 p.m., dinner 5 p.m. $$

★PARKER'S BAR-B-QUE
3109 S. Memorial Drive, Greenville, 252-756-2388
American menu. Lunch, dinner. Children's menu. Casual attire. No credit cards accepted. $

HENDERSONVILLE

Nestled in the Blue Ridge Mountain area, Hendersonville is well-known as a summer resort and popular retirement community. The nearby town of Flat Rock is also home to visit-worthy inns and restaurants.
Information: Chamber of Commerce, 330 N. King St.,
828-692-1413; www.hendersonvillechamber.org

NORTH CAROLINA

WHAT TO SEE AND DO

CARL SANDBURG HOME NATIONAL HISTORIC SITE

81 Carl Sandburg Lane, Flat Rock, 828-693-4178;
www.nps.gov-carl.com

The famous poet's 264-acre farm, Connemara, is maintained as it was when Sandburg and his family lived here from 1945 until his death in 1967. On the grounds are a house and a historic barn for the three breeds of goats that Sandburg raised, as well as a visitor center. Tours daily 9 a.m.-5 p.m.

JUMP-OFF ROCK

Hendersonville, Fifth Ave., www.historichendersonville.org

Panoramic view of the Blue Ridge Mountains from atop Jump-Off Mountain. Closed Thanksgiving, Christmas and New Year's Day.

SPECIAL EVENT

FLAT ROCK PLAYHOUSE

2661 Greenville Highway, Flat Rock, 828-693-0731;
www.flatrockplayhouse.org

Outstanding professional theater since 1939; State Theater of North Carolina since 1961. Vagabond Players offer 10 Broadway and London productions in 15 weeks. Mid-May-mid-December, Wednesday-Saturday evenings; Thursday, Saturday, Sunday matinees.

HOTELS

★COMFORT INN

206 Mitchell Drive, Hendersonville, 828-693-8800,
800-424-6423; www.comfortinn.com

85 rooms. Complimentary continental breakfast. Pets accepted, fee. $

★★ECHO MOUNTAIN INN

2849 Laurel Park Highway, Hendersonville,
828-693-9626, 800-324-6466; www.echoinn.com

45 rooms. Complimentary continental breakfast. $

★HAMPTON INN

155 Sugarloaf Road, Hendersonville, 828-697-2333,
800-426-7866; www.hamptoninn.com

118 rooms. Complimentary continental breakfast. Business center. Fitness center. Pool. $

★★★HIGHLAND LAKE INN

86 Lily Pad Lane Highland Lake Road, Flat Rock, 828-693-6812,
800-635-5101; www.hlinn.com

This hotel is just 25 minutes from Asheville, and sits on 26 acres of woods near a lake. It's a lovely country getaway in the Blue Ridge Mountains. 63 rooms. Restaurant, bar. Beach. High-speed Internet access. $$

★
★
★
★
★

SPECIALTY LODGINGS

LAKE LURE INN

2771 Memorial Highway, Lake Lure, 828-625-2525, 800-277-5873;
www.lakelureinn.com
69 rooms. Restaurant, bar. Complimentary continental breakfast. Pets accepted, fee. $

LODGE ON LAKE LURE BED & BREAKFAST

361 Charlotte Drive, Lake Lure, 828-625-2789, 800-733-2785;
www.lodgeonlakelure.com
This is an elegant bed and breakfast in the countryside. The beauty of the lake adds a wonderful backdrop to this scenic property. 16 rooms. Complimentary full breakfast. Children over 8 years only. $$

THE WAVERLY INN

783 N. Main St., Hendersonville, 828-693-9193, 800-537-8195; www.waverlyinn.com
15 rooms. Complimentary full breakfast. Restored guest house; Victorian décor, upstairs sun porch. $

RESTAURANTS

★SEASONS RESTAURANT

Highland Lake Road, Flat Rock, 828-696-9094, 800-762-1376; www.hlinn.com
American menu. Breakfast, lunch, dinner, brunch. Bar. Children's menu. Casual attire. Outdoor seating. $$

★★SINBAD

202 S. Washington St., Hendersonville, 828-696-2039; www.sinbadrestaurant.com
Mediterranean menu. American cuisine. Lunch, dinner. Closed Sunday-Monday. Bar. $$

HICKORY

Hickory is the country's center of furniture making. In a 200-mile radius of the town, 60 percent of the nation's furniture is produced and visitors often come looking for unique and interesting pieces. Golf, car racing and baseball add to the entertainment, along with a number of historical sites and museums.
Information: Catawba County Chamber of Commerce, 1055 Southgate
Corporate Park S.W., Hickory, 828-328-6111; www.hickorymetro.com

WHAT TO SEE AND DO

20 MILES OF FURNITURE

Hickory, 800-737-0782; www.20milesoffurniture.com
This area offers golf, shopping and dining, but is best known for its nearly 40 furniture stores. Plant tours are available.

CATAWBA COUNTY MUSEUM OF HISTORY

21 E. First St., Newton, 828-465-0383; www.catawbahistory.org
Exhibits include a fire engine, country doctor's office, Waugh Cabin, Barringer Cabin, a blacksmith shop, and an agriculture exhibit. Wednesday-Saturday 9 a.m.-4 p.m.; Sunday 1.30-4:30 p.m. Closed Monday and Tuesday.

NORTH CAROLINA

★
★
★
★
★

HICKORY FURNITURE MART

2220 Highway 70 S.E., Hickory, 800-462-6278; www.hickoryfurniture.com

More than 1,000 home-furnishing lines are displayed in this 1 million-square-foot complex, which includes 100 factory outlets, stores and galleries, a museum, café, shipping service, visitor center and motel.

HICKORY MUSEUM OF ART

234 Third Ave., Hickory, 828-327-8576; www.hickorymuseumofart.org

American realist 19th- and 20th-century art, including works by Gilbert Stuart; Hudson River school; American impressionists; European, Oriental and pre-Columbian pieces; changing exhibits quarterly. Tuesday-Sunday 10 a.m.-4 p.m.; Sunday 1-4 p.m. Closed Monday and holidays.

HOTELS

★HAMPTON INN HICKORY

1520 13th Ave., Hickory, 828-323-1150, 800-426-7866;
www.hamptoninn.com

119 rooms. Complimentary continental breakfast. High-speed Internet access. Swimming pool. Fitness center. Business center. Pets not accepted. **$**

★★HOLIDAY INN SELECT

1385 Lenoir Rhyne Blvd. S.E., Hickory, 828-323-1000, 800-366-5010;
www.holiday-inn.com

200 rooms. Restaurant, bar. Wireless Internet access. Business center. Fitness center. Indoor pool. **$**

RESTAURANTS

★★★1859 CAFÉ

443 Second Ave. S.W., Hickory, 828-322-1859; www.hickoryonline.com/1859cafe

The international cuisine at this restaurant includes options such as pesto-crusted scallops with mushroom risotto, sautéed duck breast with strawberry rhubarb sauce and pork tenderloin stuffed with spiced fruit and walnuts. International menu. Dinner. Closed Sunday. Bar. Casual attire. Reservations recommended. Outdoor seating. **$$**

★★★VINTAGE HOUSE

271 Third Ave. N.W., Hickory, 828-324-1210

This restaurant is a converted 100-year-old Victorian home located two blocks from the downtown center of Hickory. Dine in one of five dining rooms—two of which are enclosed porch rooms with large windows, overlooking the gardens. American menu. Dinner. Closed Sunday; first week in January, first week in July. Bar. Business casual attire. Reservations recommended. **$$$**

HIGH POINT

Furniture making has put this North Carolina city on the map. The city rests on the highest point along the North Carolina and Midland Railroad, which the state built in 1853. The plank road (finished in 1854), stretching 130 miles from Salem to Fayetteville, made it a center of trade. Mileposts on this road had carved numbers instead of painted ones so travelers could feel their way at night.

Information: Convention and Visitors Bureau, 300 S. Main St., High Point, 336-884-5255, 800-720-5255; www.highpoint.org

SPECIAL EVENT
NORTH CAROLINA SHAKESPEARE FESTIVAL
High Point Theatre, 220 E. Commerce Ave., High Point, 336-841-2273; www.ncshakes.org

Season includes three productions and *A Christmas Carol*. August-October and December.

HOTEL
★★RADISSON HOTEL HIGH POINT
135 S. Main St., High Point, 336-889-8888, 800-201-1718; www.radisson.com

252 rooms. Restaurant, bar. High-speed Internet. Pool. Fitness center. Airport transportation available. $

SPECIALTY LODGING
BOULDIN HOUSE BED AND BREAKFAST
4332 Archdale Road, High Point, 336-431-4909, 800-739-1816; www.bouldinhouse.com

Five rooms. Complimentary full breakfast. High-speed Internet access. Children over 12 years only. Pets accepted. $

RESTAURANT
★★★J. BASUL NOBLE'S
101 S. Main St., High Point, 336-889-3354; www.noblesrestaurant.com

Creative menu options are prepared in a wood-fired oven, a grille and a rotisserie, enhancing the flavors in dishes such as bacon-wrapped wood-fired grouper, grilled pork tenderloin and rotisserie half chicken. Several pizzas are offered as well as a bistro menu with lighter fare. Live jazz completes the dining experience. Italian menu. Lunch, dinner. Closed Sunday. Bar. Casual attire. Outdoor seating. Dinner Monday-Thursday 5:30-9 p.m. Friday-Saturday 5:30-10 p.m. Lunch Monday-Friday 11.30 a.m.-2 p.m.; Sunday 11 a.m.-2:30 p.m. $$

HIGHLANDS

Highlands is a summer resort near the Georgia state line. Many unusual plants are part of the primeval rain forest preserve. Completely encircled by Nantahala National Forest, the area surrounding the town is called "land of the waterfalls." A Ranger District office is located here.

Information: Chamber of Commerce, 396 Oak St., Highlands, 828-526-2114; www.highlandschamber.org

HOTELS
★HIGHLANDS SUITE HOTEL
200 Main St., Highlands, 828-526-4502, 877-553-3761; www.highlandssuitehotel.com

29 rooms, all suites. Complimentary continental breakfast. $

NORTH CAROLINA

★
★
★
★
★

★★★★OLD EDWARDS INN AND SPA

445 Main St., Highlands, 828-526-8008; www.oldedwardsinn.com

Nestled in the charming mountain town of Highlands, this historic inn on the National Register of Historic Places. Each guest room, suite and cottage is filled with period antiques and modern amenities. The luxurious 25,000-square-foot full-service spa uses herbs and botanicals from the spa's garden. 28 rooms. Restaurant, bar. Complimentary continental breakfast. Wireless Internet access. Fitness center. Children over 11 years only. $$$$

RESTAURANTS

★★★★MADISON'S RESTAURANT & WINE GARDEN

445 Main St., Highlands, 828-526-5477; www.oldedwardsinn.com

There's something old, something new, something Southern and everything delicious at Madison's Restaurant and Wine Garden at Old Edward's Inn and Spa. The chef uses local ingredients to cook up Madison's contemporary Southern cuisine, serving up Southern with a twist to locals and visitors for breakfast, dinner or just dessert and drinks. Weather permitting, pop the cork on a bottle in the Wine Garden and take in views of the lush North Carolina nature. Mountains and countryside not your thing? Dine inside on Carolina mountain trout, with a side of white truffle macaroni and cheese. And definitely save room for the plantation chocolate soufflé. American, Southern menu. Breakfast, lunch, dinner. $$$

★★NICK'S

108 North Main St., Highlands, 828-526-2706;
www.nicksfinefoods.com

American menu. Lunch, dinner. Closed Wednesday; also January-February. Children's menu. Casual attire. Reservations recommended. $$

★★ON THE VERANDAH

1536 Franklin Road, Highlands, 828-526-2338;
www.ontheverandah.com

American menu. Dinner, Sunday brunch. Closed January-mid-March; weekdays in December and March. Children's menu. Casual attire. Reservations recommended. Outdoor seating. $$$

SPA

★★★★THE SPA AT OLD EDWARDS INN AND SPA

445 Main St., Highlands, 828-526-8008; www.oldedwardsinn.com

Tucked into the mountains of the North Carolina Highlands, the Old Edwards Inn and Spa offers luxury rooms, suites and cottages for those looking to be one with nature, or one with a pedicure. Chilling out is the only task at hand at this 25,000-square-foot spa, which boasts treatments that use native North Carolina herbs and botanicals (some grown in the spa's own garden) for the signature Carolina Cocoon treatments. Or try one of the massages—go exotic with the Balinese massage or chill out with Hot Spring Stone massage—for a knot-kneading experience. But for the ultimate in relaxation, just book a Spa Suite and let the royal treatments come to you.

★
★
★
★
★

JACKSONVILLE

On the edge of the New River Marine Base (Camp Lejeune), Jacksonville has excellent fishing. The surrounding Onslow County has more than 30 miles of beaches.
Information: www.jacksonvillenc.net

HOTELS

★BEST WESTERN COURTYARD RESORT

603 N. Marine Blvd., Jacksonville, 910-455-4100; www.ramada.com
121 rooms. Complimentary continental breakfast. $

★HAMPTON INN

474 Western Blvd., Jacksonville, 910-347-6500, 800-426-7866; www.hamptoninn.com
122 rooms. Complimentary continental breakfast. Wireless Internet access. Business center. Pets not accepted. $

★HOLIDAY INN EXPRESS

2115 Highway 17 N., Jacksonville, 910-347-1900, 800-465-4329;
www.hiexpress.com
118 rooms, complimentary continental breakfast. Wireless Internet access. Business center. Outdoor pool. Fitness center. Pets not accepted. $

KILL DEVIL HILLS

Although the name Kitty Hawk is usually associated with the Wright Brothers, their early flying experiments took place on and near these dunes on the Outer Banks.
Information: Dare County Tourist Bureau, 704 US 64-264, Manteo,
252-473-2138, 800-446-6262; www.outerbanks.org

WHAT TO SEE AND DO

WRIGHT BROTHERS NATIONAL MEMORIAL

1401 National Park Drive, Kill Devil Hills, 252-441-7430; www.nps.gov
The field where the first powered flight took place on December 17, 1903 is marked, showing the takeoff point and landing place. The living quarters and hangar buildings used by the Wrights during their experiments have been replicated. The visitor center has reproductions of a 1902 glider and a 1903 flyer, with exhibits on the story of their invention. Summer daily 9 a.m.-6 p.m., September-May 9 a.m.-5 p.m. Closed Christmas Day.

★
★
★
★
★

HOTELS

★BEST WESTERN OCEAN REEF SUITES

107 Virginia Dare Court, Kill Devil Hills,
252-441-1611, 800-528-1234; www.bestwestern.com
71 rooms. Restaurants. High-speed Internet. Fitness center, pool. Spa. Beach. Pets not accepted. $$

★COMFORT INN

401 N. Virginia Dare Trail, Kill Devil Hills,
252-480-2600, 800-424-6423; www.comfortinn.com
118 rooms. Complimentary continental breakfast. Beach. Pool. Pet friendly. $

★DAYS INN

201 N. Virginia Dare Trail, Kill Devil Hills,
252-441-7211, 800-329-7466; www.daysinn.com

54 rooms. Complimentary continental breakfast. Free wireless Internet access. Pool. Beach. Pets not accepted. **$**

★★RAMADA

1701 S. Virginia Dare Trail, Kill Devil Hills,
252-441-2151, 800-635-1824; www.ramada.com

171 rooms. Restaurant, bar. High-speed Internet access. Business center. Pool. Fitness center. Beach. Pets accepted. **$$**

★★★THE SANDERLING

1461 Duck Road, Duck, 252-261-4111, 877-650-4812; www.sanderlinginn.com

Nestled on the northern reaches of the Outer Banks, the Sanderling is designed to complement the natural setting and includes an eco-center and low-rise cedar-shingled buildings. Composed of three inns and oceanside villas, the Sanderling offers secluded beaches, conference centers and a full-service spa. The restaurant is housed in a historic U.S. lifesaving station. 88 rooms. Restaurant, bar. Wireless Internet access. **$$**

RESTAURANTS

★★FLYING FISH CAFÉ

2003 S. Croatan Highway, Kill Devil Hills, 252-441-6894; www.flyingfishcafe.net

Mediterranean menu. Dinner. Bar. Children's menu. Casual attire. Reservations recommended. **$$**

★JOLLY ROGER

1836 N. Virginia Dare Trail, Kill Devil Hills, 252-441-6530; www.jollyrogerobx.com

American menu. Breakfast, lunch, dinner. Bar. Children's menu. Casual attire. **$$**

★★PORT O' CALL

504 Virginia Dare Trail, Kill Devil Hills, 252-441-7484;
www.outerbanksportocall.com

Seafood, steak menu. Dinner. Closed January-March. Bar. Children's menu. Casual attire. Reservations recommended. **$$**

LINVILLE

Linville is located in a ruggedly beautiful resort area. Several miles to the south, just off the Blue Ridge Parkway, is scenic Linville Falls, which cascade down the steep Linville Gorge. Visible from vantage points in this area are the mysterious Brown Mountain lights, a natural phenomenon observed for hundreds of years.

WHAT TO SEE AND DO

GRANDFATHER MOUNTAIN

2050 Blowing Rock Road, Linville, 828-733-4337; www.grandfather.com

The highest peak of the Blue Ridge Mountains, with spectacular views, rugged rock formations, a mile high-swinging bridge, bald eagles, gold eagles, river otters, deer, cougars, black bears, bear cubs and others in natural habitats. Hiking trails, picnic areas. Museum with exhibits on local animals, birds, flowers, geology. Daily, weather permitting. Spring 8 a.m.-6 p.m.; summer 8 a.m.-7 p.m.; fall 8 a.m.-6 p.m.; winter 9 a.m.-5 p.m.

SPECIAL EVENT
GRANDFATHER MOUNTAIN HIGHLAND GAMES
828-733-1333; www.gmhg.org
Gathering of members of more than 100 Scottish clans to view or participate in traditional Scottish sports, track-and-field events, dancing, piping and drumming, ceremonies and pageantry. Mid-July. Pets not accepted. No bicycles permitted.

RESORT
★★★THE ESEEOLA LODGE AT LINVILLE GOLF CLUB
175 Linville Ave., Linville, 828-733-4311, 800-742-6717; www.eseeola.com
The Eseeola Lodge at Linville Golf Club has an historic 18-hole golf course, eight tennis courts, a pool and a croquet lawn to keep guests busy. For children, there is a well-equipped playground and day camp. The chef prepares a daily four-course dinner of international dishes with a Southern bent. 24 rooms. Closed late October-mid-May. Two restaurants, bar. Complimentary full breakfast. Wireless Internet access. Children's activity center. **$$$**

LITTLE SWITZERLAND
Named for its sweeping panoramic views, the mountain village of Little Switzerland has been a popular resort since the early 1900s. The Blue Ridge Parkway passes through town.
Information Mitchell County Chamber of Commerce, Route 1,
Spruce Pine, 704-765-9483, 800-227-3912; www.mitchell-county.com

125

WHAT TO SEE AND DO
EMERALD VILLAGE
McKinney Mine Road and Blue Ridge Parkway, Little Switzerland,
828-765-6463, 828-765-0000; www.emeraldvillage.com
Historical area includes mines; North Carolina Mining Museum; Main Street 1920s Mining Community Museum; Gemstone Mine, where visitors can prospect for gems under shaded flumes; Mechanical Music Maker Museum; waterfall and scenic overlook; shops and deli. Daily.

MOUNT MITCHELL STATE PARK
2388 State Highway 128, Brunsville Little Switzerland, 828-675-4611; www.ncparks.gov
Adjacent to Pisgah National Forest, a natural national landmark. The road leads to the summit. At 6,684 feet, it's the highest point east of the Mississippi River. Trails, picnicking, restaurant, refreshment stands. Small-tent camping area. Observation tower, museum.

HOTEL
★★SWITZERLAND INN
86 High Ridge Road, Little Switzerland, 828-765-2153,
800-654-4026; www.switzerlandinn.com
73 rooms. Closed November-mid-April. Restaurant, bar. Complimentary full breakfast. Wireless Internet access. Pool. Pets accepted. **$**

NORTH CAROLINA

★
★
★
★
☆

LUMBERTON

Lumberton is the county seat of Robeson County and the home of many industries, including one of the largest tobacco marketing centers in the state. Hunting for quail, duck, dove and rabbit is excellent in the area. Pembroke, to the northwest, is the population center for some 30,000 Lumbee Native Americans, believed by some historians to include descendants of the "lost colonists."

Information: Visitors Bureau, 3431 Lackey St., 910-739-9999, 800-359-6971;
www.lumberton-nc.com

SPECIAL EVENT

SCOTTISH HIGHLAND GAMES

200 College St., Red Springs, 910-843-5000;
www.capefearscots.com

Celebration of Scottish heritage with music, dancing, competitions, children's events. Late September-early October.

HOTELS

★COUNTRY INN & SUITES BY CARLSON

3010 Roberts Ave., Lumberton, 910-738-2481, 888-201-1746;
www.countryinns.com

53 rooms. Complimentary continental breakfast. High-speed Internet access. Fitness center. Pool. $

★★HOLIDAY INN

101 Wintergreen Drive, Lumberton, 910-671-1166, 800-465-4329;
www.holiday-inn.com

107 rooms. Restaurant. High-speed Internet access. Fitness center. Pool. Pets not accepted. $

MAGGIE VALLEY

In 1909, Henry Setzer decided the expanding community of Plott needed a post office. He submitted the names of his three daughters to the postmaster general, who selected Maggie, aged 14. Lying in the shadow of the Great Smoky Mountains National Park, the town is 4 miles from the Soco Gap entrance to the Blue Ridge Parkway and has become a year-round resort area.

Information: Convention and Visitors Bureau/Chamber of Commerce,
2487 Soco Road, 828-926-1686, 800-624-4431; www.maggievalley.org

WHAT TO SEE AND DO

CATALOOCHEE SKI AREA

1080 Ski Lodge Road, Maggie Valley, 828-926-0285, 800-768-0285;
www.cataloochee.com

Quad, two double chair lifts, T-bar, rope tow; patrol, school, rentals; snowmaking; half-day and twilight rates; cafeteria, bar. Longest run 3,800 feet, vertical drop 740 feet. December-mid-March, daily. Monday-Friday, 9 a.m.-4:30 p.m.; Saturday, Sunday and holidays 8:30 a.m.-4:30 p.m.

★
★★
★★
★★
★

STOMPIN GROUND

3116 Soco Road, Maggie Valley, 828-926-1288; www.discovermaggievalley.com

Bluegrass and country music; clogging; exhibition dancers; square dancing. May-October, nightly.

HOTEL
★COMFORT INN

3282 Soco Road, Maggie Valley, 828-926-9106, 800-228-5150; www.comfortinn.com

68 rooms. Complimentary continental breakfast. High-speed Internet access, indoor heated pool. **$**

SPECIALTY LODGING
CATALOOCHEE SKI AREA

119 Ranch Drive, Maggie Valley, 828-926-0285, 800-768-0285;
www.cataloochee.com

Guests can relax in the lodge with a hot toddy and put their feet up around the crackling circular fireplace. Enjoy a hearty home-cooked meal or picnic on the sun-drenched deck overlooking the slopes. 26 rooms, children's activity center. Whirlpool. **$**

RESTAURANT
★★J. ARTHUR'S

2843 Soco Road, Maggie Valley, 828-926-1817; www.jarthurs.com

Seafood, steak menu. Dinner. Closed Sunday-Tuesday in November-April. Bar. Children's menu. Casual attire. Outdoor seating. **$$**

MANTEO

Found on the eastern side of Roanoke Island on the Outer Banks, the quaint town of Manteo has more bed and breakfasts than any other Outer Banks village. Fishing in the waters off Manteo is excellent. A large sport fishing fleet is available for booking at Oregon Inlet as well as on Roanoke Island.

Information: Dare County Tourist Bureau, 704 Highway 64-264,
252-473-2138, 800-446-6262; www.outerbanks.org

WHAT TO SEE AND DO
ELIZABETHAN GARDENS

1411 National Park Drive, Manteo, 252-473-3234; www.elizabethangardens.org

These 10.5 acres include Great Lawn, Sunken Garden, Queen's Rose Garden, an herb garden, a 16th-century gazebo with thatched roof and an ancient garden statuary. Plants bloom all year: spring peak, mid-April; summer peak, mid-July; fall peak, mid-October; and winter peak, mid-February. Gate House Reception Center displays period furniture, English portraits, coat of arms. Daily.

ROANOKE ISLAND FESTIVAL PARK

Manteo waterfront, 252-475-1500; www.roanokeisland.com

Representative 16th-century sailing vessel similar to those that brought the first English colonists to the New World more than 400 years ago. Living history interpretation (summer). Visitor center with exhibits and audiovisual program. February-December, daily.

SPECIAL EVENT

THE LOST COLONY OUTDOOR DRAMA

Waterside Theater, Manteo, 800-488-5012

Outdoor drama by Pulitzer Prize-winner Paul Green about the first English colony established in the New World whose curious disappearance remains a mystery to this day. Mid-June-late August. Monday-Saturday evenings. Reservations recommended.

HOTEL

★★★TRANQUIL HOUSE INN

405 Queen Elizabeth St., Manteo, 252-473-1404,
800-458-7069; www.tranquilinn.com

Built in 1988 in the style of a 19th-century Outer Banks resort, this waterfront property offers a continental breakfast and evening wine and cheese with each of its 25 rooms. Elegant dockside dining overlooking Shallowbag Bay can be found at 1587 Restaurant. 25 rooms. Complimentary continental breakfast. Restaurant. **$$**

MOREHEAD CITY

Just across the Intracoastal Waterway from Beaufort, Morehead City is the largest town in Carteret County and a year-round resort town. The port accommodates ocean-going vessels and charter boats.

Information: Crystal Coast Visitors Center, 3409 Arendell St.,
252-726-8148; www.sunnync.com

WHAT TO SEE AND DO

FORT MACON STATE PARK

E. Fort Macon Road, Atlantic Beach, 252-726-3775

This restored fort, built in 1834, was originally used as a harbor defense. Beach (lifeguards in summer), bathhouse; surf fishing; hiking, nature trails. Museum; interpretive program (summer); battle reenactments.

HOTELS

★★BUCCANEER INN

2806 Arendell St., Morehead City, 252-726-3115

91 rooms. Restaurant, bar. Complimentary full breakfast. **$**

★HAMPTON INN

4035 Arendell St., Morehead City, 252-240-2300, 800-426-7866;
www.hamptoninn.com

119 rooms. Complimentary continental breakfast. High-speed Internet access. Fitness center. **$**

★★★SHERATON ATLANTIC BEACH OCEANFRONT HOTEL

2717 W. Fort Macon Road, Atlantic Beach, 252-240-1155, 800-624-8875;
www.sheratonatlanticbeach.com

Each room at this beachfront hotel features a private balcony. There are two restaurants, two lounges and two pools as well as nearby golf, tennis. High-speed Internet access. Breakfast, Brunch. **$$**

SPECIALTY LODGINGS
EMERALD ISLE INN AND BED & BREAKFAST
502 Ocean Drive, Emerald Isle, 252-354-3222; www.emeraldisle.com
Four rooms, complimentary full breakfast. **$**

HARBOR LIGHT GUEST HOUSE
332 Live Oak Drive, Cape Carteret, 252-393-6868, 800-624-8439;
www.harborlightnc.com
Nine rooms. Complimentary full breakfast. Wireless Internet access. Children 16 and over only. **$$**

RESTAURANTS
★CAPTAIN BILL'S WATERFRONT
701 Evans St., Morehead City, 252-726-2166
Seafood menu. Lunch, dinner. Children's menu. Casual attire. Outdoor seating. **$$**

★MRS. WILLIS
3114 Bridge St., Morehead City, 252-726-3741
Seafood, steak menu. Lunch, dinner. Bar. Children's menu. Casual attire. **$$**

★SANITARY FISH MARKET
501 Evans St., Morehead City, 252-247-3111;
www.sanitaryfishmarket.com
Seafood menu. Lunch, dinner. Closed December-January. Children's menu. Casual attire. **$$**

MORGANTON
Morganton boasts a vibrant, park-filled downtown, beautiful views and access to golf, boating and other recreation, plus a thriving cultural community. It's near the site of some of the earliest evidence of European explorers to North America. In 1893, the county became a haven for the Waldenses, a religious group from the French-Italian Alps who were seeking freedom and space to expand outside their alpine homeland. They settled in nearby Valdese, and their history is part of the area's local lore.
Information: Burke County Travel and Tourism,
102 E. Union St., Morgantown

HOTELS
★★HOLIDAY INN MORGANTON
2400 S. Sterling St., Morganton, 828-437-0171, 800-465-4329;
www.holiday-inn.com
133 rooms. Restaurant, bar. High-speed Internet access. Free local calls. Fitness center. Pool. **$**

★SLEEP INN
2400 S. Sterling St., Morganton, 828-433-9000, 800-424-6423;
www.sleepinn.com
61 rooms. Complimentary continental breakfast. Free local calls. Pool. **$**

NORTH CAROLINA

★
★
★
★
★

NAGS HEAD

This is a year-round town on the Outer Banks, just south of Kill Devil Hills and at the north end of Cape Hatteras National Seashore. Swimming is good in summer. The soft sand dunes and Atlantic breezes make this a popular area for hang gliding. Offshore, partly buried in the drifting sand, are many wrecks of both old sailing ships and more modern vessels.

Information: Dare County Tourist Bureau, 704 Highway 64-264,
Manteo, 252-473-2138, 800-446-6262; www.outerbanks.org

HOTELS

★NAGS HEAD INN

4701 S. Virginia Dare Trail, Nags Head, 252-441-0454, 800-327-8881;
www.nagsheadinn.com
100 rooms, closed Sunday after Thanksgiving, December 26. Beach. $

★SURF SIDE MOTEL

6701 S. Virginia Dare Trail, Nags Head, 252-441-2105, 800-552-7873;
www.surfsideobx.com
76 rooms. Complimentary continental breakfast. Beach. Whirlpool. $

CAPE HATTERAS NATIONAL SEASHORE

★
★ ★
★ ★
★

This thin strand of islands stretches for 75 miles along the Outer Banks, and is the largest area of undeveloped coast on the Eastern Seaboard, threaded between the windy, pounding Atlantic and the shallow Pamlico Sound. Nags Head is the northern limit of the recreational area, which has three sections (separated by inlets): Bodie (pronounced *body*), Hatteras (largest of the barrier islands) and Ocracoke, the most picturesque. Bounded on three sides by the park, but separate from it, are the villages of Rodanthe, Waves, Salvo, Avon, Buxton, Fridayo, Hatteras and Ocracoke. Noted for its long expanses of sand beaches, the area is also a naturalist's paradise: wildflowers bloom most of the year, and stands of yaupon (holly), loblolly pine and live oak are common. Several freshwater ponds are found on Bodie, Hatteras and Ocracoke Islands. Many migratory and nonmigratory waterfowl, including gadwalls, greater snow and Canada geese, loons, grebes and herons winter here.

There is an information station at Whalebone Junction (Memorial Day-Labor Day, daily) south of Nags Head. Near Bodie Island Lighthouse is a bird observation platform, a nature trail and a visitor center (Good Friday-Columbus Day, daily) with natural history exhibits. There are also visitor centers with history exhibits at Ocracoke, Bodie Island Lighthouse and the Cape Hatteras Lighthouse at Buxton.

Enter from Cedar Island or Swan Quarter toll ferry. Reservations recommended. Free ferry from Ocracoke Island to Hatteras Island; 252-995-4474; www.nps.gov

SPECIALTY LODGING

FIRST COLONY INN

6720 S. Virginia Dare Trail, Nags Head, 252-441-2343, 800-368-9390;
www.firstcolonyinn.com

This beach-style bed and breakfast has welcomed Outer Banks' visitors since 1932 and is on the National Register of Historic Places. Rooms are decorated with English antiques. Wide, two-story verandas wrap around the shingled building and deliver great sunset views. 26 rooms. Complimentary full breakfast. **$**

RESTAURANTS

★★OWENS' RESTAURANT

7114 S. Virginia Dare Trail, Nags Head, 252-441-7309;
www.owensrestaurant.com

American menu. Dinner. Closed January-mid-March. Bar. Children's menu. Casual attire. **$$$**

★★PENGUIN ISLE

6708 S. Croatan Highway, Nags Head, 252-441-2637; www.penguinisle.com

American menu. Dinner. Closed January-February. Bar. Children's menu. Casual attire. Reservations recommended. Outdoor seating. **$$**

★★WINDMILL POINT

Highway 158, Nags Head, 252-441-1535; www.windmillpointrestaurant.com

American menu. Dinner, brunch. Bar. Children's menu. Casual attire. **$$$**

NEW BERN

This town, originally settled by Swiss and German immigrants, is most famous as the birthplace of Pepsi-Cola, which was first sold at a local drugstore. Many Georgian-style and Federal-style buildings give New Bern an architectural look unique in North Carolina. The Neuse and Trent rivers are ideal for swimming, boating and freshwater and saltwater fishing.

Information: Visitor Information Center, 314 S. Front St., New Bern,
252-637-9400, 800-437-5767; www.visitnewbern.com

NORTH CAROLINA

★
★
★
★
★

WHAT TO SEE AND DO

ATTMORE-OLIVER HOUSE

512 Pollock St., New Bern, 252-638-8558

This house, headquarters for the New Bern Historical Society, exhibits 18th- and 19th-century furnishings and historical objects including Civil War artifacts. Early April-mid-December, Tuesday, Thursday, Saturday; also by appointment.

TRYON PALACE HISTORIC SITES AND GARDENS

610 Pollock St., New Bern, 800-767-1560; www.tryonpalace.org

Built from 1767-1770 by Royal Governor William Tryon, this colonial building burned in 1798 and lay in ruins until it was rebuilt between 1952 and 1959. It served as the colonial and first state capital. Reconstruction, furnishings and 18th-century English gardens are beautiful and authentic. Guided tours. Daily.

PEPSI STORE
256 Middle St., New Bern, 252-636-5898; www.pepsistore.com

Site of the pharmacy in which Caleb Bradham first served his invention, "Brad's Drink," in 1858. When orders for the concoction took off, he renamed it Pepsi-Cola. Now the site is a store full of Pepsi memorabilia.

HOTELS

★★AERIE INN BED & BREAKFAST
509 Pollock St., New Bern, 252-636-5553, 800-849-5553; www.aerieinn.com

Seven rooms. Complimentary full breakfast. Wireless Internet access. $

★COMFORT INN
218 E. Front St., New Bern, 252-636-0022, 800-517-4000;
www.comfortsuitesnewbern.com

100 rooms. Complimentary continental breakfast. Wireless Internet access. Fitness center. $

★HAMPTON INN
200 Hotel Drive, New Bern, 252-637-2111, 800-426-7866; www.hamptoninn.com

101 rooms. Complimentary continental breakfast. Wireless Internet access. $

★HARMONY HOUSE INN
215 Pollock St., New Bern, 252-636-3810, 800-636-3113;
www.harmonyhouseinn.com

10 rooms. Complimentary full breakfast. Wireless Internet access. $

★★MEADOWS INN
212 Pollock St., New Bern, 252-634-1776, 877-551-1776;
www.meadowsinn-nc.com

Seven rooms. Complimentary full breakfast. Wireless Internet access. $

★ SHERATON NEW BERN HOTEL AND MARINA
100 Middle St., New Bern, 252-638-3585, 800-326-3745;
www.sheraton.com-newber

171 rooms. Wireless Internet access. Restaurant, two bars. $

OCRACOKE

Settled in the 17th century, Ocracoke was alledgedly once used as headquarters by the pirate Blackbeard. One of the Outer Bank's towns, Ocracoke is accessible only by boat or air, but the trek worth it for the beautiful beaches. The lighthouse, built in 1823, is still in use. A Cape Hatteras National Seashore visitor center is located here.

Information: www.ocracoke-nc.com

WHAT TO SEE AND DO

CEDAR ISLAND TO OCRACOKE FERRY SERVICE
3619 Cedar Island Road, Ocracoke, 252-928-3841, 800-293-3779; www.ncdot.org

Winter and summer, daily. Reservations are recommended and may be made up to one year in advance.

HOTEL
★ANCHORAGE INN
205 Highway 12, Ocracoke, 252-928-1101; www.theanchorageinn.com
37 rooms. Closed December-February. Complimentary continental breakfast. **$**

SPECIALTY LODGING
OCRACOKE ISLAND INN
100 Lighthouse Road, Ocracoke, 252-928-4351, 877-456-3466;
www.ocracokeislandinn.com
29 rooms. Restaurant. **$$**

RESTAURANT
★★BACK PORCH
110 Back Road, Ocracoke, 252-928-6401
Seafood menu. Dinner. Closed mid-November-mid-April. Casual attire. Outdoor seating. **$$**

PINEHURST

A famous year-round resort village, Pinehurst has been named the site of the 2014 U.S. Open. The eight 18-hole courses (31 miles of greens) contain 780 bunkers and the largest number of golf holes in the world at a single resort. The New England-style resort was designed more than 100 years ago by Frederick Law Olmsted, who also designed New York's Central Park and landscaped Asheville's Biltmore Estate. Handsome estates and other residences, mostly Georgian Colonial, dot the village. The Pinehurst Resort and Country Club has a 200-acre lake, 24 tennis courts and other recreational facilities that are open to members as well as to guests staying there.

Information: Convention and Visitors Bureau, Southern Pines,
910-692-3330, 800-346-5362; www.homeofgolf.com

WHAT TO SEE AND DO
SANDHILLS HORTICULTURAL GARDENS
Sandhills Community College, 3395 Airport Road, Pinehurst,
910-695-3882; www.sandhills.edu
The 25 acres include Ebersole Holly Garden; Rose Garden; Conifer Garden; Hillside Garden with bridges, waterfalls and gazebo; Desmond Native Wetland Trail Garden, a nature conservancy and bird sanctuary; and Sir Walter Raleigh Garden, a formal English garden. Daily.

HOTELS
★★★★THE CAROLINA HOTEL
1 Carolina Vista Drive, Pinehurst, 910-295-6811, 800-487-4653; www.pinehurst.com
With eight 18-hole courses designed by the sport's leading names, including Fazio, Jones, Maples and Ross, the 31 miles of golf at this property contain 780 bunkers and the largest number of golf holes in the world at a single resort. This Victorian-era hotel provides guests with handsomely furnished accommodations and first-class service. Two of the resort's nine restaurants as well as a luxurious spa are located here. 220 rooms. Two restaurants, bar. High-speed Internet access. Children's activity center. Fitness classes available. Spa. Beach. Golf, 144 holes. Tennis. Airport transportation available. **$$$**

★COMFORT INN

9801 Highway 15-501, Pinehurst, 910-215-5500, 800-831-0541; www.comfortinn.com
77 rooms. Bar. Complimentary continental breakfast. Wireless Internet access. **$**

★★★HOLLY INN

155 Cherokee Road, Pinehurst, 910-295-6811, 800-487-4653; www.pinehurst.com
The Holly Inn was the first hotel built in Pinehurst (dating to 1895) and is part of the Pinehurst Resort. The inn has dark wood paneling, fireplaces and antique furniture. The onsite 1895 restaurant features an American-Continental menu with Carolina influences. The Tavern is more casual and serves lunch and dinner. Guests at the Holly Inn have access to all the activities of the Carolina Hotel. 82 rooms. Two restaurants, bar. High-speed Internet access. Airport transportation available. **$$**

★★★MAGNOLIA

65 Magnolia Road, Pinehurst, 910-295-6900, 800-526-5562;
www.themagnoliainn.com
This historical 1896 inn is nestled in the quaint New England-style village of Pinehurst and is within walking distance of the Carolina Inn, golf courses, tennis, dining, and shopping. The rooms feature private baths with claw foot tubs, four-poster beds, cable television, and air conditioning. Two guest rooms also offer fireplaces—perfect for a romantic getaway. Rooms are casually decorated, and two offer fireplaces. 11 rooms. Restaurant, bar. Complimentary full breakfast. Wireless Internet access. **$**

RESTAURANT

★★★1895

155 Cherokee Road, Pinehurst, 910-235-8434, 800-487-4653; www.pinehurst.com
This charming restaurant is located in the historic Holly Inn and is part of the famous Pinehurst Resort. The restaurant features a Continental menu with a Carolina influence and plenty of original preparations for seafood and steak. American, Continental menu. Dinner. Closed Monday-Tuesday. Bar. Business casual attire. Reservations recommended. Valet parking. Outdoor seating. **$$$**

SPA

★★★★THE SPA AT PINEHURST

1 Carolina Vista Drive, Pinehurst, 910-235-8320, 800-487-4653; www.pinehurst.com
Featuring more than 40 different treatments, this spa is influenced by its southern location. Pine-inspired treatments dominate the menu, from the pine salt body rub to the exfoliating pine cream of the Pinehurst deluxe body treatment. The spa offers eight different massage therapies, including a special massage designed for golfers.

PITTSBORO

Just south of Chapel Hill, this small community is host to Fearrington Village, a dairy farm dating back to the 1700s and redeveloped in the 1970s. The owners turned the vast farm into a town with stores, custom real estate and award-winning lodging and restaurants.
Information: Pittsboro-Siler City Convention and Visitors Bureau, 12 East St.,
Pittsboro, 919-542-8200, 800-468-6242; visitpittsboro.com

★
★
★
★
★

HOTEL

★★★★★THE FEARRINGTON HOUSE COUNTRY INN

2000 Fearrington Village Center, Pittsboro,
919-542-2121; www.fearrington.com

The Fearrington House offers just the right mix of country style and worldly sophistication. Part of a charming village of shops, this country house hotel is located on Colonial-era farmland. The inn's former incarnation as a dairy barn is evident today in the striped Galloway cows that graze the grounds. The rooms and suites feature a country theme with authentic details like salvaged church doors used as headboards. Canopied beds and original art create a stylish look. 33 rooms. Restaurant, bar. Complimentary full breakfast. High-speed Internet access. Business center. Fitness room. Indoor pool, outdoor pool, whirlpool. Tennis. Children over 6 years only. $$$

RESTAURANTS

★★★★THE FEARRINGTON HOUSE RESTAURANT

2000 Fearrington Village Center, Pittsboro, 919-542-2121;
www.fearrington.com

This charming Victorian-style country restaurant is located on several rolling acres near Chapel Hill. The property is dotted with flower gardens and lush landscapes, and the restaurant is accented with elegant antique furnishings. Dinner lives up to the lovely surroundings. The upscale menu is American, with techniques borrowed from France and robust flavors taken from the surrounding region. The thoughtful, seasonal menu is complemented by a deep international wine list that features close to 500 selections with a focus on California varietals. American, French menu. Dinner. Bar. Jacket required. Reservations recommended. Valet parking. Outdoor seating. $$$

★MARKET CAFÉ

2000 Fearrington Village, Pittsboro, 919-542-2121; www.fearringtonvillage.com
American menu. Lunch, brunch. Children's menu. Casual attire. Reservations recommended. Outdoor seating. $

RALEIGH

The capital of North Carolina, Raleigh is also known as a center of education and technology research. The Research Triangle Park, a 6,800-acre research and development center with more than 50 companies, is located within 15 miles of Raleigh. Three major universities—North Carolina State University, Duke University in Durham and the University of North Carolina at Chapel Hill—are also here.

Named for Sir Walter Raleigh, the town was laid out in 1792, following a resolution by the North Carolina General Assembly that an "unalterable seat of government" should be established within 10 miles of Isaac Hunter's tavern. Like much of North Carolina, Raleigh was sprinkled with Union sympathizers until Fort Sumter was attacked. Lincoln's call for volunteers was regarded as an insult and North Carolina joined the Confederacy. Raleigh surrendered to General Sherman in April 1865. Legend has it that during Reconstruction, carpetbaggers controlled the Assembly, voted themselves exorbitant salaries, set up a bar in the capitol and left permanent nicks in the capitol steps from the whiskey barrels rolled up for the thirsty legislators.

Information: Greater Raleigh Convention and Visitors Bureau, 1 Hannover Square,
Raleigh, 919-834-5900, 800-849-8499; www.raleighcvb.org

★
★
★
★
★

WHAT TO SEE AND DO
MORDECAI HISTORIC PARK
1 Mimosa St., Raleigh, 919-857-4364; www.raleigh-nc.org

Preserved plantation home with many original furnishings noted for its neoclassical architecture. Also here is the house in which Andrew Johnson, 17th president of the U.S. was born. Guided tours. Tuesday-Saturday.

NORTH CAROLINA MUSEUM OF HISTORY
5 E. Edenton St., Raleigh, 919-807-7900; www.ncmuseumofhistory.org

Several innovative exhibits convey the state's history. Gift shop. Auditorium. Tuesday-Sunday.

PULLEN PARK
408 Ashe Ave., Raleigh, 919-831-6468; www.raleigh-nc.org

Scenic 72-acre park in the center of downtown featuring a 1911 carousel, train ride, paddle boats, indoor aquatic center, ball fields, tennis courts, playground and picnic shelters. Daily.

STATE CAPITOL
1 E. Edenton St., Raleigh, 919-733-4994; www.ncstatecapitol.com

A simple, stately Greek Revival-style building. The old legislative chambers, in use until 1963, have been restored to their 1840s appearance, as have the old state library room and the state geologist's office. Self-guided tours. Daily.

WILLIAM B. UMSTEAD STATE PARK
8801 Glenwood Ave., Raleigh, 919-571-4170; www.ncparks.gov

Crabtree Creek Section. On 5,480 acres with a 55-acre lake. Fishing, boating. Hiking, riding. Picnicking. Camping (March-mid-December, Thursday-Sunday). Nature study. Reedy Creek Section, 10 miles Northwest off I-40. Approximately 1,800 acres. Fishing. Hiking, riding.

HOTELS
★CANDLEWOOD SUITES
4433 Lead Mine Road, Raleigh, 919-789-4840,
888-226-3539; www.candlewoodsuites.com

122 rooms, all suites. High-speed Internet access. Health and fitness center. Pets accepted. $

★★CLARION HOTEL STATE CAPITAL
320 Hillsborough St., Raleigh, 919-832-0501,
800-424-6423; www.clarionhotel.com

202 rooms. Restaurant, bar. High-speed Internet access. $

★COURTYARD RALEIGH NORTH
1041 Wake Towne Drive, Raleigh, 919-821-3400, 800-321-2211;
www.courtyard.com

153 rooms. Restaurant. High-speed Internet access. Business center, Fitness center. $

★DAYS INN SOUTH-RALEIGH

3901 S. Wilmington St., Raleigh, 919-772-8900, 800-325-2525; www.daysinn.com

103 rooms. Complimentary continental breakfast. Wireless Internet access. **$**

★ECONO LODGE RALEIGH

2641 Appliance Court, Raleigh, 919-856-9800, 800-424-6423;
www.choicehotels.com

132 rooms. Complimentary continental breakfast. Wireless Internet access. **$**

★★EMBASSY SUITES HOTEL RALEIGH-CRABTREE VALLEY

4700 Creedmoor Road, Raleigh, 919-881-0000, 800-362-2779;
www.embassysuites.com

225 rooms, all suites. Restaurant, bar. Complimentary full breakfast. Wireless Internet access. Airport transportation available. **$$**

★FAIRFIELD INN & SUITES RALEIGH CRABTREE VALLEY

2201 Summit Park Lane, Raleigh, 919-881-9800, 800-228-2800; www.marriott.com

125 rooms. Complimentary continental breakfast. High-speed Internet access. **$**

★HAMPTON INN

6209 Glenwood Ave., Raleigh, 919-782-1112; www.hamptoninn.com

141 rooms. Complimentary continental breakfast. Wireless Internet access. Airport transportation available. **$**

★★HOLIDAY INN BROWNSTONE

1707 Hillsborough St., Raleigh, 919-828-0811, 800-331-7919;
www.brownstonehotel.com

187 rooms. Restaurant, bar. High-speed Internet access. **$**

★★★MARRIOTT RALEIGH CRABTREE VALLEY

4500 Marriott Drive, Raleigh, 919-781-7000,
800-909-8289; www.marriott.com-rdunc

Guests will enjoy comfortable accommodations at the Marriott Raleigh Crabtree Valley, and will appreciate ultramodern features like marble floors, an atrium lobby and a lush indoor tropical garden. Accessible to Interstate-440 (I-440) and Highway 70, the hotel is 15 minutes from Research Triangle Park and the airport and across the street from Crabtree Valley Mall. Nearby activities include tennis and museums of art, history and natural science. 375 rooms. High-speed Internet access. Airport transportation available. **$$**

★★★SHERATON RALEIGH CAPITAL CENTER HOTEL

421 S. Salisbury St., Raleigh, 919-834-9900, 800-325-3535;
www.sheraton.com-raleigh

The Sheraton Raleigh is located adjacent to the convention center and near the state capitol, dining, museums and entertainment. Marble floors, high ceilings and a balcony overlooking the lobby give the hotel a polished look. Guest rooms offer beds with fluffy duvets and pillows. 355 rooms. Restaurant, bar. Wireless Internet access. **$$**

NORTH CAROLINA

★
★
★
★
★

★★★★★THE UMSTEAD RESORT AND SPA

100 Woodland Pond, Cary, 919-447-4000, 866-877-4141; www.theumstead.com

Located in wooded suburban Cary, just outside of Raleigh in the Research Triangle area, this contemporary, elegant hotel offers a full-service stylish stay. Rooms are decorated in muted neutrals and feature luxury linens, fully stocked bars and plenty of room to spread out. Enjoy the full-service Umstead Spa offers or its state-of-the-art fitness center. Herons restaurant serving creative New American cuisine is a local favorite. 150 rooms. Restaurant, bar. Wireless Internet access. Spa. Pool. Pets accepted, fee. $$$

RESTAURANTS

★★42 STREET OYSTER BAR & SEAFOOD GRILL

508 W. Jones St., Raleigh, 919-831-2811; www.42ndstoysterbar.com

Seafood menu. Lunch, dinner. Bar. Children's menu. Casual attire. Reservations recommended. $$$

★ABYSSINIA ETHIOPIAN RESTAURANT

2109-146 Avent Ferry Road, Raleigh,
919-664-8151; www.abyssiniarestaurantnc.com

Middle Eastern menu. Dinner. Bar. Casual attire. $$

★★★ANGUS BARN

9401 Glenwood Ave., Raleigh, 919-787-2444, 800-277-2270; www.angusbarn.com

This steakhouse is one of the few restaurants in the country to age its own beef before it is hand cut and grilled. Also on the menu are steakhouse classics like oysters Rockefeller and chateaubriand. Two cozy, basement-level wine cellars can be reserved for private dining and hold extensive collection of bottles from around the world. A collection of antiques adds charm. Seafood, steak menu. Dinner. Bar. Children's menu. Business casual attire. Reservations recommended. Valet parking. $$$

★★CASA CARBONE RISTORANTE

6019-A Glenwood Ave., Raleigh, 919-781-8750; www.casacarbone.com

Southern Italian menu. Dinner. Closed Monday. Children's menu. Casual attire. $$

★★ENOTECA VIN RESTAURANT AND WINE BAR

410 Glenwood Ave., Raleigh, 919-834-3070; www.enotecavin.com

Italian, American menu. Dinner, Sunday brunch. Closed Monday. $$-$$$

★★★★HERONS RESTAURANT AT THE UMSTEAD HOTEL

100 Woodland Pond, Cary, 919-447-4200; www.theumstead.com/dining

It seems like an oxymoron—gourmet dining in a suburban hotel—but Herons at the Umstead Hotel is an exception. Herons puts a Southern spin on American cuisine in a fashionable setting complete with a 2,500-bottle wine cellar. A a spa menu designed for those participating in the hotel's spa program is available. Of course, decadence is too, beginning with the restaurant's homemade cinnamon bun French toast with brown sugar streusel at breakfast and ending with the luscious brownie sundae baked Alaska. Southern/American menu. Dinner. $$$

NORTH CAROLINA

★
★
★
★
★

★★IRREGARDLESS CAFÉ

901 W. Morgan, Raleigh, 919-833-8898; www.irregardless.com

American menu. Lunch, dinner, Sunday brunch. Closed Monday. Bar. Children's menu. Business casual attire. Reservations recommended. **$$**

★★★J. BETSKI'S

10 W. Franklin St., Raleigh, 919-833-7999; www.jbetskis.com

You'll see some schnitzel and some spaetzle at this unique addition to the Raleigh restaurant scene—not to mention a 'wurst or two. Owner John F. Korzekwinski brings together his German and Polish heritage to Southern cuisine, offering up traditional Old World dishes that North Carolina natives can relish in. And what better to pair the seasonal menu's pretzel dumplings and duck confit with than a hefty lager or other bubbly brew off of their beer menu? A glass of wine won't be taking away from your experience, as the list offers selections from Germany and Austria. German, Polish menu. Dinner, late-night. Closed Sunday. **$$$**

★LAS MARGARITAS

231 Timber Drive, Garner, 919-662-1030

Mexican menu. Lunch, dinner. Bar. Children's menu. Casual attire. **$$**

★★★SECOND EMPIRE

330 Hillsborough St., Raleigh, 919-829-3663; www.second-empire.com

This restaurant is housed in a renovated Second Empire Victorian home, which was built in 1879. The original heart pine floors, masonry walls and windows add to the elegant atmosphere in the upstairs dining room, which offers fine dining. For a more casual dinner, head downstairs to the Tavern or the Atrium Room, both of which offer seasonal, organic and fresh ingredients with original presentations. Contemporary American menu. Dinner. Closed Sunday. Bar. Business casual attire. Reservations recommended. **$$$**

★★★SIMPSON'S

5625 Creedmoor Road, Raleigh, 919-783-8818;
www.simpsonsrestaurant.com

Enjoy the romantic atmosphere as you dine by candlelight and listen to the pianist who plays here Friday and Saturday evenings. The restaurant, styled after an old English pub, serves an impressive steak and seafood menu (think 16-ounce lobster tails). American menu. Dinner. Closed Sunday. Bar. Business casual attire. Reservations recommended. **$$$**

★★VINNIE'S STEAKHOUSE

7440 Six Forks Road, Raleigh, 919-847-7319; www.vinniessteakhouse.com

Steak menu. Dinner. Bar. Business casual attire. Reservations recommended. Outdoor seating. **$$$**

★★WINSTON'S GRILLE

6401 Falls of Neuse Road, Raleigh, 919-790-0700; www.winstonsgrille.com

American menu. Dinner, Sunday brunch. Bar. Children's menu. Casual attire. Reservations recommended. Outdoor seating. **$$**

139

NORTH CAROLINA

★
★
★
★
★

SPA

★★★★THE UMSTEAD SPA

100 Woodland Pond, Cary, 919-447-4170; www.theumsteadspa.com

A tranquil, Asian-inspired space, the spa at the Umstead Hotel offers 14,000 square feet devoted to pampering treatments that range from hot-stone massage to milk hydrotherapy baths. Private spa suites, which accommodate four to six people, are perfect for parties and include access to a massage room, a color therapy tub and more. Guests receive fruit, Evian water and a bottle of champagne. The spa also has a fitness studio and salon services.

ROANOKE RAPIDS

Founded as a textile town, Roanoke Rapids sits on the Roanoke River and near the 5,000-acre Roanoke Lake and even more impressive 34-mile-long Gaston Lake. Plenty of boating, canoeing, rafting, hiking and bicycle trails run through the area, and significant Revolutionary war sites can be found in surrounding Halifax County.

Information: Halifax County Tourism Development Authority,
252-535-1687, 800-522-4282; www.visithalifax.com

WHAT TO SEE AND DO

HISTORIC HALIFAX STATE HISTORIC SITE

25 Saint David, Halifax, 252-583-7191;
www.nchistoricsites.org

The Halifax Resolves, the first formal sanction of American independence, were adopted here on April 12, 1776. Buildings include Owens House, Burgess Law Office, Eagle Tavern, Sally-Billy House, clerk's office, jail, Montfort Archaeology Exhibit Center. April-October, daily; rest of year, Tuesday-Sunday 9 a.m.-5 p.m. Closed holidays. Historical dramas presented in summer.

HOTELS

★BEST WESTERN ROANOKE RAPIDS

I-95 N. and Highway, 46, Roanoke Rapids,
252-537-1011, 800-832-8375; www.bestwestern.com

100 rooms. Restaurant. Complimentary continental breakfast. High-speed Internet access. $

ROCKY MOUNT

This is one of the country's largest bright-leaf tobacco marts. Cotton yarn, bolts of fabric and ready-to-wear clothing are made at the local mills. Factories produce fertilizer, furniture, chemicals, metal products, lumber and pharmaceuticals.

Information: Chamber of Commerce, 100 Coast Line St., 252-446-0323;
www.rockymountchamber.org

WHAT TO SEE AND DO

CHILDREN'S MUSEUM

270 Gay St., Rocky Mount, 252-972-1167; www.rockymountnc.gov/museum

Hands-on exhibits provide children with experiences of the latest technological advances. Tuesday-Saturday 10 a.m.-5 p.m., and Sundays 1-5 p.m. Admission is free on Wednesdays from 2-5 p.m.

HOTELS

★HAMPTON INN

530 N. Winstead Ave., Rocky Mount, 252-937-6333,
800-426-7866; www.hamptoninn.com

124 rooms. Complimentary continental breakfast. Business center, meeting rooms. Fitness room. Pool. **$**

★★HOLIDAY INN

651 Winstead Ave., Rocky Mount, 252-937-6888,
888-543-2255; www.holiday-inn.com

169 rooms. Restaurant, bar. **$**

SALISBURY

Daniel Boone spent his youth in this town and Andrew Jackson studied law in this town, which has been a trading, cultural and judicial center since 1753. During the Civil War, Salisbury was the site of a Confederate prison where 5,000 Union soldiers died. They are buried here in the National Cemetery. The area has six golf courses as well as the North Carolina Transportation Museum, which is housed in an old roundhouse and rail repair yard.

Information: Rowan County Convention and Visitors Bureau,
Salisbury, 704-638-3100, 800-332-2343; www.visitsalisburync.com

WHAT TO SEE AND DO

DR. JOSEPHUS HALL HOUSE

226 S. Jackson, Salisbury, 704-636-0103;
www.learnnc.org

Large antebellum house set amid giant oaks and century-old boxwoods, and contains most of its original Federal and Victorian furnishings. House was used as the Union commander's headquarters following the Civil War. Saturday-Sunday afternoon.

WATERWORKS VISUAL ARTS CENTER

East Liberty and North Main streets, Salisbury,
704-636-1882; www.waterworks.org

Adaptive restoration of former Salisbury Waterworks into arts center. Changing exhibits; studios, classes; courtyard; sensory garden. Guided tours. Daily.

HOTELS

★HAMPTON INN

1001 Klumac Road, Salisbury, 704-637-8000,
800-426-7866; www.hamptoninn.com

121 rooms. Complimentary continental breakfast. High-speed Internet access. **$**

★★HOLIDAY INN

530 Jake Alexander Blvd., Salisbury, 704-637-3100,
800-465-4329; www.holiday-inn.com

181 rooms. Restaurant, bar. Wireless Internet access. **$**

NORTH CAROLINA

★
★
★
★

SANFORD

This central North Carolina town is known for its production of clay bricks, made possible by its location at the topographical meeting point of coastal sand and Piedmont clay.

Information: www.sanfordnc.net

WHAT TO SEE AND DO
HOUSE IN THE HORSESHOE STATE HISTORIC SITE

324 Alston House Road, Sanford, 910-947-2051;
www.nchistoricsites.org

The house was the residence of North Carolina governor Benjamin Williams and the site of a Revolutionary War skirmish. Tuesday-Sunday.

RAVEN ROCK STATE PARK

3009 Raven Rock Road, Lillington, 910-893-4888; www.ravenrockrumble.com

A 2,990-acre park characterized by 152-foot outcrop of rock jutting over Cape Fear River. Fishing. Nature trails, interpretive programs. Picnicking.

HOTEL
★THE WINDS RESORT BEACH CLUB

310 E. First St., Ocean Isle Beach, 910-579-6275, 800-334-3581;
www.thewinds.com

86 rooms. Restaurant, bar. Complimentary full breakfast. Beach. $

SOUTH BRUNSWICK ISLANDS

The South Brunswick Islands offer wide, gently sloping beaches and beautiful scenery. Located just 50 miles from the Gulf Stream, the region has a subtropical climate and mild temperatures. Resort activities are plentiful and include fishing, swimming, tennis and golf. Shallotte is the hub of an area that includes Holden, Ocean Isle and Sunset beaches. The islands are reached by bridges across the Intracoastal Waterway.

Information: www.brunswickcountychamber.org

WHAT TO SEE AND DO
SHAW HOUSE

100 S.W. Broad St., Southern Pines, 910-692-2051; www.moorehistory.com

Antebellum house. Guided tours Tuesday-Saturday. Also on the premises are Britt Sanders Cabin and Garner House.

SOUTHERN PINES

The Sandhills are famed for golf and horses. The area first gained popularity as a resort in the 1880s, but the enthusiasm for golf in the 1920s fueled Southern Pines' growth as a resort area. Near Pinehurst and Aberdeen, it boasts more than 40 golf courses.

Information: Convention and Visitors Bureau, Southern Pines,
910-692-3330, 800-346-5362; www.homeofgolf.com

WHAT TO SEE AND DO

WEYMOUTH WOODS-SANDHILLS NATURE PRESERVE

1024 Fort Bragg Road, Southern Pines, 910-692-2167; www.sandhillsonline.com

Excellent examples of Sandhills ecology. Hiking trails along pine-covered sandridges. Natural history museum. April-October daily 9 a.m.-7 p.m.; November-March daily 9 a.m.-6 p.m.

HOTELS

★★DAYS INN

650 U.S. Highway 1, Southern Pines, 910-692-8585,
800-262-5737; www.daysinnsp.com

162 rooms. Restaurant, bar. Business center. Fitness center. Free wireless Internet access. **$**

★HAMPTON INN

1675 Highway 1 S., Southern Pines, 910-692-9266, 800-426-7866;
www.hamptoninn.com

126 rooms. Complimentary continental breakfast. High-speed Internet access. **$**

★★★MID PINES INN AND GOLF CLUB

1010 Midland Road, Southern Pines, 910-692-2114, 800-290-2334;
www.pineneedles-midpines.com

Every hole remains where Donald Ross put it in 1921, when he designed the challenging golf course at this stately inn. The large main building houses a restaurant, lounge and more than 100 nicely appointed rooms. 112 rooms. Restaurant, bar. **$**

RESORT

★★★PINE NEEDLES LODGE

1005 Midland Road, Southern Pines, 910-692-7111, 800-747-7272;
www.pineneedles-midpines.com

Legendary golfer Peggy Kirk has welcomed guests and players to Pine Needles for more than three decades. The course was designed by Donald Ross and was host to two recent U.S. Women's Opens. The rustic lodge and elegant restaurant make for a relaxing golf holiday. 78 rooms. Restaurant, bar. **$**

RESTAURANTS

★SQUIRE'S PUB

1720 Highway 1 S., Southern Pines, 910-695-1161;
www.thesquirespub.com

British menu. Lunch, dinner. Closed Sunday. Bar. Children's menu. Five dining areas. **$**

★VITO'S RISTORANTE.

615 S.E. Broad St., Southern Pines, 910-692-7815

Italian menu. Dinner. Closed Sunday; holidays. **$$**

143

NORTH CAROLINA

★
★
★
★
★

SOUTHPORT

This coastal area at the head of the Cape Fear River is a haven for saltwater and freshwater fishing. Deep-sea charter boats are available at Southport, Long Beach and Shallotte Point. There is a good yacht harbor facility for small boats and yachts, a municipal pier, three ocean piers, as well as several beaches and golf courses nearby.

Information: Southport-Oak Island Area Chamber of Commerce,
4841 Long Beach Road S.E., Southport, 910-457-6964,
800-457-6964; www.southport-oakisland.com

WHAT TO SEE AND DO
BRUNSWICK TOWN-FORT ANDERSON STATE HISTORIC SITE
8884 St. Philips Road S.E., Southport, 910-371-6613;
www.southport-oakisland.com/attractions
Brunswick, founded in 1726, thrived as a major port exporting tar and lumber. Fearing a British attack, its citizens fled when the Revolution began. In 1776, the town was burned by British sailors. Twenty three foundations have been excavated. Built across part of the town are the Civil War earthworks of Fort Anderson, which held out for 30 days after the fall of Fort Fisher in 1865. Tuesday-Saturday 10 a.m.-4 p.m.

FORT FISHER STATE HISTORIC SITE
1610 Fort Fisher Blvd. South, Kure Beach, 910-458-5538; www.nchistoricsites.org
This is the largest earthworks fort in the Confederacy. Until the last few months of the Civil War, it kept Wilmington open to blockade runners. Some of the heaviest naval bombardment of land fortifications took place here on December 24-25, 1864, and on January 13-15, 1865. Tours. Visitor center has exhibits, audiovisual shows. Reconstructed gun emplacement. Picnic area. October-March, Tuesday-Saturday 10 a.m.-4 p.m.

SPECIALTY LODGING
LOIS JANE'S RIVERVIEW INN
106 W. Bay St., Southport, 910-457-6701; www.loisjanes.com
Five rooms. Complimentary full breakfast. Built in 1892; antiques. $

STATESVILLE

Statesville is a community of many small, diversified industries, including furniture, apparel, metalworking and textiles. Visitors and locals come to nearby Lake Norman for recreation, and the downtown has several significant historic districts. The biggest event in town is the long-running hot air balloon festival in October.

Information: Greater Statesville Chamber of Commerce, 115 E. Front St.,
Statesville, 704-873-2892; www.statesvillechamber.org

WHAT TO SEE AND DO
FORT DOBBS STATE HISTORIC SITE
438 Fort Dobbs Road, Statesville, 704-873-5866; www.fortdobbs.org
Named for Royal Governor Arthur Dobbs, the now-vanished fort was built during the French and Indian War to protect settlers. Exhibits, nature trails, excavations. By appointment only.

★
★
★
★
★

CAROLINA BALLOON FESTIVAL, STATESVILLE REGIONAL AIRPORT,

Aviation Drive, Statesville, 704-873-2892;

www.carolinaballoonfest.com

This national hot air balloon festival and competition has been running for more than 30 years. Late October.

HOTEL

★★HOLIDAY INN

1215 Gardner Bagnal Blvd., Statesville, 704-878-9691,

888-465-4329; www.holiday-inn.com

134 rooms. Restaurant, bar. High-speed Internet access. $

TRYON

A temperate climate and scenic location on the southern slope of the Blue Ridge Mountains have given Tryon a reputation as one of the top places to retire in the U.S. While there are plenty of historic sites and cultural events, Tryon is best known for its equestrian events.

Information: Polk County Travel and Tourism, Visitor Information,

425 N. Trade St., Tryon, 828-859-8300, 800-440-7848;

www.nc-mountains.org

WHAT TO SEE AND DO

FOOTHILLS EQUESTRIAN NATURE CENTER

3381 Hunting Country Road, Tryon,

828-859-9021; www.fence.org

This 300-acre nature preserve has 5 miles of riding and hiking trails, wildlife programs and bird and nature walks. It's host to many equestrian events, including the Block House Steeplechase Race in April, which has happened annually for more than 60 years. Monday-Friday.

HOTEL

★★★PINE CREST INN

85 Pine Crest Lane, Tryon, 828-859-9135, 800-633-3001; www.pinecrestinn.com

Located in the foothills of the Blue Ridge Mountains, near the Foothills Equestrian Nature Center, this lovely inn evokes an English country manor. The innkeepers have restored the hardwood floors, stone fireplaces and other historic fixtures. 39 rooms, complimentary full breakfast. Restaurant. $$$

RESTAURANT

★★★PINE CREST INN RESTAURANT

85 Pine Crest Lane, Tryon, 828-859-9135, 800-633-3001; www.pinecrestinn.com

This rustic restaurant serves fusion cuisine and features beamed ceilings, a stone fireplace and heavy pine tables. There's also an award-winning wine list. American menu. Breakfast, dinner, Sunday brunch. Bar. Children's menu. Business casual attire. Reservations recommended. Outdoor seating. $$

★
★
★
★
★

WASHINGTON

Washington was rebuilt on the ashes of a town left by evacuating Union troops in April 1864. The rebels lost the town in March 1862, and because it was an important saltwater port on the Pamlico Sound tried to retake it for two years. Evidence of the shelling and burning can be seen in the stone foundations on Water Street. Water sports, including sailing, yachting, fishing and swimming, are popular.

Information: Chamber of Commerce, 252-946-9168; www.ci.washington.nc.us

WHAT TO SEE AND DO

BATH STATE HISTORIC SITE

207 Carteret St., Bath, 252-923-3971; www.nchistoricsites.org

Oldest incorporated town in the state. Buildings include Bonner House (circa 1820), Van Der Veer House (circa 1790) and Palmer-Marsh House (circa 1745) April-October, daily; rest of year, daily except Monday.

HOTEL

★COMFORT INN

1636 Carolina Ave., Washington, 252-946-4444, 800-228-5150;
www.comfortinn.com

56 rooms. Complimentary continental breakfast. Wireless Internet access. Picnic area. **$**

SPECIALTY LODGING

RIVER FOREST MANOR

738 E. Main St., Belhaven, 252-943-2151, 800-346-2151;
www.riverforestmanor.com

Nine rooms. Restaurant. Complimentary continental breakfast. Airport transportation available. **$**

WAYNESVILLE

Popular with tourists, this area offers mountain trails for riding and hiking and golf and fishing in cool mountain streams. Waynesville is 26 miles from the Cherokee Indian Reservation and Great Smoky Mountains National Park. The town of Maggie Valley, about 6 miles northwest, is in a particularly attractive area.

Information: Visitor and Lodging Information, 1233 N. Main St.,
Waynesville, 800-334-9036; www.waynesville.com

SPECIAL EVENT

INTERNATIONAL FOLK FESTIVAL

Waynesville, 828-452-2997; www.yoconafestival.org

Premier folk groups from more than 10 countries demonstrate their cultural heritage through lively music and costumed dance. Eleven days in late July.

HOTELS

★★★BALSAM MOUNTAIN INN

68 Seven Springs Drive, Balsam, 828-456-9498, 800-224-9498; www.balsaminn.com

This 100-year-old-inn sits in the Blue Ridge Mountains and features an award-winning restaurant as well as a library and access to great hiking trails. 50 rooms. Restaurant. Complimentary full breakfast. **$**

★★★THE SWAG COUNTRY INN

2300 Swag Road, Waynesville, 828-926-0430, 800-789-7672; www.theswag.com

The Swag Country Inn sits atop a 5,000-foot mountain with a private entrance to Great Smoky Mountain National Park. The rooms and suites feature handmade quilts, woven rugs and original artwork. Nature trails cover the property, and picnic baskets and brown-bag lunches are available for hikers. 15 rooms. Closed mid-November-April. Restaurant (public by reservation). Complimentary full breakfast. Children over 7 only in main building. $$$$

SPECIALTY LODGING
YELLOW HOUSE ON PLOT CREEK ROAD

89 Oakview Drive, Waynesville, 828-452-0991, 800-563-1236;
www.theyellowhouse.com

A fabulous yellow house tucked into the hills at a 3,000-foot elevation, the property has rooms with rustic décor that complements the remarkable landscape. 6 rooms. Complimentary full breakfast. $

WILLIAMSTON

Centered in Martin County on the Roanoke River, Williamston is part of a thriving river recreation community, with plenty of rafting, canoeing, fishing and hunting.

Information: www.visitmartincounty.com

WHAT TO SEE AND DO
HOPE PLANTATION

132 Hope House Road, Windsor, 252-794-3140; www.hopeplantation.org

Two-hour guided tour of Georgian plantation house (circa 1800) built by Governor David Stone. Period furnishings; outbuildings; gardens. Open Monday-Saturday, Sunday afternoon.

HOTELS
★ECONO LODGE

100 E. Blvd., Williamston, 252-792-8400; www.econolodge.com

59 rooms. Complimentary continental breakfast. High-speed Internet access. $

★★HOLIDAY INN

101 E. Blvd., Williamston, 252-792-3184, 800-792-3101; www.holidayinn.com

100 rooms. Restaurant, bar. High-speed Internet access. $

WILMINGTON

Made famous in recent years as the setting of the TV teen drama *Dawson's Creek*, Wilmington offers a small town beach atmosphere in a historic area. As the major city on North Carolina's Cape Fear Coast, it was the state's biggest town until 1910 when rail-fed industries outgrew those serviced by the harbor. In 1765, eight years before the Boston Tea Party, the citizens of Wilmington kept the British from unloading their stamps for the Stamp Act. In 1781, Cornwallis held the town as his main base of operation for almost a year. During the Civil War, blockade runners brought fortunes in goods past Federal ships lying off Cape Fear, making Wilmington the Confederacy's chief port until January 1865 when it fell. Today the town offers a steady mix of

★
★
★
★
★

industry and tourism, with historic sites, a vibrant and historic downtown and access to Cape Fear beaches.

Information: Cape Fear Coast Convention and Visitors Bureau, 24 N. Third St., Wilmington, 910-341-4030, 800-222-4757; www.cape-fear.nc.us

WHAT TO SEE AND DO
BATTLESHIP NORTH CAROLINA.
Battleship Road, Wilmington, 910-251-5797; www.battleshipnc.com
World War II vessel moored on west bank of Cape Fear River. Tour of museum, gun turrets, galley, bridge, sick bay, engine room and wheelhouse. Daily.

BURGWIN-WRIGHT HOUSE
224 Market St., Wilmington, 910-762-0570; burgwinwrighthouse.com
Restored colonial town house built on foundation of abandoned town jail. British General Cornwallis had his headquarters here in April 1781. Eighteenth-century furnishings and garden. Tours. Open Tuesday-Saturday.

MOORES CREEK NATIONAL BATTLEFIELD
40 Patriot Paul Drive, Currie, 910-283-5591; www.nps.gov/mocr
In 1776, the loosely knit colonists took sides against each other—patriots versus loyalists. Colonels Moore, Lillington and Caswell, with the blessing of the Continental Congress, broke up the loyalist forces, captured the leaders and seized gold and weapons. The action defeated British hopes of an early invasion through the South and encouraged North Carolina to be the first colony to instruct its delegates to vote for independence in Philadelphia. The 86-acre park has a visitor center near its entrance to explain the battle. Daily.

CAPTAIN J. N. MAFFITT RIVER CRUISES
Wilmington, 910-343-1611, 800-676-0162; www.cfrboats.com
Located at the foot of Market Street. Five-mile narrated sightseeing cruise covering Wilmington's harbor life and points of interest. Also river taxi service (additional fee) from Battleship *North Carolina*. May-September, daily.

POPLAR GROVE PLANTATION
10200 Highway, 17, Wilmington, 910-686-9989; www.poplargrove.com
Restored Greek Revival plantation; manor house, smokehouse, tenant house, blacksmith, loom weaver and basket weaver. Guided tours. Daily.

HOTELS
★★COURTYARD WILMINGTON
151 Van Campen Blvd., Wilmington, 910-395-8224, 800-321-2211; www.marriott.com-ilmcy
128 rooms. Wireless Internet access. $

★HAMPTON INN
1989 Eastwood Road, Wilmington, 910-256-9600, 877-256-9600; www.landfallparkhotel.com
120 rooms. Bar. Complimentary continental breakfast. High-speed Internet access. $

★
★
★
★
★

★★HOLIDAY INN

5032 Market St., Wilmington, 910-392-1101, 800-833-4721;
www.holiday-inn.com

124 rooms. Restaurant. Complimentary continental breakfast. High-speed Internet access. **$**

★★★HILTON WILMINGTON RIVERSIDE

301 N. Water St., Wilmington, 910-763-5900, 800-445-8667;
www.wilmingtonhilton.com

This hotel is a short walk from shops, restaurants, cultural attractions and the city's riverwalk. Guest rooms are comfortable and offer magnificent views of Cape Fear River. 274 rooms. Restaurant, bar. Wireless Internet access. **$**

★★★THE WILMINGTONIAN

101 S. Second St., Wilmington, 910-343-1800, 800-525-0909;
www.thewilmingtonian.com

Located in downtown Wilmington, just two blocks from Cape Fear River and a 40-minute drive to the beaches on the Atlantic Coast, this renovated inn caters to both leisure and business travelers with roomy suites and plentiful amenities. 40 rooms, all suites. Restaurant, bar. Complimentary continental breakfast. Wireless Internet access. **$**

SPECIALTY LODGINGS

C. W. WORTH HOUSE

412 S. Third St., Wilmington, 910-762-8562, 800-340-8559;
www.worthhouse.com

Seven rooms. Children over 12 years only. Complimentary full breakfast. High-speed wireless Internet access. **$**

DARLINGS BY THE SEA—OCEANFRONT WHIRLPOOL SUITES

329 Atlantic Ave., Kure Beach, 910-458-8887, 800-383-8111;
www.darlingsbythesea.com

Best described as a quaint honeymooners' cottage, each suite has a wonderful terrace overlooking the ocean. Five rooms, all suites. No children allowed. Complimentary continental breakfast. Beach. **$$**

FRONT STREET INN

215 S. Front St., Wilmington, 910-762-6442, 800-336-8184; www.frontstreetinn.com
12 rooms, all suites. Complimentary continental breakfast. Wireless Internet access. Bar. **$$**

THE GRAYSTONE INN

100 S. Third St., Wilmington, 910-763-2000, 888-763-4773;
www.graystoneinn.com

The antique-filled inn includes a music room with a grand piano, a mahogany-paneled library and a chandelier lit dining room. Rooms are decorated in period furnishings, some with claw-foot tubs. Nine rooms. Complimentary full breakfast. Wireless Internet access. Children over 12 years only. **$$**

NORTH CAROLINA

★
★
★
★
★

ROSEHILL INN

114 S. Third St., Wilmington, 910-815-0250,
800-815-0250; www.rosehill.com

This elegant Victorian home was built in 1848. Each of the large, luxurious guest rooms has its own individual charm and is perfect for a romantic retreat. Six rooms, children over 14 years only. Complimentary full breakfast. Wireless Internet access. **$$**

THE VERANDAS

202 Nun St., Wilmington, 910-251-2212; www.verandas.com

This 8,500-square-foot, Victorian-Italianate mansion sits two blocks from the Cape Fear River. Climb the spiral staircase to the enclosed cupola for a spectacular sunset view. Eight rooms. Complimentary full breakfast. Children over 12 years only. **$$**

RESTAURANTS

★CAFÉ PHOENIX

9 S. Front St., Wilmington, 910-343-1395; www.thecaffephoenix.com

Mediterranean menu. Lunch, dinner. Bar. Children's menu. Casual attire. Reservations recommended. Outdoor seating. **$$**

★DRAGON GARDEN

341-52 S. College Road, Wilmington, 910-452-0708

Chinese, sushi, Thai menu. Lunch, dinner. Casual attire. Reservations recommended. **$**

★★EDDIE ROMANELLI'S

5400 Oleander Drive, Wilmington, 910-799-7000; www.romanellisrestaurant.com

Italian, American menu. Lunch, dinner, late-night. Bar. Children's menu. Casual attire. **$$**

★★ELIJAH'S

2 Ann St., Wilmington, 910-343-1448; www.elijahs.com

American menu. Lunch, dinner, Sunday brunch. Bar. Children's menu. Casual attire. Reservations recommended. Outdoor seating. **$$**

★★FREDDIE'S

111 K Ave., Kure Beach, 910-458-5979; www.freddieskurebeach.com

Italian, American menu. Dinner. Children's menu. Casual attire. Reservations recommended. **$$**

★HIERONYMUS SEAFOOD

5035 Market St., Wilmington, 910-392-6313; www.hieronymusseafood.com

Seafood menu. Dinner. Bar. Children's menu. Casual attire. Reservations recommended. Outdoor seating. **$$$**

★★PILOT HOUSE

2 Ann St., Wilmington, 910-343-0200; www.pilothouserest.com

American menu. Lunch, dinner, Sunday brunch. Bar. Children's menu. Casual attire. Outdoor seating. **$$$**

NORTH CAROLINA

★
★★
★
★
★

★★PORT CITY CHOP HOUSE

1981 Eastwood Road, Wilmington, 910-256-4955; www.chophousesofnc.com

Seafood, steak menu. Lunch, dinner. Closed Sunday. Bar. Children's menu. Business casual attire. Reservations recommended. Outdoor seating. **$$$**

★★ROY'S RIVERBOAT LANDING

2 Market St., Wilmington, 910-763-7227;
www.theunioncafe.com

International-Fusion menu. Lunch, dinner, Sunday brunch. Closed four days in December. Bar. Casual attire. Reservations recommended. Outdoor seating. **$$$**

★WATER STREET

5 S. Water St., Wilmington, 910-343-0042; www.5southwaterstreet.com

American. Lunch, dinner. Bar. Children's menu. Casual attire. Outdoor seating. Riverfront dining in old warehouse. **$$**

WILSON

Located just off Interstate 95 (I-95), midway between New York and Florida, Wilson is most often visited by snowbirds heading south. It is also one of the Southeast's leading antique markets and has one of the nation's largest tobacco markets.

Information: www.wilson-nc.com

HOTELS

★BEST WESTERN LA SAMMANA

817 Ward Blvd., Wilson, 252-237-8700, 800-937-8376;
www.bestwestern.com

78 rooms. Complimentary continental breakfast. High-speed Internet access. Pool. Pets accepted. **$**

★COMFORT INN

4941 Highway 264 W., Wilson, 252-291-6400, 800-424-6423;
www.choicehotels.com

76 rooms. Complimentary continental breakfast. Free wireless Internet access. Free local calls. Pets accepted. **$**

★HAMPTON INN

5606 Lamm Road, Wilson, 252-291-0330; www.hamptoninn.com

100 rooms. Complimentary continental breakfast. High-speed Internet access. **$**

WINSTON-SALEM

One of the South's biggest industrial cities, Winston-Salem is a combination of two communities. Salem, with the traditions of its Moravian founders, and Winston, an industrial center, matured together. Tobacco markets, large banks and arts and crafts galleries contribute to this thriving community.

Information: Convention and Visitors Bureau, 601 W. 4th St., Winston-Salem, 336-728-4200, 800-331-7018; www.wvb.com

★
★
★
★
☆

WHAT TO SEE AND DO

BOWMAN GRAY STADIUM

1250 S. Martin Luther King Jr. Drive, Winston-Salem, 336-727-2748;
www.bowmangrayracing.com

Bowman Gray Stadium is a multiuse public arena that hosts Winston-Salem State Rams college football games as well as NASCAR short track and (1/4-mile asphalt oval). Part of the city's Lawrence Joel Veterans Memorial Coliseum Complex, Bowman Gray has hosted races for more than 50 years, making it the longest operating NASCAR short track in the country.

HISTORIC OLD SALEM

900 Old Salem Road, Winston-Salem, 336-721-7300,
888-653-7253; www.oldsalem.org

Restoration of a planned community that Moravians, with their old-world skills, turned into the 18th-century trade and cultural center of North Carolina's Piedmont. Many of the sturdy structures built for practical living have been restored and furnished with original or period pieces. Early crafts are demonstrated throughout the town. A number of houses are privately occupied. Nine houses and the outbuildings are open to the public. Tours (self-guided) start at the visitor center on Old Salem Road. Special events are held during the year. Tuesday-Sunday.

REYNOLDA HOUSE, MUSEUM OF AMERICAN ART

2250 Reynolda Road, Winston-Salem,
336-758-5150; www.reynoldahouse.org

On the estate of the late R. J. Reynolds of the tobacco dynasty. American paintings, original furniture, art objects, costume collection. Adjacent is Reynolda Gardens, 125 acres of open fields and naturalized woodlands; formal gardens, greenhouse. Tuesday-Saturday, also Sunday afternoon.

WAKE FOREST UNIVERSITY

1834 Wake Forest Road, Winston-Salem, 336-758-5000;
www.wfu.edu

Established in 1834, Wake Forest has 5,600 students. Sites to visit on campus include the Fine Arts Center, Museum of Anthropology and Reynolda Village, a complex of shops, offices and restaurants. Bowman Gray School of Medicine is on Medical Center Boulevard.

HOTELS

★★HOLIDAY INN

5790 University Parkway, Winston-Salem, 336-767-9595, 800-553-9595;
www.holiday-inn.com

150 rooms. Restaurant, bar. Wireless Internet access. Outdoor pool. **$**

★QUALITY INN

5719 University Parkway, Winston-Salem, 336-767-9009,
800-426-7866; www.qualitywinstonsalem.com

113 rooms. Complimentary continental breakfast. Outdoor pool. **$**

SPECIALTY LODGINGS

AUGUSTUS T. ZEVELY

803 S. Main St., Winston Salem, 336-748-9299, 800-928-9299;
www.winston-salem-inn.com
12 rooms. Children over 12 years only. Complimentary continental breakfast. Built in 1844, restored to its mid-19th century appearance. **$**

BROOKSTOWN INN

200 Brookstown Ave., Winston-Salem, 336-725-1120, 800-845-4262;
www.brookstowninn.com
This historic inn was built in 1837 as a textile mill. The conversion preserved the original handmade brick and exposed beam construction. The romantic rooms include European-style breakfast. 70 rooms. Complimentary continental breakfast. Free wireless Internet access. **$$**

TANGLEWOOD PARK

4061 Clemmons Road, Clemmons, 336-778-6370;
www.forsyth.cc/tanglewood
28 rooms. Complimentary continental breakfast. Golf. Tennis. Picnic, clubhouse facilities of Tanglewood Park available. **$**

RESTAURANTS

★★6TH AND VINE

209 W. Sixth St., Winston-Salem, 336-725-5577; www.6thandvine.com
Mediterranean menu. Lunch, dinner, late-night, brunch. Closed Monday. Bar. Children's menu. Casual attire. Outdoor seating. Tuesday-Saturday 11 a.m.-late, Sunday brunch 11 a.m.-3 p.m. **$$**

★★★RYAN'S RESTAURANT

719 Coliseum Drive, Winston-Salem, 336-724-6132; www.ryansrestaurant.com
An inviting brick pathway surrounded by philodendron and with a cascading waterfall leads guests to Ryan's. The décor here is simple yet elegant, and tables offer a view of the woods and brook below. The menu features steakhouse standards, along with a wide selection of seafood dishes such as pepper seared tuna with red cabbage slaw. Seafood, steak menu. Dinner. Closed Sunday. Bar. Business casual attire. Reservations recommended. Outdoor seating. **$$$**

★★SWEET POTATOES

529 N. Trade St., Winston-Salem, 336-727-4844;
www.sweetpotatoes-arestaurant.com
American, Southern menu. Lunch, dinner. Closed Sunday; also last week in August. Bar. Casual attire. **$$**

★★VINEYARD

120 Reynolda Village, Winston-Salem,
336-748-0269; www.thevineyards120restaurant.com
Continental menu. Dinner. Closed Sunday; week of July 4. Bar. Business casual attire. Reservations recommended. Outdoor seating. **$$$**

★
★
★
★
★

★★ZEVELY HOUSE

901 W. Fourth St., Winston-Salem, 336-725-6666; www.zevelyhouse.com

American, French menu. Dinner, Sunday brunch. Closed Monday; holidays. Bar. Business casual attire. Reservations recommended. Outdoor seating. **$$**

WRIGHTSVILLE BEACH

A pleasant, family-oriented resort town, Wrightsville Beach offers swimming, surfing, fishing and boating. The public park has facilities for tennis, basketball, soccer, softball, volleyball, shuffleboard and other sports.

Information: www.wrightsville.com

HOTEL

★★HOLIDAY INN SUNSPREE RESORT

1706 N. Lumina Ave., Wrightsville Beach, 910-256-2231, 877-330-5050;
www.holiday-inn.com

184 rooms. Three restaurants, bar. Indoor pool, outdoor pool. **$**

RESTAURANTS

★★BRIDGE TENDER

1414 Airle Road, Wrightsville Beach, 910-256-4519; www.thebridgetender.com

Seafood, steak menu. Lunch, dinner. Bar. Casual attire. Reservations recommended. Outdoor seating. **$$$**

★DOCKSIDE

1308 Airlie Road, Wrightsville Beach, 910-256-2752; www.thedockside.com

American menu. Lunch, dinner. Bar. Children's menu. Casual attire. Outdoor seating. **$$**

★★KING NEPTUNE

11 N. Lumina Ave., Wrightsville Beach, 910-256-2525; www.kingneptunewb.com

Seafood, steak menu. Dinner. Bar. Children's menu. Casual attire. **$$**

★★OCEANIC

703 S. Lumina Ave., Wrightsville Beach, 910-256-5551; www.oceanicrestaurant.com

Seafood, steak menu. Lunch, dinner, Sunday brunch. Bar. Children's menu. Casual attire. Outdoor seating. **$$**

NORTH CAROLINA

★
★
★
★

SOUTH CAROLINA

LOVELY BEACHES, A TEMPERATE YEAR-ROUND CLIMATE AND GOLF COURSES TO RIVAL THE world's best have made tourism one of South Carolina's most important industries. Hilton Head resorts are packed with families when the weather is warm, while Myrtle Beach is the town of choice for golf lovers. The surrounding area has more than 100 courses.

This state's turbulent and romantic history tells a story that is deeply rooted in its people and the history of the U.S. During the American Revolution, almost 200 battles and skirmishes were fought in South Carolina. The first overt act of revolution occurred at Fort Charlotte on July 12, 1775, making it was the first British property seized by American Revolutionary forces. Less than 100 years later on December 20, 1860, South Carolina became the first state to secede from the Union. And, the clash that started the Civil War began on South Carolina soil when Confederate soldiers bombed and seized Fort Sumter in 1861, holding onto the fort until the evacuation of Charleston in 1865. Impoverished and blackened by the fires of General Sherman's "March to the Sea," South Carolina emerged from the difficult Reconstruction days and was readmitted to the Union in 1868.

Economic problems have plagued South Carolina in the past, but in recent decades, diversified industries have brought greater prosperity. South Carolina is a major producer of tobacco, cotton, pine lumber, corn, oats, sweet potatoes, soybeans, peanuts, peaches, melons, beef cattle and hogs, and power projects have been created by damming the Santee, Saluda, Savannah, and other rivers. Tourism is part of this growing economy, and the state is known for its water sports, deep sea fishing, car racing and, of course, golf.

Information: www.discoversouthcarolina.com

FUN FACTS

South Carolina was named for King Charles II of England.

South Carolina's Strom Thurmond was the first U.S. senator elected by write-in vote.

The state is the top producer of peaches in the country.

The first battle of the Civil War took place at Fort Sumter in Charleston.

155

SOUTH CAROLINA

★
★
★
★
★

AIKEN

A popular social and sports center, Aiken is known for its equestrian sports including flat-racing training, steeplechase and harness racing, polo, fox hunts and drag hunts. There is also good tennis and golf. The University of South Carolina-Aiken is located here.

Information: Chamber of Commerce, 121 Richland Ave.,
803-641-1111; www.aikenchamber.net

TRAVELING THE LOW COUNTRY

The 100-mile stretch of coastline between Charleston and Savannah, Georgia, is known as South Carolina's "low country," a region of remote marshlands and subtropical barrier islands of palmetto, live oak and Spanish moss. Peppered with cozy beach towns, the area is a great place for a road trip.

Head west from Charleston along Highway 17 south (the old Atlantic Coast Highway) taking every opportunity to detour east. The first side trip takes you 24 miles south along Highway 174 to Edisto Beach, a low-key island beach town with seafood restaurants and a wide white-sand beach with campgrounds and state park cabins. Return to Highway 17 and continue south 22 miles to the Highway 21 turnoff to Beaufort, 18 miles east. A modest, quiet village, Beaufort serves as the unofficial capital of the low country. Downtown, tidy Victorian houses and a small set of storefronts and restaurants overlook a beautiful marshland landscape. Cross the marsh on the Highway 21 bridge east to St. Helena Island. Visit the Penn Center, where you can see exhibits documenting the efforts of federal troops who in 1861 tried to free 10,000 slaves working on local cotton plantations. Female religious leaders from Philadelphia started the Penn Center in 1862 as one of the first schools for African-Americans in the nation. Just beyond St. Helena are Hunting Island and an impeccable white sand beach, perfect for camping, swimming or crabbing.

Retrace your path to return to Beaufort, but take Highway 170 southeast through Chelsea to Highway 278 south. This route juts east to the highly developed Hilton Head Island. Before the Civil War, the island was rich with Sea Island cotton, rice and indigo. Now it's filled here with tourists who come for the golf courses, beaches and resorts.

From the southern tip of Hilton Head, a passenger ferry makes the trip over to neighboring Daufuskie Island, home of the Gullah community which descended from African-Americans. The island was so isolated they were able to maintain many more African traditions than more assimilated mainlanders.

Return west on Highway 278 to Highway 170 and connect back up with Highway 17 going south to Savannah. When heading back north, take a speedy trek up Interstate-95 (I-95), or retrace your steps and enjoy the low country's beauty one more time. Approximately 100 miles.

WHAT TO SEE AND DO

AIKEN COUNTY HISTORICAL MUSEUM

433 Newberry St., Southwest, Aiken, 803-642-2015; www.aikencountysc.gov

Period room settings and displays in a late 1800s home. Log cabin and one-room schoolhouse on grounds. Special features include an archaeology exhibit and a 1950s drug store. Museum store. Tuesday-Friday 9:30 a.m.-4:30 p.m., Saturday-Sunday 2-5 p.m.

REDCLIFFE

181 Redcliffe Road, Beech Island, 803-827-1473; www.southcarolinaparks.com

Built in the 1850s, this Greek Revival mansion is furnished with Southern antiques, art collections, historic documents and books. Picnic area. Thursday-Monday 9 a.m.-6 p.m.; House: noon-4 p.m.

THOROUGHBRED RACING HALL OF FAME

135 Dupree Place, Aiken, 803-642-7631; www.aikenracinghalloffame.com

Dedicated to champion horses trained in Aiken. September-May, Tuesday-Sunday 2-5 p.m.; June-August, Saturday-Sunday 2-5 p.m.

HOTEL

★★★THE WILLCOX

100 Colleton Ave., Southeast, Aiken, 803-648-1898, 877-648-2200; www.thewillcox.com

This distinguished mansion set on 2,000 acres of the Hitchcock Woods offers some of the best of South Carolina's horse country. Guest rooms and suites are decorated with antiques, Oriental rugs and feather-topped four-poster beds. Most accommodations have working fireplaces. The onsite spa offers everything from massages to rejuvenating facials. 22 rooms. Complimentary full breakfast. Restaurant. Spa. $$$

BEAUFORT

The second-oldest town in the state, Beaufort is the unofficial capital of South Carolina's low country and is filled with antebellum homes and churches. The town has rebuilt itself several times, first after Native Americans destroyed it in 1715, then after the British attacked in 1812 and finally after Northern troops forced the evacuation of almost the entire town during the Civil War.

Information: Greater Beaufort Chamber of Commerce, 1106 Carteret St., Beaufort, 843-986-5400; www.beaufort.org

WHAT TO SEE AND DO

JOHN MARK VERDIER HOUSE MUSEUM

801 Bay St., Beaufort, 843-524-6335; www.historic-beaufort.org

Federal period house built in 1790 and once known as the Lafayette Building; the Marquis de Lafayette is said to have spoken here from the piazza in 1825. Monday-Saturday 11 a.m.-4 p.m.

ST. HELENA'S EPISCOPAL CHURCH

505 Church St., Beaufort, 843-522-1712; www.sthelenas1712.org

Tombstones from surrounding burial ground became operating tables when the church was used as a hospital during the Civil War. Tuesday-Friday 10 a.m.-4 p.m., Saturday 10 a.m.-1 p.m.

HOTELS

★★★BEAUFORT INN

809 Port Republic St., Beaufort, 843-379-4667; www.beaufortinn.com

Built in 1897, this romantic low-country inn offers rooms, suites and a private, two-bedroom cottage. The dining room offers seasonal, Southern cuisine and an

★
★
★
★
★

extensive wine list. 21 rooms. Children over 8 years only in the inn. Complimentary full breakfast. Restaurant. High-speed Internet access. **$$$**

★BEST WESTERN SEA ISLAND INN

1015 Bay St., Beaufort, 843-522-2090, 800-780-7234;
www.bestwestern.com

43 rooms. Complimentary continental breakfast. High-speed Internet access. Exercise room. Meeting rooms. Pool. **$**

★★★THE RHETT HOUSE INN

1009 Craven St., Beaufort, 843-524-9030, 888-480-9530;
www.rhetthouseinn.com

One block from the Intracoastal Waterway, the Rhett House Inn, a plantation dating back to 1820, has rooms decorated with floral fabrics, fireplaces, four-poster beds and antiques. Children over 5 years only. Wireless Internet access, Complimentary continental breakfast. **$$**

RESTAURANTS

★★BEAUFORT INN

809 Port Republic St., Beaufort, 843-379-4667; www.beaufortinn.com

American menu. Breakfast, lunch, dinner, Sunday brunch. Bar. Casual attire. Outdoor seating. Reservation recommended. **$$$**

★★BREAKWATER RESTAURANT & BAR

205 W. St., Beaufort, 843-379-0052; www.breakwaterrestaurantandbar.com

French menu. Dinner. Closed Sunday. Bar. Casual attire. Outdoor seating, Reservation recommended. **$$**

★★BRITISH OPEN PUB OF BEAUFORT

8 Waveland Cat Island, Beaufort, 843-524-4653; www.britishopenpub.net

American menu. Lunch, dinner, Sunday brunch. Bar. Casual attire. Outdoor seating. **$$**

★★PLUMS

904 Bay St., Beaufort, 843-525-1946; www.plumsrestaurant.com

American menu. Lunch, dinner. Bar. Children's menu. Casual attire. Outdoor seating. **$$**

CAMDEN

During the Revolution, General Cornwallis occupied Camden, the oldest inland town in the state, and made it the principal British garrison and the interior command post for the South. Although several battles were fought in and near the town, including the Battle of Camden, the town was never recaptured by Americans. Instead, it was evacuated and burned by the British in 1781. Today, Camden is famous for its horseback riding, horse shows, hunt meets, polo and steeplechase races. There are 200 miles of bridle paths in the area and three race tracks. Springdale Course is an extremely difficult and exciting steeplechase run.

Information: Kershaw County Chamber of Commerce and Visitor Center,
724 S. Broad St., 803-432-2525, 800-968-4037; www.camden-sc.org

WHAT TO SEE AND DO
BETHESDA PRESBYTERIAN CHURCH
502 DeKalb St., Camden, 803-432-4593; www.bethesdapresbyterianchurch.org
Designed by the architect of the Washington Monument, Robert Mills, the church is considered a masterpiece. Monday-Friday 9 a.m.-4 p.m.

HISTORIC CAMDEN REVOLUTIONARY WAR SITE
222 S. Broad St., Camden, 803-432-9841; www.historic-camden.net
Archaeological site of South Carolina's oldest inland town. Visitor area includes two early 19th-century log cabins and a restored 18th-century townhouse. Trails lead to the reconstructed foundation of a pre-Revolutionary War powder magazine, the Kershaw-Cornwallis House and two reconstructed British fortifications. The site of the Battle of Camden, a National Historic Landmark, is 5 miles north of town. Self-guided and guided tours, Tuesday-Saturday 10 a.m.-5 p.m., Sunday 2-5 p.m.

SPECIAL EVENTS
CAROLINA CUP STEEPLECHASE
Springdale Race Course, 200 Knights Hill Road, Camden, 803-432-6513,
800-780-8117; www.carolina-cup.org
This annual 'rites of spring' draws more than 70,000 fans every year to enjoy the sport of steeplechase horse racing alongside spring fashions and elaborate tailgate parties. Early April.

COLONIAL CUP INTERNATIONAL STEEPLECHASE
Springdale Race Course, 200 Knights Hill Road, Camden, 803-432-6513,
800-780-8117; www.carolina-cup.org
The Colonial Cup draws more than 15,000 fans and horsemen from around the world and provides the season's grand finale—often deciding all the national titles including jockey of the year, trainer of the year and horse of the year. Mid-November.

SPECIALTY LODGING
GREENLEAF INN
1308 Broad St., Camden, 803-425-1806, 800-437-5874;
www.greenleafinnofcamden.com
Located in the historic district. Its guesthouses were built in 1805 and 1890 and are decorated in Victorian style. 10 rooms. Complimentary full breakfast. Wireless Internet access. Restaurant. **$**

CHARLESTON
This aristocratic and storied American city lives up to its reputation for cultivated manners. Charleston's homes, historic shrines, old churches, lovely gardens, winding streets and intricate iron-laced gateways exude charm.

The Charleston of today is a survivor of siege, flood, hurricane and epidemic. Capital of the province until 1786 and the first permanent settlement in the Carolinas, Charles Towne, as it was first called, was established as a tiny colony by Anthony Ashley Cooper, Earl of Shaftesbury. At the same time, he established the only American nobility in history, with barons, landgraves (dukes) and caciques (earls), each owning great plantations.

SOUTH CAROLINA

★
★
★
★
★

This nobility lasted less than 50 years, but it was the foundation for an aristocratic tradition that still exists. Although many of the colonists moved to the Carolina low country and established plantations, every year on May 10 the planters and their families moved back to Charleston to escape the mosquitoes and malarial heat. From spring to frost, these planters created a season of sport, theater and socials. Charleston had the first playhouse, the first museum, the first public school in the colony, the first municipal college in America and the first fire insurance company on the continent. (It was a victim the next year of a fire that destroyed half the city.)

In 1780, Charleston was captured and occupied by the British for two and a half years. The city was almost the last point in the state to be cleared of British troops. With peace came prosperity, but rivalry between the small farmers of the interior and the merchants and plantation owners of the lowlands resulted in the capital's creation in Columbia.

The Ordinance of Secession was passed by convention in Charleston in 1860, and the bombing at Fort Sumter began the Civil War. Today, the beautiful city retains outstanding architecture in its large historic downtown. With a rich mix of styles from early Colonial, Georgian, Federal, Greek Revival and Italianate to Victorian as well as ample historic artifacts, Charleston is a wonderful place to explore on foot.

Information: Visitor Reception and Transportation Center, 375 Meeting St.,
843-853-8000, 800-868-8118; www.charlestoncvb.com

WHAT TO SEE AND DO
AIKEN-RHETT HOUSE
48 Elizabeth St., Charleston, 843-723-1159; www.historiccharleston.org
Built around 1818, this palatial residence was added on to and redecorated by Governor and Mrs. William Aiken Jr. in the mid-1800s. The house remained in the family until 1975, and many original pieces of furniture are still in the rooms for which they were purchased. On the National Register of Historic Places. Daily.

BOONE HALL PLANTATION
1235 Long Point Road, Mount Pleasant, 843-884-4371;
www.boonehallplantation.com
This 738-acre estate has a 1935 Georgian-style house similar to the original plantation house that fell into ruin, a cotton gin house, a pecan grove, nine slave cabins and gardens of antique roses. The property has been used to film many TV shows and movies. Battle reenactments are held during the summer and draw Civil War buffs. April-Labor Day, Monday-Saturday 8:30 a.m.-6:30 p.m., Sunday 1-5 p.m.; Labor Day-March, Monday-Saturday 9 a.m.-5 p.m., Sunday 1-4 p.m.

CHARLESTON MUSEUM
360 Meeting St., Charleston, 843-722-2996; www.charlestonmuseum.org
Founded in 1773 and first opened to the public in 1824, the Charleston Museum is America's oldest museum. Key artifacts in the collection include an impressive early silver display (George Washington's christening cup is among the pieces), an Egyptian mummy, South Carolina ceramics, a skeleton of a primitive toothed whale, the chairs that delegates sat in to sign South Carolina's Ordinance of Secession and firearms used in the Civil War. Children will enjoy the museums hands-on exhibits. Monday-Saturday 9 a.m.-5 p.m., Sunday 1-5 p.m.

SOUTH CAROLINA

★
★
★
★
★

CHARLES TOWNE LANDING

1500 Old Town Road, Charleston, 843-852-4200; www.southcarolinaparks.com

In 1670, colonists established the first permanent English settlement in the Carolinas at this location. Today, visitors find archaeological investigations, reconstructed fortifications, formal gardens, as well as nature trails, a colonial village and a replica of *Adventure*, a 17th-century trading ketch. Tram tours are available, and there also is a natural habitat zoo of indigenous animals onsite. Daily 8:30 a.m.-5 p.m.

THE CITADEL, MILITARY COLLEGE OF SOUTH CAROLINA

171 Moultrie St., Charleston, 843-225-3294; www.citadel.edu

Established in 1842 by an act of the South Carolina General Assembly, the Citadel was originally located on Marion Square in downtown Charleston near the Revolutionary War rampart. In 1922, the college was moved to a picturesque setting on the bank of the Ashley River. The site houses 24 major buildings, including Summerall Chapel, a shrine of patriotism and remembrance. Citadel parades on Friday afternoons are said to be the best free show in Charleston. Visitors may take self-guided campus tours. Cadet-led tours for groups of eight or more are available through the Public Affairs Office, 843-953-6779. Closed Saturday-Sunday.

DOCK STREET THEATRE

135 Church St., Charleston, 843-577-7183, 800-454-7093;
www.charlestonstage.com

In 1736, a building on this site opened as the very first in America constructed specifically for theatrical productions. Later, the street name changed to Queen, but the Dock Street Theatre name stuck. Today's theater is on the site of the original and presents productions of the Charleston Stage Company during the spring and fall. Dock Street Theatre is a performance venue for Charleston's Spoleto Festival.

DRAYTON HALL

3380 Ashley River Road, Charleston, 843-769-2600; www.draytonhall.org

One of the oldest surviving pre-American Revolution plantation houses in the area, this Georgian Palladian house is surrounded by live oaks and is located on the Ashley River. Held in the Drayton family for seven generations before its donation to the National Trust, the mansion has been maintained in near original condition. Tours daily. November-February. Main Gates: 8:30 a.m.-4 p.m.; Museum Shop: 8:30 a.m.-5 p.m.

EDMONDSTON-ALSTON HOUSE

4300 Ashley River Road, Charleston, 843-556-6020, 800-782-3608;
www.middletonplace.org

Greek Revival style house with an uninterrupted view across the harbor. Guided tours, daily; closed first full week in February. Tuesday-Saturday 10 a.m.-4:30 p.m., Sunday and Monday 1:30-4:30 p.m.

FRENCH HUGUENOT CHURCH

44 Queen St., Charleston, 843-722-4385; www.frenchhuguenotchurch.org

As early as 1687, French Huguenots were worshipping in a church on this site. The current church is a National Historic Landmark. Completed in 1845, it was the first

SOUTH CAROLINA

Gothic Revival building in Charleston. Constructed of brick covered with stucco, the church features distinctive windows, buttresses and unusual ironwork.

GIBBES MUSEUM OF ART

135 Meeting St., Charleston, 843-722-2706; www.gibbesmuseum.org

The more than 100-year-old museum houses an eclectic collection that includes Japanese woodblock prints as well as miniature rooms depicting traditional American and French architecture, decorative arts and design. This museum is also known for its portraits of famous South Carolinians by notable artists, including Thomas Sully, Benjamin West and Rembrandt Peale. Don't miss the Charleston Renaissance Gallery, which showcases works by Charleston artists responsible for the city's cultural renaissance in the 1920s and 1930s. Tours available. Tuesday-Saturday 10 a.m.-5 p.m., Sunday 1-5 p.m.

HEYWARD-WASHINGTON HOUSE

360 Meeting St., Charleston, 843-722-2996; www.charlestonmuseum.org

This brick double house, noteworthy for its collection of Charleston-made furniture, was built in 1772 during the Revolutionary era. Rice planter Daniel Heyward gave the house to his son Thomas Heyward Jr., a signer of the Declaration of Independence. George Washington stayed here during his weeklong visit to the city in 1791. Dubose Heyward used the neighborhood in which the house stands as the setting for *Porgy and Bess.* Monday-Saturday 10 a.m.-5 p.m., Sunday 1-5 p.m.

JOSEPH MANIGAULT HOUSE

360 Meeting St., Charleston, 843-722-2996; www.charlestonmuseum.org

This home was designed by Gabriel Manigault for his brother Joseph. The brothers were descendants of a French Huguenot family. This elegant neoclassical three-story brick town house, a National Historic Landmark, reflects the wealthy lifestyle of the Manigault family, as well as living conditions of the slaves who worked there. Monday-Saturday 10 a.m.-5 p.m., Sunday 1-5 p.m.

MAGNOLIA PLANTATION AND GARDENS

3550 Ashley River Road, Charleston, 843-571-1266, 800-367-3517;
www.magnoliaplantation.com

These internationally famous gardens are America's oldest (circa 1676). They now cover 50 acres with camellias, azaleas, magnolias and hundreds of other flowering species. Also on the grounds are a 125-acre waterfowl refuge, a tri-level observation tower, a 16th-century maze, an 18th-century herb garden, nature trails and a petting zoo. Canoe and bicycle rentals are available. Plantation home and local art gallery. March-October, 8 a.m.-dusk; November-February, call for hours.

MIDDLETON PLACE PLANTATION

4300 Ashley River Road, Charleston, 843-556-6020, 800-782-3608;
www.middletonplace.org

Once the home of Arthur Middleton, a signer of the Declaration of Independence, Middleton Place has America's oldest landscaped gardens and a restored House Museum. Laid out in 1741, the gardens feature ornamental butterfly lakes, sweeping terraces and a wide variety of flora and fauna. Daily from 9 a.m.

NATHANIEL RUSSELL HOUSE

51 Meeting St., Charleston, 843-724-8481; www.historiccharleston.org

Regarded as Charleston's grandest neoclassical house museum, this house (circa 1808) features period antiques, lavish plasterwork, oval drawing rooms and a magnificent "free-flying" staircase. Daily Monday-Saturday 10 a.m.-5 p.m., Sunday 2-5 p.m.

OLD EXCHANGE AND PROVOST DUNGEON

122 E. Bay St., Charleston, 843-727-2165, 1-888-763-0448; www.oldexchange.com

Completed in 1771, the Royal Exchange and Custom House is one of the most historically significant buildings of Colonial and Revolutionary America. The upper levels were designed to accommodate heavy export and import trade and as a place to conduct business, and the lower level held common prisoners, pirates and suspected rebels. In 1788, South Carolina delegates gathered in the building to ratify the U.S. Constitution. George Washington was a guest of honor here at a grand ball in 1791. Daily 9 a.m.-5 p.m.

ST. PHILIP'S EPISCOPAL CHURCH

142 Church St., Charleston, 843-722-7734; www.stphilipschurchsc.org

Established in 1670, this is the oldest congregation in Charleston and the first Episcopal church in the Carolinas. Today's building was completed in 1838. During the Civil War, its bells were removed and converted into cannons for the Confederacy. New bells were placed in the steeple on July 4, 1976.

SPECIAL EVENTS

FALL HOUSE AND GARDEN CANDLELIGHT TOURS

147 King St., Charleston, 843-722-4630, 800-968-8175;
www.preservationsociety.org

The annual Candlelight Tours of Homes and Gardens allows visitors a peek at some of the city's best residential architecture of the 18th, 19th and 20th centuries. Tours are self-paced and self-guided (although there are volunteer guides at each site). Late September-late October.

FESTIVAL OF HOUSES AND GARDENS

40 E. Bay St., Charleston, 843-722-3405; www.historiccharleston.org

The welcome mats are out at 150-historic private homes in 11 colonial and antebellum neighborhoods during this annual festival. Also available are lectures, luncheons featuring low-country foods, afternoon teas, wine tastings and book signings. Early reservations are essential—most events sell out well in advance. Mid-March-Mid-April.

SPOLETO FESTIVAL USA

Gaillard Municipal Auditorium, 77 Calhoun St., Charleston,
843-579-3100; www.spoletousa.org

One of the best arts festivals in the country, Spoleto USA is a counterpart to the arts festival held in Spoleto, Italy, which was founded by composer Gian Carlo Menotti. The Charleston festival offers opera, dance, chamber music, theater, symphonic music, jazz, solo voice, choral performance, visual arts and special events, including conversations with the artists—more than 120 offerings in total. Venues include the

SOUTH CAROLINA

★
★
★
★
★

Gaillard Auditorium and historic Dock Street Theatre in Charleston, as well as less-conventional locales such as Middleton Place and Mepkin Abbey Monastery. Late May-early June.

HOTELS

★★★ANCHORAGE INN

26 Vendue Range, Charleston, 843-723-8300, 800-421-2952;
www.anchoragencharleston.com

Afternoon tea, English toiletries and period furnishings make for a sophisticated stay at this inn in the downtown historic district. 19 rooms. Complimentary continental breakfast. Free High-speed Internet access. Business center. **$**

★BEST WESTERN KING CHARLES INN

237 Meeting St., Charleston, 843-723-7451, 866-546-4700; www.kingcharlesinn.com

91 rooms. Restaurant. Pool with sundeck. High-speed Internet access. Business center. Fitness facility. **$**

★BEST WESTERN SWEETGRASS INN

1540 Savannah Highway, Charleston, 843-571-6100,
800-937-8376; www.bestwestern.com

87 rooms. Complimentary continental breakfast. Pool. Fitness facility. Business center. High-speed Internet access. Pets accepted. **$**

★
★★
★★
★

FORT SUMTER NATIONAL MONUMENT

South Carolina, the first state to leave the union, passed its Ordinance of Secession on December 20, 1860. The Confederacy demanded surrender of Fort Sumter on April 11, 1861. This demand was refused by Major Robert Anderson, who was in command of Union forces at the fort. At 4:30 a.m. on April 12, Confederate firing began, and the fort was surrendered after 34 hours of intense bombardment. This attack compelled President Lincoln to call for 75,000 volunteers to put down the rebellion, beginning the Civil War. The monument includes Fort Sumter and Fort Moultrie, located one mile east of Fort Sumter on Sullivan's Island, and a key fort during the Revolutionary War. Both forts were active through World War II and have been modified through the years.

A pivotal location in the Civil War, the Fort Sumter National Monument sits on an island three miles southeast of Charleston in Charleston Harbor, and is accessible by private boat or by Fort Sumter tour boat, leaving from the City Marina (on Lockwood Drive, Charleston) and from Patriots Point Naval Museum, Mount Pleasant.

Fort Moultrie has been restored by the National Park Service. Fort Sumter's ruins have been partially excavated, and a museum has been established. The visitor center has an audiovisual program depicting the evolution of seacoast defense. Self-guided tour. Daily.

Information: 1214 Middle St., Sullivan's Island, 843-883-3123; www.nps.gov/fosu

★★★★CHARLESTON PLACE

205 Meeting St., Charleston, 888-635-2350;
www.charlestonplace.com

Located in Charleston's historic district, this hotel is within an easy stroll to antebellum mansions, luscious gardens and colonial markets. Guest rooms are traditional and attractively appointed with colonial furnishings. A fitness center, pool with retractable roof and shops such as Godiva and Gucci make this a perfect base for travelers who appreciate modern luxuries. 440 rooms. High-speed Internet access. Two restaurants, two bars. Fitness classes available, spa. Business center. $$$

★★★CHARLESTON'S VENDUE INN

19 Vendue Range, Charleston, 843-577-7970, 800-845-7900;
www.vendueinn.com

With its polished pine floors, Oriental rugs, period furniture and other historic accents, this romantic inn offers a memorable Charleston stay. Many of the individually decorated rooms overlook the Charleston Harbor and Waterfront Park. 65 rooms. Complimentary full breakfast. Restaurant, bar. Fitness room. Wireless Internet access. $

★★★FRANCIS MARION HOTEL

387 King St., Charleston, 843-722-0600, 877-756-2121;
www.francismarioncharleston.com

Originally opened in 1924, this European-style hotel was named for an American Revolution war hero who evaded British troops by winding through swampland. Rooms are cozy, but the hotel's amenities and its prompt, courteous service make for a comfortable stay. 230 rooms. Restaurant, two bars. Free wireless Internet access. Spa. Fitness center. $$

★HAMPTON INN CHARLESTON-HISTORIC DISTRICT

345 Meeting St., Charleston, 843-723-4000, 888-759-4001;
www.hamptoninn.com

171 rooms. Complimentary continental breakfast. Free High-speed Internet access. $

★★★HARBOUR VIEW INN

2 Vendue Range, Charleston, 843-853-8439, 888-853-8439;
www.harbourviewcharleston.com

Enjoy spectacular vistas of Charleston's East Harbor from this historic inn. Located near some of the city's best restaurants, rooms have four-poster beds, flatscreen TVs and plush beds with luxury bedding. 57 rooms. Business center. $$

★★★HILTON CHARLESTON HARBOR RESORT AND MARINA

20 Patriot's Point Road, Charleston, 843-856-0028, 888-856-01028;
www.charlestonharborresort.com

This luxurious resort sits on an 18-hole private championship golf course, private beach and 450-slip marina. Beautiful sunsets across the Charleston Harbor and historic skyline, with many antebellum buildings and churches, are visible from most rooms. Water sports from charter fishing to parasailing are available. 129 rooms. Pets accepted, fee. High-speed Internet access. Two restaurants, bar. Whirlpool, pool. $$

★THE INN AT MIDDLETON PLACE

4290 Ashley River Road, Charleston, 843-556-0500, 800-543-4774;
www.theinnatmiddletonplace.com

53 rooms. Complimentary full breakfast. Restaurant, bar. Children's activity center. Outdoor pool, wireless Internet access. $$

★★★MARKET PAVILION HOTEL

225 E. Bay St., Charleston, 843-723-0500, 877-440-2250;
www.marketpavilion.com

Luxury meets Southern hospitality at this downtown Charleston hotel. Guest rooms feature cashmere blankets, four-poster beds, marble baths and fluffy bathrobes. As Charleston's only USDA Prime steakhouse, Grill 225, the hotel's signature restaurant, is a popular setting for lunch and dinner. Afterward, everyone heads upstairs to the rooftop bar for drinks. 66 rooms. Complimentary continental breakfast. High-speed Internet access. Two restaurants, two bars. $$$

★★★PLANTERS INN

112 N. Market St., Charleston, 843-722-2345, 800-845-7082; www.plantersinn.com

This delightful inn, located right on the Market, carefully blends historic references with modern amenities. The spacious rooms and suites feature period furnishings, whirlpool baths and fireplaces. The Inn's Peninsula Grill gets kudos from locals and guests alike for its artfully presented and palate-pleasing food. 64 rooms. Complimentary continental breakfast. Restaurant. $$

★★★RENAISSANCE CHARLESTON HOTEL HISTORIC DISTRICT

68 Wentworth St., Charleston, 843-534-0300; www.renaissancehotels.com

The Renaissance Charleston offers luxury in the middle of the city's historic district. Guest accommodations feature baths with granite vanities, beds with plush down comforters and fluffy pillows, plus extras like wireless Internet access and PlayStation. The hotel's signature restaurant, Wentworth Grill, serves fresh, seasonal Southern-influenced cuisine perfect for business meetings or a dinner. 166 rooms. Wireless Internet access. Restaurant, bar. Pets not accepted. Outdoor pool. Spa. Fitness center. $$

★★★WENTWORTH MANSION

149 Wentworth St., Charleston, 843-853-1886, 888-466-1886;
www.wentworthmansion.com

Once a private home, this stunning mansion in the city's historic center has handcarved marble fireplaces, ornate plasterwork and Tiffany stained-glass windows. Guest rooms offer gas fireplaces and charming views. The full European breakfast is served on the sun porch each morning, and the Rodgers Library is a great spot for evening drinks. 21 rooms. Complimentary full breakfast. Restaurant. Wireless Internet access. whirlpools. $$$

SPECIALTY LODGINGS

ANSONBOROUGH INN

21 Hasell St., Charleston, 843-723-1655, 800-522-2073; www.ansonboroughinn.com

37 rooms, all suites. Complimentary continental breakfast. Bar. $$

BARKSDALE HOUSE INN

27 George St., Charleston, 843-577-4800, 888-577-4980;
www.barksdalehouse.com

Built as a town house in 1778 by wealthy Charlestonian George Barksdale, this stately bed and breakfast is filled with period furnishings and modern conveniences. 14 rooms. Children over 10 years only. Complimentary continental breakfast. $

BATTERY CARRIAGE HOUSE INN

20 S. Battery, Charleston, 843-727-3100, 800-775-5575;
www.batterycarriagehouse.com

Hidden within the flowering gardens of the Steven-Lathers Mansion, an exquisite private home, this 1843 bed and breakfast offers private entrances, romantic décor and a view of Charleston Harbor. 11 rooms. Children over 12 years only. Complimentary continental breakfast. Whirlpool. Wireless Internet access. $

THE GOVERNOR'S HOUSE INN

117 Broad St., Charleston, 843-720-2070, 800-720-9812;
www.governorshouse.com

A National Landmark, this inn is the former home of Edward Rutledge, national statesman, patriot and youngest signer of the Declaration of Independence who later served as U.S. Senator and governor of South Carolina. Rooms and common areas are exquisitely detailed. 11 rooms. Bar. Wireless Internet access. $$$

INDIGO INN

1 Maiden Lane, Charleston, 843-577-5900, 800-845-7639;
www.indigoinn.com

Housed in an 1850 warehouse once used to store indigo for dying textiles, this colorful inn is located in the middle of the historic district, just one block from City Market. 40 rooms. Complimentary continental breakfast. $

JOHN RUTLEDGE HOUSE INN

116 Broad St., Charleston, 843-723-7999, 866-720-2609;
www.johnrutledgehouseinn.com

19 rooms. Complimentary continental breakfast. Free wireless Internet access. $$

KINGS COURTYARD INN

198 King St., Charleston, 843-723-7000, 866-720-2949;
www.kingscourtyardinn.com

This three-story, antebellum, Greek Revival structure was built in 1854 and remains one of the gems of Charleston's historic district. 44 rooms. Complimentary continental breakfast. Restaurant, bar. Free wireless Internet access. $

MAISON DU PRE

317 E. Bay St., Charleston, 843-723-8691, 800-844-4667;
www.maisondupre.com

The main house dates to 1804. Located in historic downtown, adjacent to the Gaillard Auditorium, this inn is decorated in period furniture and art made by the family that runs it. 15 rooms. Complimentary continental breakfast. $

SOUTH CAROLINA

★
★
★
★
★

MEETING STREET INN

173 Meeting St., Charleston, 843-723-1882, 800-842-8022;
www.meetingstreetinn.com

Each room in this classic, single-house inn opens onto the piazza and courtyard. Rooms are individually decorated with period furniture. 56 rooms. Complimentary continental breakfast. Bar. Free wireless Internet access. **$**

VICTORIA HOUSE INN

208 King St., Charleston, 843-720-2946, 866-720-2946;
www.thevictoriahouseinn.com

Built in the late 1880s, this Romanesque-style Victorian house now serves as a lovely inn. Located in the downtown historic district, the inn offers amenities such as a bedside champagne breakfast. 22 rooms. Complimentary continental breakfast. Wireless Internet access. **$**

RESTAURANTS

★★82 QUEEN

82 Queen St., Charleston, 843-723-7591,
800-849-0082; www.82queen.com

Southern menu. Lunch, dinner, Sunday brunch. Bar. Children's menu. Business casual attire. Reservations recommended. Outdoor seating. **$$$**

★★ANSON

12 Anson St., Charleston, 843-577-0551; www.ansonrestaurant.com

Southern menu. Dinner. Bar. Children's menu. Business casual attire. Reservations recommended. **$$$**

★★AW SHUCKS

70 State St., Charleston, 843-723-1151; www.a-w-shucks.com

American, seafood menu. Lunch, dinner. **$$$**

★★BASIL

460 King St., Charleston, 843-724-3490;
www.basilthairestaurant.com

Charlestonians consider Basil restaurant the finest place to get their Thai food fixes. They praise Basil's deep-fried duck and zesty pad thai. And we're not talking mere take-out Thai here. Basil serves up sophisticated Thai fare that stays true to its roots, thanks to Chef Suntorn Cherdchoongarm, who insists on cooking everything from scratch and using freshly made sauces. At Basil, you'll find traditional curries, both green and red, along with savory chicken satay and spicy volcano shrimp. Don't forget to start off with the fresh Basil Roll, wrapped in light, soft rice paper and filled with crisp lettuce, bean sprouts, shrimp and of course, tender leaves of fragrant basil. Thai menu. Lunch (Monday-Friday), dinner. **$$$**

★★BLOSSOM CAFÉ

171 E. Bay St., Charleston, 843-722-9200; www.magnolias-blossom-cypress.com

Seafood menu. Lunch, dinner, Sunday brunch. Bar. Children's menu. Casual attire. Outdoor seating. **$$**

★
★
★
★
★

★★★CAROLINA'S

10 Exchange St., Charleston, 843-724-3800, 888-486-7673;
www.carolinasrestaurant.com

Located on a quiet, sleepy stretch of Exchange Street, Carolina's is the place to go for honest, straightforward low-country cuisine. The restaurant is divided into three distinct dining areas: the romantic Sidewalk Room, the relaxed Bar Room and the Perditas Room, an homage to the restaurant that used to occupy this space. Perditas' famous Fruits de Mer dish is always on the menu, alongside standout items such as the jumbo lump crab cake and the pan-roasted lamb rack. American menu. Dinner. Lunch Bar. Business casual attire. Reservations recommended. Complimentary valet parking. $$$

★★★★CHARLESTON GRILL

224 King St., Charleston, 843-577-4522; www.charlestongrill.com

The Charleston Grill is a clubby spot located in the Charleston Place Hotel. Stained-glass French doors, dark wood-paneled walls and marble floors create a classy, old-world atmosphere. Rich dishes like shrimp and catfish hoecakes with fried oysters and tartar remoulade provide a hint of the kind of low-country fare served at this sophisticated restaurant. Live jazz draws locals. American menu. Dinner. Bar. Children's menu. Business casual attire. Reservations recommended. Valet parking. Outdoor seating. $$$$

★★★★CIRCA 1886

149 Wentworth St., Charleston, 843-853-7828; www.circa1886.com

169

Located behind the historic Wentworth Mansion, this restaurant offers classic Charleston charm. The 280-bottle wine list complements the local cuisine on the menu, which is created by talented chef Marc Collins using regional ingredients. Try the Carolina crabcake soufflé, a cheese course made from Appalachian raw cow milk's cheese or the catfish with lobster and white cheddar grits. Desserts are traditional and rich, from gingerbread pudding with orange blossom honey ice cream to sweet potato butterscotch soufflé. The classic presentation of each dish adds an elegant flourish to the meal. The staff is also polished and friendly. American menu. Dinner. Closed Sunday. Bar. Business casual attire. Reservations recommended. Valet parking. $$$

★★★CYPRESS: A LOWCOUNTRY GRILLE

167 E. Bay St., Charleston, 843-727-0111;
www.magnolias-blossom-cypress.com

This restaurant offers a daring take on classic low-country food (traditionally defined by hearty dishes with plenty of rice, shrimp and unique seasonings). The wood-burning grill adds additional flavor to entrées like reconstruction lamb T-bone. American menu. Dinner. Bar. Children's menu. Business casual attire. Reservations recommended. $$$

★★FULTON FIVE

5 Fulton St., Charleston, 843-853-5555

Italian menu. Dinner only from 5:30 p.m. Closed Sunday and week before Labor Day. Bar. Business casual attire. Reservations recommended. Outdoor seating. $$

SOUTH CAROLINA

★★GAULART & MALICLET FRENCH CAFÉ

98 Broad St., Charleston, 843-577-9797; www.fastandfrench.org

French menu. Breakfast, lunch. Monday-Saturday; dinner. Tuesday-Saturday. Closed Sunday. Casual attire. $$

★★HANK'S SEAFOOD RESTAURANT

10 Hayne St., Charleston, 843-723-3474; www.hanksseafoodrestaurant.com

Seafood menu. Dinner. Bar. Children's menu. Casual attire. $$

★★★HIGH COTTON

199 E. Bay St., Charleston, 843-724-3815; www.high-cotton.net

"High cotton" is an old Southern saying that means living large. The menu at this casually elegant restaurant echoes that sentiment with boldly flavored dishes such as cornbread-crusted flounder with sweet pea and corn succotash, or bourbon-glazed pork with white cheddar jalapeno grits. American menu. Lunch Saturday, dinner, Sunday brunch. Bar. Children's menu. Business casual attire. $$

★★HOMINY GRILL

207 Rutledge Ave., Charleston, 843-937-0930; www.hominygrill.com

Low-country Southern menu. Breakfast, lunch, dinner, brunch. Closed late December. Casual attire. Outdoor seating. $$

★★LA FOURCHETTE

432 King St., Charleston, 843-722-6261; www.lafourchettecharleston.com

Totally French and utterly divine, this bistro on Upper King has locals pouring in for their signature pommes frites fried twice in duck fat. This method transforms ordinary hand-cut fries into perfectly delectable, crispy frites that are served with housemade mayonnaise for dipping. Cozy, dimly lit and convincingly Parisian, La Fourchette keeps it charmingly modest with a 40-seat dining room and a simple, authentically French menu. Start with a classic salade vert made of Boston lettuce to whet your appetite before the fries and finish off a steaming bowl of mussels cooked in white wine or the coquilles St. Jacques, a dish of rich chopped scallops in baked cream. C'est magnifique! French menu. Dinner. $$

★★★MAGNOLIA'S

185 E. Bay St., Charleston, 843-577-7771; www.magnolias-blossom-cypress.com

This smart, uptown restaurant specializes in updated Southern food. Chef Donald Barickman uses Southern ingredients in mouth-watering combinations. American menu. Lunch, dinner, Sunday brunch. Bar. $$

★★★MCCRADY'S

2 Unity Alley, Charleston, 843-577-0025; www.mccradysrestaurant.com

Housed in a beautifully restored building opened and operated as a tavern since 1778, this restaurant is the playground of young rising star chef Sean Brock. Brock's love for fresh, first-rate ingredients shines in dishes such as the spice-roasted rack of lamb with cauliflower, bok choy and huckleberries. The dessert menu features unusual combinations like peanut butter cake with popcorn ice cream and salted caramel. International menu. Dinner. Bar. Business casual attire. Reservations recommended. $$$

SOUTH CAROLINA

★
★
★
★
★

★★★★PENINSULA GRILL

112 N. Market St., Charleston, 843-723-0700; www.peninsulagrill.com

Located in the Planter's Inn, this restaurant has the sophisticated feel of an urban eatery without losing sight of its Southern charm. The menu is inventive, offering boldly flavored dishes spiced up with low-country accents like collards, hushpuppies, grits and black-eyed peas. Chef Robert Carter's famous coconut layer cake is worth the splurge. There's also a champagne bar menu of decadent little treats like oysters, lobster, foie gras, caviar and duck pâté. American menu. Dinner. Bar. Business casual attire. Reservations recommended. Outdoor seating. **$$$**

★★SERMET'S CORNER

276 King St., Charleston, 843-853-7775

Mediterranean menu. Lunch, dinner. Bar. Children's menu. **$$**

★★SLIGHTLY NORTH OF BROAD

192 E. Bay St., Charleston, 843-723-3424;
www.slightlynorthofbroad.net

Low-country menu. Lunch, dinner. Bar. Children's menu. Casual attire. **$$**

★★★SOCIAL WINE BAR

188 E. Bay St., Charleston, 843-577-5665; www.socialwinebar.com

Social Wine Bar's collection of wine extends beyond wine titans Napa Valley and Burgundy, France. Here, you'll find bottles from Spain and Italy to pinots from Oregon's Willamette Valley and syrahs from France's Cotes du Rhone. Why go to West Coast vineyards when they can come to you? Social Wine Bar even offers a selection of choice sake, Japan's rice wine. With such a dizzying array of wine to choose from, any vino lover in Charleston will have to make a stop at this popular venue that serves not only wine but also sophisticated, tapas-style small plates. Try the warm spinach salad with grilled pears or the rich, oxtail rillette napoleon from the "hot" menu to start. American menu. Dinner, late-night. **$$$**

CLEMSON

Home of Clemson University, this community also hosts vacationers attracted to the huge lake formed by the Hartwell Dam on the Savannah River.

Information: Clemson Area Chamber of Commerce, Clemson, 864-654-1200,
800-542-0746; www.clemsonchamber.org

WHAT TO SEE AND DO

CLEMSON UNIVERSITY

109 Daniel Drive, Clemson, 864-656-3311; www.clemson.edu

Named for Thomas G. Clemson, son-in-law of John C. Calhoun, who bequeathed the bulk of his estate Fort Hill for establishment of a scientific college. Clemson University was founded in 1889 and has 17,000 students. Guided tours: Monday-Saturday 9:45 a.m. and 1:45 p.m., Sunday 1:45 p.m. Closed school holidays and exam week.

FORT HILL
Clemson University, Fort Hill Street and Calhoun Drive, Clemson,
864-656-2475; www.clemson.edu

An 1803 mansion on 1,100 acres acquired by John C. Calhoun during his first term as vice president. House has many original furnishings belonging to Calhoun. Daily.

HANOVER HOUSE
South Carolina Botanical Garden, Clemson University, 102 Garden Trail,
864-656-2475; www.clemson.edu

This French Huguenot house was relocated here from its original site in Berkeley County to prevent submersion by Lake Moultrie. Saturday-Sunday by appointment only.

SOUTH CAROLINA BOTANICAL GARDEN
150 Discovery Lane, Clemson, 864-656-3405; www.clemson.edu

This 250-acre area includes azalea and camelia trails, ornamental plantings, large collection of shrubs, dwarf conifer flower and turf display gardens and a wildflower garden labeled in Braille. Daily.

HOTEL
★COMFORT INN
1305 Tiger Blvd., Clemson, 864-653-3600, 877-424-6423; www.comfortinn.com

122 rooms. Complimentary continental breakfast. Whirlpool. Pets accepted. Exercise room. Outdoor pool. High-speed Internet access. $

SPECIALTY LODGING
SUNRISE FARM BED & BREAKFAST INN
325 Sunrise Drive, Salem, 864-944-0121, 888-991-0121;
www.bbonline.com/sc/sunrisefarm/

Eight rooms. Built in 1890; Victorian country farmhouse. Complimentary full breakfast. Pets accepted. Golf. $

COLUMBIA

Located within three miles of the geographic center of the state, Columbia was laid out as the capital in a compromise between the contending up-country and low-country farmers. One of the nation's first planned cities, Columbia rarely departs from a checkerboard pattern. The streets are sometimes 150 feet wide, planned that way originally to discourage malaria.

The University of South Carolina, founded in 1801 as South Carolina College, is based here and is a leading influence in the city. Historical sites abound, as Columbia has a rich revolutionary and Civil War history. In 1865, General William T. Sherman's troops reduced Columbia to ashes, destroying 84 blocks and 1,386 buildings. Today, a city of stately buildings, a rejuvenated downtown and a thriving economy based on government, higher education and a mix of industries make South Carolina's biggest city a popular place to visit and a great town to live in.

Information: Columbia Metropolitan Visitors Center, 803-254-0479,
800-264-4884; www.columbiacvb.com

COLUMBIA MUSEUM OF ART

Main and Hampton streets, Columbia, 803-799-2810;
www.columbiamuseum.org

Galleries house Renaissance paintings, 19th- and 20th-century American, emphasizing Southeast and European paintings. Concerts, films, lectures and special events accenting exhibitions. Wednesday-Thursday, Saturday 10 a.m.-5 p.m.; Friday 10 a.m.-5 p.m. in December; Sunday 1-5 p.m.

CONFEDERATE RELIC ROOM AND MUSEUM

Columbia Mills Building, 301 Gervais St., Columbia,
803-737-8095; www.crr.sc.gov

Relic collection from the Colonial period through the space age with special emphasis on South Carolina's Confederate period. Tuesday-Saturday 10 a.m-5 p.m. First Sunday of the Month 1-5 p.m.

FIRST BAPTIST CHURCH

1306 Hampton St., Columbia, 803-256-4251; www.fbccola.com

The site of the first Secession Convention, which marked the beginning of the Civil War, on December 17, 1860. Monday-Friday, Sunday.

FIRST PRESBYTERIAN CHURCH

1324 Marion St., Columbia, 803-799-9062; www.firstprescolumbia.org

First congregation organized in Columbia; President Woodrow Wilson's parents are buried in churchyard. Daily.

173

FORT JACKSON

Fort Jackson, 4394 Strom Thurmond Blvd., Columbia, 803-751-1742;
www.jackson.army.mil

The most active initial entry training center for the U.S. Army, with 16,000 soldiers assigned. The museum on Jackson Boulevard has displays on the history of the fort and today's army. Monday-Friday 8:30 a.m.-4:30 p.m.

GOVERNOR'S MANSION

800 Richland St., Columbia, 803-737-1710;
www.scgovernorsmansion.org

Built in 1855 as the officers' quarters for Arsenal Academy. Tours every half-hour. Tuesday-Wednesday 10-11 a.m. Reservations required.

HAMPTON-PRESTON MANSION

1615 Blanding St., Columbia, 803-252-7742;
www.historiccolumbia.org

Purchased by Wade Hampton I and occupied by the Hamptons and the family of his daughter, Mrs. John Preston. In February 1865, the house served as headquarters for Union General J. A. Logan. Many Hampton surviving family furnishings and decorative arts of the antebellum period on display. Tours on the hour. Tuesday-Sunday.

SOUTH CAROLINA

★
★
★
★
★

RIVERBANKS ZOO AND GARDEN

500 Wildlife Parkway, Columbia, 803-779-8717;
www.riverbanks.org

Exhibits of animals in natural habitat areas; aquarium-reptile complex with diving demonstrations; demonstrations at Riverbanks Farm; penguin and sea lion feedings. Daily 9 a.m.-5 p.m. April-September, Saturday-Sunday to 6 p.m.

ROBERT MILLS HISTORIC HOUSE AND PARK

1616 Blanding St., Columbia, 803-252-7442;
www.historiccolumbia.org

One of a few residences designed by Robert Mills, Federal architect and designer of the Washington Monument; mantels, art, furnishings of Regency period. Tours on the hour. Tuesday-Saturday 10 a.m.-4 p.m., Sunday 1-5 p.m.

TRINITY CATHEDRAL

1100 Sumter St., Columbia, 803-771-7300;
www.trinityepiscopalcathedral.org

Reproduction of Yorkminster, England; the oldest church building in Columbia and one of the largest Episcopal congregations in the U.S. Hiram Powers baptismal font, box pews, English stained glass. Three Wade Hamptons (a politically prominent South Carolina family) are buried in the churchyard; graves of seven governors and six bishops are also here. Daily.

UNIVERSITY OF SOUTH CAROLINA

McKissick Visitor Center, 816 Bull St., Columbia, 803-777-0169, 800-922-9755;
www.sc.edu/visitorcenter

Located downtown. For campus tour information, stop at the University of South Carolina Visitor Center. Monday-Friday, select weekends.

HOTELS

★★EMBASSY SUITES HOTEL COLUMBIA-GREYSTONE

200 Stoneridge Drive, Columbia, 803-252-8700, 800-362-2779;
www.embassysuites.com

214 rooms, all suites. Complimentary full breakfast. High-speed Internet access. Restaurant, bar. Airport transportation available. Business center. Fitness room. $$

★HAMPTON INN-DOWNTOWN HISTORIC DISTRICT

822 Gervais St., Columbia, 803-231-2000, 800-426-7866;
www.hamptoninncolumbia.com

122 rooms. Complimentary continental breakfast. Wireless Internet access. Business center. Fitness center. Pool. $

★★RAMADA COLUMBIA

7510 Two Notch Road, Columbia, 803-736-3000, 877-308-4986; www.ramada.com
251 rooms. Wireless Internet access. Restaurant, bar. Fitness center. Pets accepted. Pool. $

RESTAURANTS

★★HAMPTON STREET VINEYARD

1201 Hampton St., Columbia, 803-252-0850;
www.hamptonstreetvineyard.com

American menu. Lunch, dinner. Closed Sunday. Bar. Casual attire. Reservations recommended. Outdoor seating. $$$

★★HENNESSY'S

1649 Main St., Columbia, 803-799-8280; www.hennessyssc.com

American menu. Lunch, dinner. Closed Sunday. Bar. Business casual attire. Reservations recommended. $$

★★★RISTORANTE DIVINO

803 Gervais St., Columbia, 803-799-4550; www.ristorantedivino.com

Ristorante Divino is located in Columbia's historic downtown district, within walking distance to a variety of shops. The wine cellar features more than 3,000 bottles of wine and includes 400 varieties to complement the classic Italian dishes on the menu, which feature an emphasis on seafood. Northern Italian menu. Dinner. Closed Sunday. Bar. Business casual attire. Reservations recommended. Valet parking. $$$

DARLINGTON

Any true fan of stock car racing knows Darlington. It is the state's stock car racing center and home to the Stock Car Hall of Fame as well as what is said to be the nation's largest automobile auction market.

Information: Greater Darlington Chamber of Commerce,
843-393-9511; www.visitdarlingtoncounty.org

WHAT TO SEE AND DO

DARLINGTON RACEWAY

1301 Harry Byrd Highway, Darlington, 866-459-7223; www.darlingtonraceway.com

Remembered as the original "Super Speedway," the track first opened in 1950 and is famous for its unique egg shape. Hundreds of miles raced, millions of fans and numerous legends have left their mark here. Major races in May; check for ongoing events and racing schools on Web site. Monday-Friday 9 a.m.-5 p.m.

JOE WEATHERLY STOCK CAR MUSEUM AND NATIONAL MOTORSPORTS PRESS ASSOCIATION STOCK CAR HALL OF FAME

1301 Harry Byrd Highway, Darlington, 843-395-8499; www.darlingtonraceway.com

Darlington Raceway, the oldest super-speedway in the country, also houses the sport's hall of fame. The museum details NASCAR's storied Darlington history and features everyone from NASCAR's first champion, Red Byron, to David Pearson and Dale Earnhardt. Several rooms are filled with stock cars that once sped across the raceway, including the blue Plymouth that Richard Petty drove to victory in 10 races back in 1967. Daily 9 a.m.-5 p.m.

FLORENCE

This community has grown from a sparsely settled crossroads into a major retail and wholesale distribution center. The economy is no longer dependent on agriculture.

Florence is also the home of Francis Marion College and Florence-Darlington Technical College.

Information: Greater Florence Chamber of Commerce, 610 W. Palmetto St., Florence, 843-665-0515; www.florencechamber.com

WHAT TO SEE AND DO

FLORENCE STOCKADE

Stockade and National Cemetery roads, Florence

The stockade was a Civil War prison that housed Union soldiers transferred from the notorious Andersonville prison. Roughly 2,800 soldiers died there, including Florena Budwin, whom Friends of the Florence Stockade say is the only female Civil War prisoner to die in captivity. The site is a Civil War Heritage Site.

WAR BETWEEN THE STATES MUSEUM

107 S. Guerry St., Florence, 843-669-1266; www.florenceweb.com/warmuseum.htm

Explore artifacts, pictures and stories from the Civil War. Wednesday, Saturday 10 a.m.-5 p.m.

HOTEL

★★★ABINGDON MANOR

307 Church St., Latta, 843-752-5090, 888-752-5090; www.abingdonmanor.com

This opulent Greek Revival building is listed on the National Register of Historic Places. The grand entry hall and luxurious guest rooms are only part of the charm. An excellent restaurant, full breakfast and nightly cocktails make this hotel a true luxury. Seven rooms. Children over 10 years only. Complimentary full breakfast. Wireless Internet access. Restaurant, bar. $$

RESTAURANT

★★★ABINGDON MANOR RESTAURANT

307 Church St., Latta, 843-752-5090, 888-752-5090; www.abingdonmanor.com

This elegant restaurant, located inside a charming inn of the same name, offers a creative menu of American fare using fresh ingredients from the onsite garden. American menu. Dinner. Closed Sunday. Bar. Business casual attire. Reservations recommended. $$$

GAFFNEY

On I-85, just outside of town, stands the Gaffney Peachoid, an elevated tank that resembles a gigantic peach and holds a million-gallon water supply. Gaffney is home to textile and metal working centers and is also a center for agriculture, particularly peaches.

Information: Cherokee County Chamber of Commerce, 225 S. Limestone St., 864-489-5721; www.cherokeechamber.org

WHAT TO SEE AND DO

COWPENS NATIONAL BATTLEFIELD

4001 Chesnee Highway, Gaffney, 864-461-2828; www.nps.gov/cowp

This was the scene of the victory of General Daniel Morgan's American Army over superior British forces on January 17, 1781. The battle wounded the British Army substantially enough to help set the stage for Cornwallis' surrender. Features an 843-acre tract with exhibits, an information and visitor center, a self-guided tour road and a walking trail with audio stations and a restored 1830 historic house. Daily 9 a.m.-5 p.m.

PRIME OUTLETS GAFFNEY

1 Factory Shops Blvd., Gaffney, 864-902-9900, 888-545-7194;
www.primeoutlets.com

An open-air, village-style manufacturers' outlet, featuring 65 outlet shops. Daily.

SPECIAL EVENT
SOUTH CAROLINA PEACH FESTIVAL

225 S. Limestone St., Gaffney, 864-489-5716; www.scpeachfestival.org

Arts and crafts, sports events, entertainment. July.

GEORGETOWN

Georgetown sits on the shore of Winyah Bay, the site of the first European settlement on the North American mainland outside of Mexico. In 1526, a group of Spaniards settled here, only to be driven out within a year by disease and Native American attacks. Rice and indigo plantations were established along nearby rivers around 1700, helping Georgetown thrive as a seaport. Known as a sawmill city during the first three decades of this century, Georgetown currently boasts several manufacturing industries as well as a booming tourist industry anchored by its historic plantations, gardens and beaches.

Information: Georgetown County Chamber of Commerce, 1001 Front St.,
Georgetown, 843-546-8436, 800-777-7705; www.georgetownchamber.com

WHAT TO SEE AND DO
HAMPTON PLANTATION STATE PARK

1950 Rutledge Road, McClellanville, 843-546-9361;
www.discoversouthcarolina.com

This restored 18th-century mansion was the center of a large rice plantation. Guided tours on the hour, special programs. Grounds: Memorial Day-Labor Day, daily 9 a.m-6 p.m.; rest of the year, Thursday-Monday 9 a.m.-6 p.m.; mansion: Memorial Day-Labor Day, daily 11 a.m.-4 p.m.; rest of the year, Thursday-Monday 1-4 p.m.

HOPSEWEE PLANTATION

494 Hopsewee Road, Georgetown, 803-546-7891; www.hopsewee.com

Preserved 1740 rice plantation house on the North Santee River. Birthplace of Thomas Lynch Jr., a signer of the Declaration of Independence. March-October, Monday-Friday 10 a.m.-4 p.m.; rest of year, Thursday-Friday 10 a.m.-4 p.m.; and by appointment.

PRINCE GEORGE WINYAH CHURCH

708 Broad St., Georgetown, 843-546-4358; www.pgwinyah.org

The English stained-glass window behind the altar was originally a part of St. Mary's Chapel for Negroes at Hagley Plantation on Waccamaw. The church has been in continuous use since it was constructed, except during the American Revolution and the Civil War. Tours are available. Memorial Day-October, Monday-Friday 11:30 a.m.-4:30 p.m.

TOWN CLOCK BUILDING

633 Front St., Georgetown

Tablet marks the landing of Lafayette at North Island in 1777. Federal troops came ashore on the dock at the rear of the building in an attempt to capture the town.

HOTEL
★CAROLINIAN INN

706 Church St., Georgetown, 843-546-5191, 800-722-4667;
www.carolinianinn.com

89 rooms. Complimentary continental breakfast. **$**

RESTAURANTS
★★RICE PADDY

732 Front St., Georgetown, 843-546-2021; www.ricepaddyrestaurant.com

American menu. Lunch, dinner. Closed Sunday. Bar. Children's menu. Casual attire. Monday-Saturday 11:30 a.m.-2:30 p.m. and 6-10 p.m. **$$**

★★RIVER ROOM

801 Front St., Georgetown, 843-527-4110; www.riverroomgeorgetown.com

Seafood menu. Lunch, dinner. Closed Sunday. Bar. Children's menu. **$$**

GREENVILLE

Best known for its textile industry, Greenville has several hundred manufacturing plants producing clothing, nylon, chemicals, plastic film and machinery. Beautiful trees line the streets and there are many forested parks in the area. The Reedy River, passing over falls in the heart of Greenville, originally provided the city's power. Pleasant streets now border the twisting Sylvan Stream. Furman University, a small liberal arts college, is located in Greenville.

Information: Convention and Visitors Bureau, 631 S. Main St., Greenville,
864-233-0461, 800-717-0023; www.greatergreenville.com

WHAT TO SEE AND DO
CAESARS HEAD STATE PARK

8155 Geer Highway, Cleveland, 864-836-6115; www.southcarolinaparks.com

Approximately 7,000 acres overlooking a valley of almost impenetrable brush and dense forest. One side of the mountain resembles Caesar's head. Hiking trails. Picnicking (shelter). Trailside camping, store, special programs.

GREENVILLE COUNTY MUSEUM

420 College St., Greenville, 864-271-7570; www.greenvillemuseum.org

Permanent collection of American art, featuring historical and contemporary works. Rotating exhibits include painting, sculpture, photography. Lectures, tours. Tuesday-Sunday.

GREENVILLE ZOO

150 Cleveland Park Drive, Greenville, 864-467-4300; www.greenvillezoo.com

Wildlife from around the world on display in natural, open-air exhibits. Lighted tennis courts, ball field; nature, jogging, hiking and bicycle trails; park. Daily. Children under 13 years must be accompanied by an adult.

PARIS MOUNTAIN STATE PARK

2401 State Park Road, Greenville, 864-244-5565; www.southcarolinaparks.com

Approximately 1,300 acres with three lakes. Thick forest setting with swiftly flowing streams. Lake swimming, fishing, pedal boats (rentals); nature, hiking trail, picnicking, playground, camping. Daily 11 a.m.-5 p.m.

TABLE ROCK STATE PARK

158 E. Ellison Lane, Pickens, 864-878-9813; www.southcarolinaparks.com

Approximately 3,000 acres. Extends over Table Rock Mountain (elevation 3,124 feet) and valleys. Lake swimming; fishing; boating, canoeing (rentals). Hiking trail; carpet golf. Picnicking, restaurant, store. Camping (hookups, dump station), cabins; recreation building. Nature center; nature and recreation programs. Daily 7 a.m.-9 p.m.

HOTELS

★★COURTYARD GREENVILLE HAYWORD MALL

70 Orchard Park Drive, Greenville, 864-234-0300, 800-321-2211;
www.courtyard.com

146 rooms. High-speed Internet access. Restaurant. $

★DAYS INN

60 Roper Mountain Road, Greenville, 864-297-9996, 800-329-7466;
www.daysinn.com

121 rooms. Complimentary continental breakfast. Wireless Internet access. $

★★EMBASSY SUITES HOTEL GREENVILLE GOLF RESORT AND CONFERENCE CENTER

670 Verdae Blvd., Greenville, 864-676-9090, 800-362-2779;
www.embassysuites.com

268 rooms, all suites. Complimentary full breakfast. High-speed Internet access. Restaurant, bar. Golf, 18 holes. Airport transportation available. Business center. $

★★★GREENVILLE MARRIOTT

1 Parkway East, Greenville, 864-297-0300, 800-833-2221; www.marriott.com

This Marriott has a contemporary theme with marble floors and leather chairs in the lobby and yellow-striped wall coverings and light wood furniture in guest rooms. 204 rooms. Wireless Internet access. Restaurant, bar. Spa. Airport transportation available. $$

★HAMPTON INN

246 Congaree Road, Greenville, 864-288-1200, 800-426-7866;
www.hamptoninn.com

123 rooms. Complimentary continental breakfast. Wireless Internet access. $

SOUTH CAROLINA

★
★
★
★
☆

★★★HILTON GREENVILLE

45 W. Orchard Park Drive, Greenville, 864-232-4747, 800-445-8667; www.hilton.com

This modern hotel, located on Greenville's suburban East side, has been updated with comfortable beds with luxury bedding and instated a new smoke-free policy. Upscale touches in rooms include Cuisinart coffeemakers with Lavazza coffee, alarm clocks with CD players and MP3 hookups and Crabtree & Evelyn bath products. 256 rooms. Wireless Internet access. Restaurant, bar. Airport transportation available. **$$**

★★★HYATT REGENCY GREENVILLE

220 N. Main St., Greenville, 864-235-1234, 800-233-1234; www.hyatt.com

Nestled in the heart of downtown Greenville, this Hyatt property is within walking distance of the Bi-Lo Center. Also nearby are the Peace Center for the Performing Arts and Furman University. Spacious rooms feature desks and other amenities designed for business travelers. 328 rooms. Wireless Internet access. Restaurant, bar. Airport transportation available. **$$**

★★★THE WESTIN POINSETT

120 Main St., Greenville, 864-421-9700, 800-937-8461; www.westin.com

This historic hotel, built in 1925, is located among many of Greenville's boutique shops and dining spots and is near Furman University. The lobby features plaster ceilings, crystal chandeliers and terrazzo floors. Guest rooms are decorated in warm beige hues and feature the chain's signature Heavenly beds. 200 rooms. Wireless Internet access. Restaurant, bar. Connecting rooms available. Satellite channels. Airport transportation available. **$$**

RESTAURANT

★★★STAX'S PEPPERMILL

30 Orchard Park Drive, Greenville, 864-288-9320; www.staxs.com

This contemporary restaurant features a wine room, an enclosed porch with window views, and a lounge with inviting soft sofas and plush booths. Features a continental menu with steak and seafood options, as well as sushi. International menu. Dinner. Closed Sunday. Bar. Casual attire. Reservations recommended. **$$$**

GREENWOOD

Located at the junction of highways and railways, Greenwood was originally the plantation of Green Wood. The city later became known as the community of Woodville before adopting its present name. Greenwood's Main Street is one of the widest (316 feet) in the nation. The area has historic sites related to the Revolutionary War, but the city is best known for its sports and recreation. Rolling hills, year-round temperate climate and lots of undeveloped wooded land have made this a haven for golfers.

Information: Chamber of Commerce, 110 Phoenix St., Greenwood,
864-223-8431; www.greenwoodchamber.org

WHAT TO SEE AND DO

BAKER CREEK STATE PARK

863 Baker Creek Road, McCormick, 864-443-2457; www.discoversouthcarolina.com

Approximately 1,300 acres. Lake swimming, bathhouse; lake fishing; boating (ramps). Nature, bridle trails; 'carpet golf.' Picnicking, playground. Camping. Daily 6 a.m.-6 p.m., to 9 p.m. during daylight savings time.

HICKORY KNOB RESORT

Highway 4, McCormick, 864-391-2450, 800-491-1764;
www.southcarolinaparks.com

Nature trails; 18-hole golf course, putting green, field archery course, skeet range, field trial area. Waterskiing, lake fishing, boating equipment and supplies available. Camping, lodge, cabins. Recreation and nature programs. Convention facilities. Playground. Restaurant.

NINETY SIX NATIONAL HISTORIC SITE

1103 Highway 248 S., Ninety Six, 864-543-4068; www.nps.gov/nisi

Site of old Ninety Six, an early village in South Carolina backcountry, so named because it is 96 miles away from the Cherokee Village of Keowee on the Cherokee Path. The South's first land battle of the American Revolution in 1775 and the 28-day siege of Ninety Six in 1781 occurred here. The earthworks of the British-built Star Fort remain, along with reconstructed siege works and other fortifications of the period. Also here are subsurface remains of two village complexes, a trading post-plantation complex and a network of 18th-century roads. Visitor center; museum. Daily 8 a.m.-5 p.m.

SPECIALTY LODGING
BELMONT INN

104 E. Pickens St., Abbeville, 864-459-9625, 877-459-8118; www.belmontinn.net

25 rooms. Complimentary continental breakfast. Restaurant, bar. **$**

HARDEEVILLE

This small low country town is located 15 miles from Savannah and Hilton Head and 20 miles from historic Beaufort. The Savannah River runs through Hardeeville, providing a scenic spot for fishing and angling.

Information: www.cityofhardeeville.com

WHAT TO SEE AND DO
SAVANNAH NATIONAL WILDLIFE REFUGE

1000 Business Center Drive, Hardeeville, 912-652-4415; www.fws.gov/savannah

Approximately 25,600 acres. More than half the acreage consists of bottomland hardwoods reminiscent of the great cypress and tupelo swamps that once extended along the Carolina and Georgia Low Country. Argent Swamp can only be reached by boat; wild azaleas, iris, spider lilies and other flowers bloom in succession, beginning in spring. Laurel Hill Wildlife Drive is open to cars and allows viewing of wildlife, especially waterfowl from December to February. Migrating songbirds are abundant in spring and fall. Tupelo-Swamp Walk (mid-March-September) is best for bird-watchers and photographers. Daily; some areas closed October-November for hunting; impoundments north of Highway 17 closed November-mid-March; Laurel Hill Drive hours posted at gate.

HILTON HEAD

This year-round resort island attracts all travelers from families who want an easy, kid-friendly atmosphere to high-end travelers and everyone. Hilton Head, reached by a bridge on Highway 278, is bordered by one of the few remaining unpolluted

SOUTH CAROLINA

★
★
★
★
★

marine estuaries on the East Coast and is the largest sea island between New Jersey and Florida. The island has 12 miles of beaches, numerous golf courses and tennis courts, swimming, miles of bicycle paths, horseback riding, four nature preserves and deep-sea, sound and dockside fishing. There are also nine marinas and a paved 3,700-foot airstrip, 3,000 hotel and motel rooms, more than 200 restaurants and 28 shopping centers, plus many art galleries and numerous sporting and cultural events.

Information: Chamber of Commerce, 843-785-3673; www.hiltonheadisland.org

WHAT TO SEE AND DO
DAUFUSKIE ISLAND RESORT GOLF
421 Squire Pope Road, Hilton Head, 843-341-4810, 800-648-6778;
www.daufuskieresort.com
Rates for both resort guests and day players are relatively low for the two 18-hole courses on the property (the Melrose, designed by Jack Nicklaus, and the Bloody Point, designed by Tom Weiskopf and Jay Morrish), both of which offer challenging holes and great views of the Atlantic Ocean.

HARBOUR TOWN GOLF LINKS
Sea Pines Resort, 32 Greenwood Drive, Hilton Head Island,
888-807-6873; www.seapines.com
Pete Dye designed the courses, featuring the designer's signature red-and-white-striped lighthouse, which serves as a backdrop for the course's 18th hole. The par-71 layout is less than 7,000 yards from the back tees, but the fairways can be narrow and the greens small. Two other courses at the resort, Ocean and Sea Pines, add 36 more holes to the offerings.

HOTELS
★★★CROWNE PLAZA
130 Shipyard Drive, Hilton Head Island, 843-842-2400, 800-334-1881;
www.cphiltonhead.com
Located in Shipyard Plantation, this 11-acre resort is a paradise for golfers and tennis players. The beachfront location is set on miles of sandy oceanfront great for trying sailboats, boogie boards and beach trikes. 340 rooms. Three restaurants, one bar. Children's activity center. Beach. $$

★★★DAUFUSKIE ISLAND RESORT AND BREATHE SPA
421 Squire Pope Road, Hilton Head Island, 843-341-4820,
800-648-6778; www.daufuskieresort.com
The full-service resort, which has vacation cottages and villas, offers a range of activities from 36 holes of golf to horseback riding, croquet and tennis. 192 rooms. Three restaurants, four bars. Children's activity center. Spa. Beach. Children's pool, whirlpool. $$

★HAMPTON INN
1 Dillon Road, Hilton Head Island, 843-681-7900, 800-426-7866;
www.hamptoninn.com
115 rooms. Complimentary continental breakfast. $

★★HILTON HEAD MARRIOTT BEACH AND GOLF RESORT

1 Hotel Circle at Palmetto Dunes, Hilton Head Island, 843-686-8400,
800-228-9290; www.hiltonheadmarriott.com

This beachfront Marriott is located at Palmetto Dunes, within walking distance of the
Shelter Cove Marina shops and attractions. Nicely appointed rooms plus beach access
and several pools provide reasons to stay within the resort's walls. 513 rooms. Three
restaurants, two bars. Children's activity center. Fitness classes available. Outdoor
pools, indoor pool, whirlpools, children's pool. Beach. **$**

★★HILTON OCEANFRONT RESORT HILTON HEAD ISLAND

23 Ocean Lane, Hilton Head Island, 843-842-8000, 800-845-8001;
www.hiltonheadhilton.com

Enjoy the widest beach on the island at this luxe, self-contained resort. Manicured
gardens and lagoons adorn the property. 324 rooms. Three restaurants, two bars. High-
speed Internet access. Children's activity center. Fitness classes available. Beach. Two
outdoor pools, children's pool, two whirlpools. **$$$**

★★★★THE INN AT PALMETTO BLUFF

476 Mount Pilla Road, Bluffton, 843-706-6500, 866-706-6565;
www.palmettobluffresort.com

This Low Country inn, a sister to California's famed Auberge du Soleil, delivers
luxury accommodations, fine dining and pure relaxation in a riverfront setting.
Rooms offer plenty of luxury touches such as plasma televisions, wet bars with Sub-
Zero refrigerators and deep soaking tubs. Enjoy the Jack Nicklaus-designed golf
course or full-service spa. The River House restaurant serves Southern-influenced
recipes such as she-crab bisque laced with aged sherry and cast-iron fried quail with
bacon, eggs, arugula and warm ricotta pudding. 50 rooms, all suites. Restaurant,
bar. **$$$$**

★★★MAIN STREET INN

2200 Main St., Hilton Head Island, 843-681-3001, 800-471-3001;
www.mainstreetinn.com

The Main Street Inn is a beacon of sophistication. The 32 rooms are individually
designed, yet all feature luxurious velvet and silk linens, unique artwork and distinc-
tive furnishings. Afternoon tea is a daily tradition. 33 rooms. Children over 12 years
only. Complimentary full breakfast. **$**

★★QUALITY INN & SUITES

200 Museum St., Hilton Head Island, 843-681-3655, 800-784-1180;
www.qualityinn.com

127 rooms. Restaurant, bar. Wireless Internet access. Pets accepted, fee. **$**

★★★THE WESTIN RESORT, HILTON HEAD ISLAND

2A Grasslawn Ave., Hilton Head Island, 843-681-4000; www.westin.com/hiltonhead

This self-contained beachfront resort is a standout with its roster of leisure activities
from golf, tennis and swimming to a fully stocked Reebok gym with yoga, Pilates
and fitness machines. Rooms have plush beds with fluffy duvets, soaking tubs and

SOUTH CAROLINA

★
★
★
★
★

balconies. 412 rooms. High-speed Internet access. Three restaurants, bar. Children's activity center. Fitness classes available. Spa. Indoor pool, two outdoor pools, whirlpool. Beach. Airport transportation available. $$

RESTAURANTS

★★ALEXANDER'S

76 Queens Folly Road, Hilton Head Island, 843-785-4999;
www.alexandersrestaurant.com

American, seafood menu. Dinner. Bar. Children's menu. Casual attire. $$

★AUNT CHILADAS EASY STREET CAFÉ

69 Pope Ave., Hilton Head, 843-785-7700; www.auntchiladashhi.com

Mexican, seafood, steak menu. Lunch, dinner, late-night, brunch. Bar. Children's menu. Casual attire. $

★★CHARLIE'S L'ETOILE VERTE

8 New Orleans Road, Hilton Head Island, 843-785-9277;
www.charliesofhiltonhead.com

French menu. Lunch Tuesday-Saturday, dinner. Closed Sunday. Bar. Casual attire. Reservations recommended. $$

★★★HARBOURMASTER'S OCEAN GRILL

1 Shelter Cove Lane, Hilton Head Island, 843-785-3030;
www.oceangrillrestaurant.com

Located on the waterway entrance to Shelter Cove Harbour, this restaurant offers creative and sumptuous seafood cuisine. Exceptional service, unmatched ambience and dramatic views. Seafood menu. Dinner. Closed January. Bar. Children's menu. Casual attire. Reservations recommended. Outdoor seating. $$$

★★LITTLE VENICE

2 Shelter Cove Lane, Hilton Head Island, 843-785-3300

Italian menu. Dinner. Bar. Casual attire. Reservations recommended. Outdoor seating. $$

★★OLD OYSTER FACTORY

101 Marshland Road, Hilton Head Island, 843-681-6040; www.oldoysterfactory.com

Seafood menu. Dinner. Bar. Children's menu. Outdoor seating. $$

★★PRESTO KITCHEN

45 Pembroke Drive, Hilton Head Island, 843-342-2400

International menu. Dinner. Closed Sunday-Monday. Bar. Business casual attire. Reservations recommended. $$$

★★★RED FISH

8 Archer Road, Hilton Head Island, 843-686-3388;
www.redfishofhiltonhead.com

Red Fish offers a menu of unique Caribbean dishes made with creatively blended house-made seasonings, vegetables and tropical fruits. Grilled grouper, Latin ribs

★
★
★
★
★

and crispy Ashley Farms free-range brick chicken are among many enticing menu choices. An extensive wine list has more than 1,000 bottles. Warm, terra-cotta walls accented with framed pictures and dark wood chairs set around white-clothed tables add to the casual atmosphere. Caribbean menu. Lunch, dinner. Bar. Children's menu. Business casual attire. Reservations recommended. Outdoor seating. $$

★SCOTT'S FISH MARKET

1 Shelter Cove Lane, Hilton Head Island, 843-785-7575
Seafood menu. Dinner. Closed January. Bar. Children's menu. Casual attire. Outdoor seating. $$

★STEAMERS SEAFOOD COMPANY

28 Coligny Plaza, Hilton Head, 843-785-2070; www.steamerseafood.com
Seafood menu. Lunch, dinner. Bar. Children's menu. Casual attire. Outdoor seating. $$

SPA

★★★★SPA AT PALMETTO BLUFF

476 Mount Pilla Road, Bluffton, 843-706-6500, 866-706-6565; www.palmettobluffresort.com
Plantation shutters, willowing white drapery and the surrounding verdant countryside heighten the serenity of true Southern hospitality. Treatments for golfers include the Masters (hydrating massage and facial for sun-damaged skin) and the 20th Hole (private steam and sports massage). Everyone—not just golfers—will de-stress with treatments such as the Aromatherapy massage, which uses a personalized mix of flower-, herb- and root-based essential oils.

ISLE OF PALMS

This coastal barrier island just north of Charleston and only 20 minutes from downtown was originally home to the Seewee tribe of Native Americans. It's now a popular resort destination.
Information: www.isle-of-palms.us

HOTEL

★★★BOARDWALK INN AT WILD DUNES RESORT

5757 Palm Blvd., Isle of Palms, 843-886-6000, 888-778-1876; www.wilddunes.com
Beachy elegance defines the atmosphere at this resort. The property includes two 18-hole Tom Fazio-designed golf courses, a 17-court tennis center, a marina and a fitness center. The Sea Island Grill specializes in Low Country cooking. 93 rooms. High-speed Internet access. Two restaurants, two bars. Children's activity center. Fitness classes available. $$

RESTAURANT

★★THE BOATHOUSE RESTAURANT

101 Palm Blvd., Isle of Palms, 843-886-8000; www.boathouserestaurants.com
Seafood menu. Dinner, Sunday brunch. Bar. Children's menu. Casual attire. Outdoor seating. $$$

★
★
★
★
★

KIAWAH ISLAND

Kiawah Island is one of the richest natural environments on the eastern seaboard. Named for the Native Americans who once hunted and fished here, the island is separated from the mainland by the Kiawah River and a mile-wide salt marsh. Separate resort areas and private residential neighborhoods ensure a minimum of automobile traffic and leave much of the island untouched. The Kiawah Island Resort offers activities such as golf, tennis and nature programs that take advantage of the island's natural beauty.

Information: Visitor Center, 22 Beachwalker Drive, 843-768-5116, 843-768-5117; www.charlestoncvb.com

HOTEL

★★★★★THE SANCTUARY HOTEL AT KIAWAH ISLAND

1 Sanctuary Beach Drive, Kiawah Island, 843-768-6000, 877-683-1234; www.thesanctuary.com

With five championship courses just outside its door, the Sanctuary hotel at Kiawah Island is a natural choice for golfers. This elegant resort also offer fine dining, a first-class spa and a beautiful setting. Rooms blend traditional early-American furnishings with a crisp coastal ambience and offers ocean views. Service is spectacular, with a friendly staff attending to every need. 255 rooms. Wireless Internet access. Three restaurants, three bars. Children's activity center. Fitness classes available, spa. Beach. Indoor pool, children's pool, whirlpool. Airport transportation available. **$$$$**

RESTAURANT

★★★★OCEAN ROOM

1 Sanctuary Beach Drive, Kiawah Island, 843-768-6253, 877-683-1234; www.thesanctuary.com

Plates sparkle at this fine-dining spot with New American entreés such as seared Hudson Valley foie gras with sautéed snow peas, sweet soy and snow pea sorbet, or seared rare ahi tuna with crispy shrimp dumplings, wilted wasabi leaves and lavender-scented jasmine rice. If you're feeling especially indulgent, order a side of the Iranian osetria caviar, priced at $220 per ounce. Seafood menu. Dinner. Bar. Jacket required. Reservations recommended. **$$$**

SPA

★★★★★SPA AT THE SANCTUARY

1 Sanctuary Beach Drive, Kiawah Island, 843-768-6340; www.thesanctuary.com

Located inside the Sanctuary at Kiawah Island, the Spa resembles a grand Southern seaside mansion. Inside, the hospitable staffs greet guests with herbal tea and fresh fruit before leading the way to one of 12 rooms for nature-based treatments, which feature botanical extracts, natural enzymes and a signature Southern touch. If exercise is on your mind, head downstairs to the fitness center, which features latest cardiovascular and resistance equipment, a 65-foot-long indoor pool and Pilates and yoga studios.

MOUNT PLEASANT

Founded 1680, Mount Pleasant is now part of suburban Charleston, and its main point of interest is the *U.S.S. Yorktown.*

Information: Mount Pleasant-Isle of Palms Visitor Center, 311 Johnnie Dodds Blvd., 843-884-8517; www.townofmountpleasant.com

PATRIOTS POINT NAVAL AND MARITIME MUSEUM

40 Patriots Point Road, Mount Pleasant, 843-884-2727;
www.patriotspoint.org

This is an amazing assemblage of naval equipment and lore, appropriately located in Charleston Harbor. The star is the famed World War II aircraft carrier, the *U.S.S. Yorktown*. Onboard the *Yorktown* are numerous displays, including the Congressional Medal of Honor Society's museum and headquarters, the World War II Fast Carrier exhibit, the Battle of Midway Torpedo Squadrons memorial and a World War II cruiser room. Other vessels include the *Savannah*, the world's first nuclear-powered merchant ship; the *Laffey*, a World War II destroyer; the *Clamagore*, a World War II submarine; and the *Ingham*, a Coast Guard cutter. April-September 9 a.m.-7:30 p.m.; October-March 9 a.m.-6:30 p.m.

RESTAURANT
★THE WRECK

106 Haddrell St., Mount Pleasant, 843-884-0052; www.wreckrc.com

Seafood menu. Dinner. Outdoor seating. Closed Sunday. No credit cards accepted. **$**

MURRELLS INLET

Located just 10 miles south of Myrtle Beach, Murrells Inlet calls itself the seafood capital of South Carolina. Besides restaurants, there is a beautiful stretch of beach in the area known as the Grand Strand called Huntington Beach with amazingly well-preserved marshland and coastline.

Information: www.murrellsinletsc.com

187

WHAT TO SEE AND DO
BROOKGREEN GARDENS

1931 Brookgreen Drive, Murrells Inlet, 843-235-6000, 800-849-1931;
www.brookgreen.org

On the site of former rice and indigo plantations, these gardens contain more than 500 pieces of American sculpture, boxwood, massive moss-hung oaks and native plants, as well as a wildlife park with native animals. Creek and all-terrain vehicle excursions take visitors through forests, creeks, old plantation homes and rice fields. Daily 9:30 a.m.-5 p.m.; until 9 p.m. Wednesday-Friday in summer; closed Monday in December.

HUNTINGTON BEACH STATE PARK

16148 Ocean Highway, Georgetown, 803-237-4440; www.southcarolinaparks.com

Approximately 2,500 acres. Ocean swimming, surf fishing. Hiking, nature trails; marsh boardwalk. Picnicking (shelters); playground. Camping.

SPECIAL EVENT
ANNUAL ATALAYA ARTS AND CRAFTS FESTIVAL, HUNTINGTON BEACH STATE PARK

16148 Ocean Highway, Murrells Inlet, 843-237-4440; www.atalayafestival.com

This juried art show has been running annually for more than three decades. Fine art, quality crafts and Low Country food, along with live music. Mid-late September.

SOUTH CAROLINA

RESTAURANT
★★CAPTAIN DAVE'S DOCKSIDE
4037A Highway 17 Business, Murrells Inlet, 843-651-5850;
www.captdavesdockside.com
Seafood menu. Lunch, dinner. Bar. Children's menu. Casual attire. Reservations recommended. Outdoor seating. **$$**

★★HOT FISH CLUB
4911 Highway 17 Business, Murrells Inlet, 843-357-9175; www.hotfishclub.com
American menu. Dinner. Closed Monday-Tuesday. **$$**

MYRTLE BEACH
With the warm Gulf Stream only a few miles offshore and dunes to shelter the miles of white sand, Myrtle Beach is one of the most popular seaside resorts on the Atlantic Coast. Named for the many myrtle trees in the area it lures millions of vacationers each summer with swimming, fishing, golf, tennis and its boardwalk.
Information: Myrtle Beach Area Chamber of Commerce, 1200 N. Oak St.,
Myrtle Beach, 843-626-7444, 800-356-3016; www.myrtlebeachlive.com

WHAT TO SEE AND DO
BAREFOOT LANDING
4898 Highway 17 S., Myrtle Beach, 843-272-8349, 800-272-2320; www.bflanding.com
With a mixture of specialty shops and factory stores, Barefoot Landing appeals to a variety of shoppers. There are also more than a dozen eateries and a variety of entertainment options, including the House of Blues and a video arcade. Daily, hours vary by season.

BAREFOOT RESORT
4980 Barefoot Resort Bridge Road, North Myrtle Beach,
843-390-3200, 800-320-6536; www.barefootgolf.com
Maybe the best place in Myrtle Beach to play golf, Barefoot Resort features four courses designed by some of the sport's biggest names—Davis Love III, Tom Fazio, Greg Norman and Pete Dye all took a piece of the land and crafted courses.

BROADWAY AT THE BEACH
1325 Celebrity Circle, Myrtle Beach, 843-444-3200, 800-386-4662;
www.broadwayatthebeach.com
This 350-acre complex, billed as the largest venue of its kind in South Carolina, features a wide variety of shops, dining and nightclubs. Also onsite are a 16-screen movie theater, an IMAX theater, a NASCAR SpeedPark, a miniature golf course, a water park and an aquarium. Broadway at the Beach is also home to the Myrtle Beach Pelicans, a Class A affiliate of the Atlanta Braves. Daily, hours vary by season.

HOTELS
★★BEACH COVE RESORT
4800 S. Ocean Blvd., North Myrtle Beach, 843-918-9000, 800-369-7043;
www.beachcove.com
330 rooms, all suites. Restaurant, two bars. Children's activity center. Beach. Indoor pool, three outdoor pools, children's pool, four whirlpools. **$**

★
★
★
★
★

★★COMPASS COVE OCEANFRONT RESORT

2311 S. Ocean Blvd., Myrtle Beach, 843-448-8373, 800-331-0934;
www.compasscove.com

532 rooms, all suites. Two restaurants, bar. Children's activity center. Beach. Two indoor pools, 16 outdoor pools, three children's pools, whirlpool. Airport transportation available. **$$**

★★COURTYARD MYRTLE BEACH BAREFOOT LANDING

1000 Commons Blvd., Myrtle Beach, 843-361-1730, 877-502-4653;
www.courtyard.com

157 rooms. Restaurant. Indoor pool, whirlpool. **$**

★★★THE CYPRESS INN

16 Elm St., Conway, 843-248-8199, 800-575-5307;
www.acypressinn.com

This 12-room bed and breakfast in the quiet town of Conway is located alongside a quaint marina. Go deep-sea fishing or simply walk the beautiful stretches of South Carolina beaches, located only 15 minutes away. 12 rooms. Complimentary full breakfast. Spa. **$**

★★★EMBASSY SUITES

9800 Queensway Blvd., Myrtle Beach, 843-449-0006, 800-876-0010;
www.kingstonplantation.com

Modern and inviting, this Embassy Suites is located close to Myrtle Beach's best theaters, restaurants, water parks and shopping. The hotel itself has six outdoor pools, golf and tennis. 385 rooms. Complimentary full breakfast. Restaurant, bar. Children's activity center. Indoor pool, outdoor pools, children's pool, whirlpool. **$$**

★FAIRFIELD INN

1350 Paradise Circle, Myrtle Beach, 843-444-8097, 800-217-1511;
www.fairfieldinn.com

111 rooms. Complimentary continental breakfast. Wireless Internet access. Outdoor pool, whirlpool. Business center. **$**

★HAMPTON INN

1140 Celebrity Circle, Myrtle Beach, 843-916-0600, 800-426-7866;
www.hamptoninn.com

141 rooms. Complimentary continental breakfast. High-speed Internet access. Children's activity center. Indoor pool, outdoor pool, whirlpool. Airport transportation available. **$**

★HAMPTON INN & SUITES OCEANFRONT

1803 S. Ocean Blvd., Myrtle Beach, 843-946-6400, 877-946-6400;
www.hamptoninnoceanfront.com

116 rooms. Complimentary continental breakfast. High-speed Internet access. Beach. Indoor pool, outdoor pool, children's pool, whirlpool. Airport transportation available. **$$**

★★★HILTON MYRTLE BEACH RESORT

10000 Beach Club Drive, Myrtle Beach, 843-449-5000,
877-887-9549; www.hilton.com

This oceanfront hotel has great views of the Atlantic Ocean and inviting guest rooms decorated in bright hues of gold, blue, green and terracotta. Nearby activities include the shops at Broadway at the Beach, the NASCAR Speedway, the Palace Theater, as well as many dining options. 385 rooms. High-speed Internet access. Three restaurants, two bars. Beach. Indoor pool, outdoor pool, children's pool, whirlpool. Golf, 18 holes. $$$

★LA QUINTA INN

1561 21st Ave. N., Myrtle Beach, 843-916-8801, 800-687-6667; www.laquinta.com

128 rooms. Complimentary continental breakfast. High-speed Internet access. Airport transportation available. $

★★OCEAN CREEK RESORT

10600 N. Kings Highway, Myrtle Beach, 843-272-7724, 877-844-3800;
www.oceancreek.com

410 rooms. Restaurant, bar. Children's activity center. Beach. $

★★★SHERATON MYRTLE BEACH CONVENTION CENTER HOTEL

2101 N. Oak St., Myrtle Beach, 843-918-5000;
www.starwoodhotels.com/sheraton

Situated in the center of Myrtle Beach, within walking distance to the Broadway at the Beach shopping area, this contemporary Sheraton offers an ideal location. The hotel's signature beds come decked out with down comforters and pillow-top mattresses, which are also available in a version designed for canine travelers. 402 rooms. High-speed Internet access. Restaurant, bar. Fitness room. Indoor pool, whirlpool. Airport transportation available. Business center. $$

SPECIALITY LODGING

SERENDIPITY INN

407 71st Ave., N., Myrtle Beach, 843-449-5268, 800-762-3229;
www.serendipityinn.com

This quaint inn located near the beach offers rooms decorated with country quilts and four poster beds. 15 rooms. Complimentary full breakfast. Whirlpool. $

RESTAURANTS

★CAGNEY'S OLD PLACE

9911 N. Kings Highway, Myrtle Beach, 843-449-3824;
www.cagneysoldplace.com

American menu. Dinner. Closed Sunday; also January and December. Bar. Children's menu. Casual attire. Reservations recommended. $$

★CAPTAIN GEORGE'S SEAFOOD

1401 29th Ave., Myrtle Beach, 843-916-2278; www.captaingeorges.com
Seafood menu. Lunch Sunday, dinner. Bar. Children's menu. Casual attire. $$

★
★
★
★
★

★★CHESTNUT HILL RESTAURANT

9922 Highway 17 N., Myrtle Beach, 843-449-3984; www.chestnuthilldining.com

American menu. Dinner, Sunday brunch. Bar. Children's menu. Casual attire. **$$**

★★COLLECTORS CAFÉ

7726 N. Kings Highway, Myrtle Beach, 843-449-9370;
www.collectorscafeandgallery.com

Mediterranean menu. Lunch, dinner. Closed Sunday; also two weeks in January. Bar. Casual attire. Reservations recommended. **$$$**

★DIRTY DON'S OYSTER BAR & GRILL

408 21st Ave. N., Myrtle Beach, 843-448-4881; www.dirtydonsoysterbar.com

American, seafood menu. Lunch, dinner, late-night. Bar. Children's menu. Casual attire. Outdoor seating. **$$**

★★JOE'S BAR AND GRILL

810 Conway Ave., North Myrtle Beach, 843-272-4666; www.dinejoes.com

American menu. Dinner. Bar. Children's menu. Casual attire. Outdoor seating. **$$**

★★★THE PARSON'S TABLE

4305 McCorsley Ave., Little River, 843-249-3702;
www.parsonstable.com

Not only can you get a juicy roast prime rib at the Parson's Table, but you can eat it inside a church, too. The location remains very much the same structure that it was in 1885, when Little River Methodist Church was built. The cherished establishment first opened its church doors as a restaurant in the late 1970s and has been serving exquisite American steakhouse fare ever since. The restaurant's décor is positively Southern-charm antique, complete with dark wooden walls, stained glass windows and an original Tiffany glass lamp in the main dining room. A thorough wine list graces The Parson's Table as well as a good seafood selection on top of the traditional beef. American, steakhouse menu. Dinner. Closed Sunday. **$$$**

★★SEA CAPTAIN'S HOUSE

3002 N. Ocean Blvd., Myrtle Beach, 843-448-8082; www.seacaptains.com

Seafood menu. Breakfast, lunch, dinner. Bar. Children's menu. Casual attire. **$$$**

★★★SEABLUE TAPAS

503 Highway 17 North, North Myrtle Beach, 843-249-8800;
www.seablueonline.com

SeaBlue Tapas is located in a shopping center across the street from a Home Depot and a TGIF, but step inside its doors and you're suddenly and quite literally transported into ultra chic, impossibly cool blues. The bar, the walls and the glowing aquarium all emanate blue light. At times, you'll feel like you're in an underwater lounge instead of a restaurant. As for the tapas, try the SeaBlue shrimp and grits, sizzling in a garlicky sauce, or the braised baby-back ribs. If you need a break from all that blue, try the Raspberry Flirtini. American menu. Dinner. Closed Sunday **$$$**

★
★
★
★
★

ORANGEBURG

Named for the Prince of Orange, this town is the seat of Orangeburg County, one of the most prosperous farm areas in the state. Manufacturing plants for wood products, ball bearings, textiles, textile equipment, chemicals, hand tools, and lawn mowers are all located within the county.

Information: Orangeburg County Chamber of Commerce,
1570 John C. Calhoun Drive, 803-534-6821; www.orangeburg.net

WHAT TO SEE AND DO
EDISTO MEMORIAL GARDENS

367 Green St., Orangeburg, 803-533-6020, 800-545-6153; www.orangeburgsc.net
City-owned 110-acre site. Seasonal flowers bloom all year; more than 3,200 rose bushes, camellias, azaleas; also many flowering trees. Gardens daily, dawn-dusk.

PAWLEYS ISLAND

A beach community halfway between Myrtle Beach and Georgetown, Pawleys Island has less than 500 year-round residents but thousands of visitors who come for its easy-going atmosphere and beach and golf access.

Information: www.townofpawleysisland.com

HOTEL
★★★LITCHFIELD PLANTATION

King's River Road, Pawleys Island, 843-237-9121, 800-869-1410;
www.litchfieldplantation.com

192

This former plantation house from the 1750s has been beautifully restored and converted into an elegant country inn. Guests will find uniquely decorated rooms with private baths and suites with antique sleigh beds, fireplaces and double Jacuzzis. The resort has direct beach access via Litchfield Plantation's beach club on Pawleys Island, plus onsite dining at the Carriage House Club. 38 rooms. Complimentary full breakfast. Restaurant, bar. Pool. $$

SPECIALTY LODGING
SEAVIEW INN

414 Myrtle Ave., Pawleys Island, 843-237-4253; www.seaviewinn.com
20 rooms. Closed November-mid-April. Children over three years only. Beach. $$

RESTAURANT
★★CARRIAGE HOUSE CLUB

Kings River Road, Litchfield Plantation, Pawleys Island,
843-237-9322; www.litchfieldplantation.com

Set in the serene backdrop of the Litchfield Plantation, the brick structure that houses the Carriage House Club restaurant is a Southern jewel to be sure. The former English carriage house is now a choice establishment for classic gourmet cuisine with a Southern twist. Must-orders are two chef specialties: the Carriage House grouper, lightly battered and served with a beurre blanc sauce and the goat cheese-dijon mustard crusted rack of lamb. If that doesn't do you in, take a look at the dessert list, which features good ol' pecan and key lime pies. American menu. Breakfast, dinner. Closed Sunday-Monday. $$$

SOUTH CAROLINA

★
★
★
★

ROCK HILL

Both a college and an industrial town, Rock Hill takes its name from the flint rock that had to be cut when a railroad was built through town. Today it is home to Winthrop University and flanked by state parks.

Information: York County Convention & Visitors Bureau, 201 E. Main St., 803-329-5200, 800-866-5200; www.yccvb.com

WHAT TO SEE AND DO

ANDREW JACKSON STATE PARK

196 Andrew Jackson Park Road, Lancaster, 803-285-3344; www.southcarolinaparks.com

Approximately 360 acres. Lake fishing, boating (rentals). Nature trail. Picnicking (shelters). Camping. Recreation building, outdoor amphitheater. Log house museum contains documents, exhibits of Jackson lore. One-room hool with exhibits.

CATAWBA CULTURAL CENTER

1536 Tom Steven Road, Rock Hill, 803-328-2427; www.ccppcrafts.com

Located on the Catawba Indian Reservation, this center strives to preserve the heritage of the Catawbas' culture. Tours and programs are available by appointment. Monday-Saturday 9 a.m.-5 p.m.

HISTORIC BRATTONSVILLE

1444 Brattonsville Road, McConnells, 803-684-2327; www.chmuseums.org

Learn about local history in this restored village of more than two dozen structures, including Backwoodsman Cabin, Colonel Bratton Home, Homestead House and Brick Kitchen. Gift shop. Guided tours (by appointment). Self-guided audio tour. Monday-Saturday 10 a.m.-5 p.m., Sunday 1-5 p.m.

MUSEUM OF YORK COUNTY

4621 Mount Gallant Road, Rock Hill, 803-329-2121; www.chmuseums.org

Contains a large collection of mounted African hoofed mammals; large African artifacts collection. Hall of Western Hemisphere contains mounted animals from North and South America. Art galleries and planetarium. Catawba pottery sold here. Nature trail, picnic area. Monday-Saturday 10 a.m.-5 p.m., Sunday 1-5 p.m.

HOTELS

★HAMPTON INN

2111 Tabor Drive, Rock Hill, 803-325-1100, 800-426-7866; www.hamptoninn.com

162 rooms. Complimentary continental breakfast. Wireless Internet access. **$**

★MICROTEL INN & SUITES CHARLOTTE-ROCK HILL

1047 Riverview Road, Rock Hill, 803-817-7700; www.microtelinn.com

77 rooms. Business center. Wireless Internet access. **$**

SPECIALTY LODGING
EAST MAIN GUEST HOUSE
600 E. Main St., Rock Hill, 803-366-1161; www.bbonline.com/sc/eastmain
Built in 1916, this gray brick Cape Cod features tastefully decorated rooms and a common area equipped with a TV, refrigerator, snacks and games. The garden area is a nice spot to relax. Three rooms. Children over 12 years only. Complimentary full breakfast. $

RESTAURANT
★TAM'S TAVERN
1027 Oakland Ave., Rock Hill, 803-329-2226
Cajun, seafood menu. Lunch, dinner. Closed Sunday. Bar. Business casual attire. Reservations recommended. $$

SANTEE
This community serves as the gateway to the Santee-Cooper lakes recreation area, created by the Pinopolis and Santee dams on the Santee and Cooper rivers. There are numerous marinas and campgrounds on the Santee-Cooper lakes.
Information: 803-854-2131, 800-227-8510; www.santeecoopercountry.org

WHAT TO SEE AND DO
EUTAW SPRINGS BATTLEFIELD SITE
Santee, 12 miles Southeast off Highway 6
Site where ragged colonials fought the British on September 8, 1781 in what is considered to be the last major engagement in South Carolina. Both sides claimed victory. Three acres maintained by state.

FORT WATSON BATTLE SITE AND INDIAN MOUND
Santee, 803-478-2217; www.discoversouthcarolina.com
A 48-foot-high mound that is the site of an American Revolution battle on April 15-23, 1781, during which General Francis Marion attacked and captured a British fortification, its garrison, supplies and ammunition. Three acres maintained by state. Observation point has view of Santee-Cooper waters.

SANTEE NATIONAL WILDLIFE REFUGE
Secondary State Road, Summerton, 803-478-2217;
www.discoversouthcarolina.com
Attracts many geese and ducks during winter. Observation tower, self-guided nature trail; visitor information center with exhibits. Tuesday-Sunday 8 a.m.-4 p.m. Seasonal hunting and fishing, wildlife observation and photography.

HOTEL
★★BEST WESTERN
Highway 95, Santee, 803-854-3089; www.bestwestern.com
108 rooms. Complimentary continental breakfast. Restaurant. Outdoor pool, whirlpool. $

★
★
★
★
☆

SUMMERVILLE

Long a resort escape for wealthy plantation owners fleeing the mosquitoes of the Low Country, Summerville has a quintessentially Southern charm and history. More than 700 homes and buildings are on the National Register of Historic Places.

Information: Summerville-Dorchester County Chamber of Commerce and Visitor Center, 402 N. Main St., 866-875-8535; www.summervilletourism.com

WHAT TO SEE AND DO

FRANCIS BEIDLER FOREST

336 Sanctuary Road, Summerville, 843-462-2150;
www.audubon.org/local/sanctuary/beidler

Located in the heart of the Low Country, this 11,000-acre site in Four Holes Swamp encompasses the largest remaining virgin stand of bald cypress and tupelo gum trees in the world. Oak, ash and blackgum also grow here, as do 300 varieties of wildlife and numerous flowers, ferns, vines and other plants. A National Audubon Society sanctuary, the forest is named for a lumberman who championed conservation on both public and private lands. A 6,500-foot boardwalk into the swamp leads out from and back to the visitor center. Guided walks and canoe trips are available. Tuesday-Sunday 9 a.m.-5 p.m.

OLD DORCHESTER STATE HISTORIC SITE

300 State Park Road, Summerville, 843-873-1740; www.southcarolinaparks.com

This 325-acre park is on the site of a colonial village founded in 1697 by a group representing the Congregational Church of Dorchester, Massachusetts. The town prospered, but it was seized by the British during the American Revolution. By the time the war was over, the town had been abandoned. Overlooking the Ashley River, the site today includes remnants of a fort, a cemetery and the bell tower of St. Georges Parish Church. Archaeological excavations are ongoing. Thursday-Monday 9 a.m.-6 p.m.

HOTEL

★★★★★WOODLANDS RESORT & INN

125 Parsons Road, Summerville, 843-875-2600, 800-774-9999;
www.woodlandsinn.com

The 1906 Greek Revival Main House has casual, refined and lavishly appointed guest rooms designed by interior designer David Eskell-Briggs. Guests can dip their toes in the pool, volley on the two clay tennis courts, play croquet matches on the lawn and ride bikes to the nearby town of Summerville. Sandalwoods Day Spa features Aveda products in all of its treatments. The Dining Room turns out delicious dishes in a cozy space. 19 rooms. Pets accepted. High-speed Internet access. Restaurant, bar. Children's activity center. Outdoor pool. Tennis. Airport transportation available. Business center. Spa. $$$

RESTAURANT

★★★★★THE DINING ROOM AT WOODLANDS

125 Parsons Road, Summerville, 843-308-2115, 800-774-9999;
www.woodlandsinn.com

Perfecting the atmosphere of Southern charm, the Dining Room offers menus that change daily and feature flavorful, regional American dishes. Chef Tarver King and

★
★
★
★
★

his staff showcase local ingredients. Standout dishes include hay-smoked duckling with crispy pomme darphin and Maine lobster with morels and English pea-acquerello risotto. With wine pairings by sommelier Stephane Peltier and desserts like chocolate napoleon with fleur de sel caramel, the end of a meal is as memorable as the beginning. American menu. Breakfast, lunch, dinner, Sunday brunch. Bar. Jacket required at dinner. Reservations recommended. Valet parking. Outdoor seating. $$$$

SUMTER

Long the center of a prosperous agricultural area, Sumter has in recent years become an industrial center. Both the city and county are named for General Thomas Sumter, the "fighting gamecock" of the American Revolution. As a tourism spot, Sumter offers a unique contrast of antebellum mansions and modern facilities. Shaw Air Force Base, headquarters of the 9th Air Force and the 363rd Tactical Fighter Wing, is nearby.

Information: Convention and Visitors Bureau, 32 E. Calhoun St.,
803-778-5434, 800-688-4748; www.sumter-sc.com

WHAT TO SEE AND DO

CHURCH OF THE HOLY CROSS

335 N. Kings Highway, Statesburg, 803-494-8101, 800-688-4748;
www.discoversouthcarolina.com

Built of *pise de terre* (rammed earth); unusual architectural design and construction. Also noted for stained-glass windows set to catch the rays of the rising sun. Many notable South Carolinians from the 1700s are buried in the old church cemetery, including Joel R. Poinsett.

★
★★
★★
★
☆

OPERA HOUSE

21 N. Main St., Sumter, 803-436-2500, 888-688-4748; www.sumter-sc.com

Today the 1893 Opera House stands not only as a symbol of the past but also as an active sign of the ongoing progressive spirit of the people of Sumter. The 600-seat auditorium is used for concerts, school events and other local happenings. Many performances are free.

POINSETT STATE PARK

6660 Poinsett Park Road, Wedgefield, 803-494-8177;
www.southcarolinaparks.com

Approximately 1,000 acres of mountains and swamps named for Joel R. Poinsett, who introduced the poinsettia (which originated in Mexico) to the U.S. Spanish moss, mountain laurel, rhododendron. Fishing, boating (rentals). Hiking, nature trails; picnicking (shelters). Nature center.

SUMTER COUNTY MUSEUM

122 N. Washington St., Sumter, 803-775-0908; www.sumtercountymuseum.org

Two-story Edwardian house depicting Victorian lifestyle; period rooms, historical exhibits, war memorabilia, economic and cultural artifacts, artwork and archives (genealogical research). Museum is surrounded by formal gardens designed by Robert Marvin; several outdoor exhibits of farm implements, rural life; carriage house. Tuesday-Saturday 10 a.m.-5 p.m. Closed holidays.

SUMTER GALLERY OF ART

200 Hasel St., Sumter, 803-775-0543; www.sumtergallery.org

Located in the 24,000-square-foot facility at the Sumter County Cultural Center, regional artwork features paintings, drawings, sculpture, photography and pottery; permanent collection of touchable works for the blind and changing exhibits. Tuesday-Saturday 11 a.m.-5 p.m., Sunday 1:30-5 p.m.

SWAN LAKE IRIS GARDENS

822 W. Liberty St., Sumter, 803-436-2640; www.sumter-sc.com

150 acres of Kaempferi and Japanese iris, seasonal plantings, nature trails; ancient cypress, oak and pine trees; 45-acre lake with all eight species of swan. Picnicking, playground. Daily 7:30 a.m.-dusk. Home to the Iris Festival held every May.

SPECIAL EVENT
SUMTER IRIS FESTIVAL

Swan Lake Iris Gardens, 822 W. Liberty St., Sumter,
803-436-2640, 800-688-4748; www.sumtersc.gov

Fireworks display, parade, art show, golf and tennis tournaments, barbecue cook-off, local talent exhibition, square dance, iris gardens display. Late May.

HOTEL
★FAIRFIELD INN

2390 Broad St., Sumter, 803-469-9001, 800-228-2800; www.qualityinn.com

124 rooms. Complimentary continental breakfast. Seasonal outdoor pool with sundeck. $

WALTERBORO

Settled in 1784 by Charleston plantation owners as a summer resort area, Walterboro has retained its charm of yesterday despite its growth. The town boasts a casual pace and rural lifestyle where people can enjoy fishing and hunting, early 19th-century architectural designs, plantations and beach and recreational facilities.

Information: Walterboro-Colleton Chamber of Commerce, 109-C Benson St.,
843-549-9595; www.walterboro.org

SOUTH CAROLINA

WHAT TO SEE AND DO
COLLETON COUNTY COURTHOUSE

101 Hampton St., Walterboro

Building designed by Robert Mills; the first public nullification meeting in the state was held in 1828.

★
★
★
★
☆

OLD COLLETON COUNTY JAIL

239 N. Jefferies Blvd., Walterboro, 843-549-2303;
www.southcarolinamuseums.org

Neo-Gothic 1855 structure resembles a castle and is home to the Colleton Museum and the Chamber of Commerce. Served as the Walterboro jail until 1937.

SOUTH CAROLINA ARTISANS CENTER

334 Wichman St., Walterboro, 843-549-0011; www.southcarolinaartisanscenter.org

Features handcrafted art and gifts by regional artists. Craftspeople demonstrate their skills. Educational programs and special events also offered. Monday-Saturday 9 a.m.-6 p.m., Sunday 1-6 p.m.

HOTEL

★★COMFORT INN & SUITES

97 Downs Lane, Walterboro, 843-538-5911, 877-424-6423; www.comfortinn.com

96 rooms. Complimentary continental breakfast. High-speed Internet access. Restaurant. $

198

SOUTH CAROLINA

★
★
★
★
★

INDEX

Numbers

17 Hundred 90 Inn & Restaurant (Savannah), 72

17 Hundred 90 Inn and Restaurant (Savannah), 70

1810 West Inn (Thomson), 41

1859 Café (Hickory), 120

1884 Paxton House Inn (Thomasville), 75

1895 (Pinehurst), 134

1906 Pathway Inn Bed & Breakfast, 13

20 Miles Of Furniture (Hickory), 119

42 Street Oyster Bar & Seafood Grill (Raleigh), 138

6th and Vine (Winston-Salem), 153

82 Queen (Charleston), 168

A

Abingdon Manor (Latta), 176

Abingdon Manor Restaurant (Latta), 176

Abyssinia Ethiopian Restaurant (Raleigh), 138

Aerie Inn Bed & Breakfast (New Bern), 132

Aiken County Historical Museum (Aiken), 156

Aiken-Rhett House (Charleston), 160

Albany Museum of Art (Albany), 12

Albemarle Inn (Asheville), 84

Alexander's (Hilton Head Island), 184

Allen & Son Barbeque (Chapel Hill), 93

Alpine Village Inn (Blowing Rock), 88

Amalfi's (Charlotte), 99

American Dance Festival (Durham), 106

Anchorage Inn (Charleston), 164

Anchorage Inn (Ocracoke), 133

The Andersonville Trail (Perry), 61

Andrew Jackson State Park (Lancaster), 193

Andrew Low House (Savannah), 67

Angus Barn (Raleigh), 138

Anna Ruby Falls (6 miles north of Helen), 50

Annual Atalaya Arts and Crafts Festival, Huntington Beach State Park (Murrells Inlet), 187

Anson (Charleston), 168

Ansonborough Inn (Charleston), 166

Anthony's (Atlanta), 26

Appalachian Cultural Museum (Blowing Rock), 90

Appalachian National Scenic Trail, 50

Appalachian Ski Mountain (Blowing Rock), 88

Applewood Manor Inn (Asheville), 84

Aria (Atlanta), 27

Arrowhead Inn Bed & Breakfast (Durham), 106

Asheville Art Museum (Asheville), 81

Atlanta Botanical Garden (Atlanta), 16

Atlanta Braves (MLB) (Atlanta), 16

Atlanta Cyclorama (Atlanta), 16

Atlanta Dogwood Festival (Atlanta), 20

Atlanta Falcons (NFL) (Atlanta), 16

Atlanta Fish Market (Atlanta), 27

Atlanta Hawks (NBA) (Atlanta), 16

Atlanta History Center (Atlanta), 17

Atlanta Marriott Marquis (Atlanta), 20

Attmore-Oliver House (New Bern), 131

Au Pied De Cochon (Atlanta), 27

Augusta Marriott Hotel & Suites (Augusta), 40

Augusta Symphony Orchestra (Augusta), 40

Augustus T. Zevely (Winston Salem), 153

Aunt Chiladas Easy Street Café (Hilton Head), 184

AW Shucks (Charleston), 168

B

Babette's Café (Atlanta), 27

Bacchanalia (Atlanta), 27

Back Porch (Ocracoke), 133

Baker Creek State Park (McCormick), 180

The Ballantyne Resort, A Luxury Collection Hotel (Charlotte), 96

199

INDEX

Ballastone Inn & Townhouse (Savannah), *71*

Balsam Mountain Inn (Balsam), *146*

Barber House (Valdosta), *76*

Barefoot Landing (Myrtle Beach), *188*

Barefoot Resort (North Myrtle Beach), *188*

Barksdale House Inn (Charleston), *167*

Barnsley Gardens Resort (Adairsville), *45*

Basil (Charleston), *168*

Basil's Mediterranean Café (Atlanta), *28*

Bath State Historic Site (Bath), *146*

Battery Carriage House Inn (Charleston), *167*

Battleship North Carolina. (Wilmington), *148*

Beach Cove Resort (North Myrtle Beach), *188*

Beaufort Historic Site (Beaufort), *87*

The Beaufort House Victorian Inn (Asheville), *84*

Beaufort Inn (Beaufort), *157, 158*

Bed & Breakfast Inn (Savannah), *71*

Beef Barn (Andrews Drive), *117*

Belford's (Savannah), *72*

Belmont Inn (Abbeville), *181*

Bennett Place State Historic Site (Durham), *105*

Bennie's Red Barn (Simons Island), *66*

Berry College (Berry), *64*

Best Cellar (Blowing Rock), *90*

Best Western (Santee), *194*

Best Western Brunswick Inn (Brunswick), *43*

Best Western Colonial Inn (Athens), *14*

Best Western Columbus (Columbus), *48*

Best Western Courtyard Resort (Jacksonville), *123*

Best Western Great Smokies Inn (Cherokee), *102*

Best Western Hilltop Inn (Forsyth), *53*

Best Western Inn Of Dalton (Dalton), *51*

Best Western Island Inn (St. Simons Island), *65*

Best Western King Of The Road (Valdosta), *77*

Best Western La Sammana (Wilson), *151*

Best Western Ocean Reef Suites (Kill Devil Hills), *123*

Best Western Riverside Inn (Macon), *60*

Best Western Roanoke Rapids (Roanoke Rapids), *140*

Best Western Skyland Inn (Durham), *106*

Bethesda Presbyterian Church (Camden), *159*

Biltmore Estate (Asheville), *81*

Bistro Savannah (Savannah), *72*

Bistro Sofia (Greensboro), *116*

Bistro VG (Roswell), *38*

Blackbeard's (Island), *58*

Blossom Café (Charleston), *168*

Blowing Rock (Blowing Rock), *88*

Blowing Rock Inn (Blowing Rock), *88*

Bludau's Goetchius House (Columbus), *49*

Bluepointe (Atlanta), *28*

Boardwalk Inn at Wild Dunes Resort (Isle of Palms), *185*

The Boathouse Restaurant (Isle of Palms), *185*

Bone's Restaurant (Atlanta), *28*

Bonne Soirée (Chapel Hill), *94*

The Bonner House (Carrollton), *46*

Bonterra (Charlotte), *99*

Boone Hall Plantation (Mount Pleasant), *160*

Botanical Gardens at Asheville (Asheville), *81*

Bouldin House Bed and Breakfast (High Point), *121*

Bowman Gray Stadium (Winston-Salem), *152*

The Boyhood Home of President Woodrow Wilson (Augusta), *40*

Brasstown Bald Mountain-Visitor Information Center (Hiawassee), *56*

Brasstown Valley Resort (Young Harris), *56*

Breakwater Restaurant & Bar (Beaufort), *158*

Brenau University (Gainesville), *53*

Bridge Tender (Wrightsville Beach), *154*

British Open Pub of Beaufort (Beaufort), *158*

Brixx Pizza (Charlotte), *99*

Broadway at the Beach (Myrtle Beach), *188*

Brogen's South (Simons Island), *67*

Brookgreen Gardens (Murrells Inlet), *187*

Brookstown Inn (Winston-Salem), *153*

Brunswick Town-
Fort Anderson
State Historic Site
(Southport), *144*
Buccaneer Inn
(Morehead City), *128*
Bull Durham Blues
Festival (Durham),
106
Bulloch House (Warm
Springs), *78*
Burgwin-Wright House
(Wilmington), *148*

C
C. W. Worth House
(Wilmington), *149*
Caesars Head State Park
(Cleveland), *178*
The Café (Atlanta), *28*
Café Phoenix
(Wilmington), *150*
Cagney's Old Place
(Myrtle Beach), *190*
CALHOUN, *45*
Calverts (Augusta), *41*
Candlewood Suites
(Raleigh), *136*
Canoe (Atlanta), *28*
Cape Fear Botanical
Garden (Fayetteville),
111
Cape Lookout National
Seashore (Harkers
Island), *87*
Captain Bill's Waterfront
(Morehead City), *129*
Captain Dave's Dockside
(Murrell Inlet), *188*
Captain George's
Seafood (Myrtle
Beach), *190*
Captain J. N. Maffitt
River Cruises
(Wilmington), *148*
Captain Joe's
(Brunswick), *44*
Captain's Quarters Inn
(Edenton), *109*
Carl Sandburg Home
National Historic Site
(Flat Rock), *118*

Carolina Balloon
Festival, Statesville
Regional Airport,
(Statesville), *145*
Carolina Crossroads
(Chapel Hill), *94*
Carolina Cup
Steeplechase
(Camden), *159*
The Carolina Hotel
(Pinehurst), *133*
The Carolina Inn (Chapel
Hill), *92*
Carolina's (Charleston),
169
Carolinian Inn
(Georgetown), *178*
Carriage House Club
(Litchfield Plantation,
Pawleys Island), *192*
The Carriage House
Restaurant (Jefferson),
57
Casa Carbone
Ristorante (Raleigh),
138
Castle Inn (Helen), *55*
Cataloochee Ski Area
(Maggie Valley), *126,
127*
Catawba County
Museum of History
(Newton), *119*
Catawba Cultural Center
(Rock Hill), *193*
Cedar Crest Victorian Inn
(Asheville), *84*
Cedar Island to Ocracoke
Ferry Service
(Ocracoke), *132*
The Cedars Inn
(Beaufort), *87*
Centennial Olympic Park
(Atlanta), *17*
Charles Towne
Landing (Charleston),
161
Charleston Grill
(Charleston), *169*
Charleston Museum
(Charleston), *160*
Charlie Tripper's
(Valdosta), *77*

Charlie's L'Etoile Verte
(Hilton Head Island),
184
Charlotte Hawkins
Brown Memorial
State Historic Site
(Sedalia), *114*
The Charlotte Museum of
History and Hezekiah
Alexander Homesite
(Charlotte), *95*
Chart House (Savannah),
72
Charter House Inn
(Bainbridge), *42*
Chateau Elan Winery
And Resort
(Braselton), *42*
Chateau Elan's Le Clos
(Braselton), *43*
Chattahoochee
National Forest
(Dahlonega), *50*
Chelsea (Simons Island),
67
Cherokee Heritage
Museum and Gallery
(Cherokee), *102*
Cherry Blossom Festival
(Macon), *60*
Chestnut Hill Restaurant
(Myrtle Beach), *191*
Chetola Resort At
Blowing Rock
(Blowing Rock), *89*
Chief Vann House
State Historic Site
(Chatsworth), *47*
Chieftains Museum
(Rome), *64*
Children's Museum
(Rocky Mount), *140*
Chimney Rock Park
(Asheville), *81*
Chops (Atlanta), *29*
Christ Episcopal Church
(Savannah), *68*
Church of the Holy Cross
(Stateburg), *196*
Church-Waddel-Brumby
House (Athens), *14*
Circa 1886 (Charleston),
169

The Citadel, Military College of South Carolina (Charleston), *161*

City Grill (Atlanta), *29*

City Hall (Macon), *59*

City Hall (Savannah), *68*

Clarion Hotel Atlanta Airport (College Park), *37*

Clarion Hotel State Capital (Raleigh), *136*

Clemson University (Clemson), *171*

Cliff Dwellers Inn (Blowing Rock), *89*

Cliffs of the Neuse State Park (Seven Springs), *113*

The Cloister (Sea Island), *73*

The Cloister spa (Sea Island), *74*

CNN Studio Tour (Atlanta), *17*

Coheelee Creek Covered Bridge (Blakely), *42*

Cohutta Dining Room (Chatsworth), *47*

Cohutta Lodge & Conference Center (Chatsworth), *47*

Collectors Café (Myrtle Beach), *191*

Colleton County Courthouse, *197*

Colonial Cup International Steeplechase (Camden), *159*

Colonial Park Cemetery (Savannah), *68*

The Colonnade (Atlanta), *29*

Colt & Alison (Sea Island), *73*

Columbia Museum of Art (Columbia), *173*

The Columbus Museum (Columbus), *48*

Comfort Inn & Suites (Walterboro), *198*

Comfort Inn (Cartersville), *47*

Comfort Inn (Cherokee), *103*

Comfort Inn (Clemson), *172*

Comfort Inn (Fayetteville), *111*

Comfort Inn (Hendersonville), *118*

Comfort Inn (Kill Devil Hills), *123*

Comfort Inn (Maggie Valley), *127*

Comfort Inn (New Bern), *132*

Comfort Inn (Perry), *62*

Comfort Inn (Pinehurst), *134*

Comfort Inn (Valdosta), *77*

Comfort Inn (Villa Rica), *46*

Comfort Inn (Washington), *146*

Comfort Inn (Wilson), *151*

Comfort Inn and Suites (Norcross), *37*

Comfort Inn Greensboro (Greensboro), *115*

Comfort Suites (Albany), *12*

Comfort Suites Biltmore Square Mall (Asheville), *82*

Compass Cove Oceanfront Resort (Myrtle Beach), *189*

Concord Mills (Concord), *103*

Concord Motorsport Park (Concord), *103*

Confederate Relic Room and Museum (Columbia), *173*

Consolidated Gold Mines (Dahlonega), *50*

Converse Dalton Ferrell House (Valdosta), *77*

Country Inn & Suites By Carlson (Lumberton), *126*

Country's North (Columbus), *49*

Courtyard Augusta (Augusta), *41*

Courtyard by Marriott (College Park), *37*

Courtyard by Marriott Durham (Durham), *106*

Courtyard Charlotte City Center (Charlotte), *97*

Courtyard Charlotte University Research Park (Charlotte), *97*

Courtyard Greenville Hayword Mall (Greenville), *179*

Courtyard Myrtle Beach Barefoot Landing (Myrtle Beach), *189*

Courtyard Raleigh North (Raleigh), *136*

Courtyard Savannah Midtown (Savannah), *70*

Courtyard Wilmington (Wilmington), *148*

Cowpens National Battlefield (Gaffney), *176*

Cowtippers (Atlanta), *29*

Crippen's (Blowing Rock), *90*

Crippen's Country Inn (Blowing Rock), *89*

Crooked River State Park (Marys), *64*

Crown Garden & Archives (Dalton), *51*

Crowne Plaza (Hilton Head Island), *182*

Cumberland Falls Bed & Breakfast (Asheville), *83*

The Cypress Inn (Conway), *189*

Cypress: A Lowcountry Grille (Charleston), *169*

D

Dahlonega Courthouse Gold Museum State Historic Site (Dahlonega), *50*

Dailey's (Atlanta), *29*

Dale Earnhardt Tribute (Kannapolis), *103*

Dalton Depot (Dalton), *51*

Dan'l Boone Inn (Boone), *90*

Dante's Down the Hatch (N.E.), *29*

Darlings By The Sea— Oceanfront Whirlpool Suites (Kure Beach), *149*

Darlington Raceway (Darlington), *175*

Daufuskie Island Resort and Breathe Spa (Hilton Head Island), *182*

Daufuskie Island Resort Golf (Hilton Head), *182*

Davenport House (Savannah), *68*

Davidson Village Inn (Davidson), *104*

Days Inn (Asheville), *83*

Days Inn (Cartersville), *47*

Days Inn (Greenville), *179*

Days Inn (Kill Devil Hills), *124*

Days Inn (Rome), *64*

Days Inn (Savannah), *70*

Days Inn (Southern Pines), *143*

Days Inn South-Raleigh (Raleigh), *137*

The Dining Room (Atlanta), *29*

The Dining Room at Woodlands (Summerville), *195*

Dirty Don's Oyster Bar & Grill (Myrtle Beach), *191*

Discovery Place (Charlotte), *96*

Dock Street Theatre (Charleston), *161*

Dockside (Wrightsville Beach), *154*

Dominick's (Norcross), *38*

Doubletree Guest Suites Raleigh-Durham (Durham), *106*

Doubletree Hotel (Charlotte), *97*

Doubletree Hotel (Roswell), *37*

Doubletree Hotel Biltmore-Asheville (Asheville), *83*

Doubletree Hotel Charlotte Airport (Charlotte), *97*

Dr. Josephus Hall House (Salisbury), *141*

Dragon Garden (Wilmington), *150*

Drayton Hall (Charleston), *161*

Dublin-Laurens Museum (Dublin), *52*

Duke Homestead State Historic Site (Durham), *105*

The Duke Mansion (Charlotte), *97*

Duke University (Durham), *105*

Duke's Wallace Wade Stadium (Durham), *105*

The Dunhill Hotel (Charlotte), *97*

Durham Bull Athletic Park (Durham), *105*

Dusty's Barbecue (Atlanta), *30*

E

East Bay Inn (Savannah), *70*

East Main Guest House (Rock Hill), *194*

Ecco (Atlanta), *30*

Echo Mountain Inn (Hendersonville), *118*

Econo Lodge (Helen), *56*

Econo Lodge (Williamston), *147*

Econo Lodge Raleigh (Raleigh), *137*

Eddie Romanelli's (Wilmington), *150*

Edisto Memorial Gardens (Orangeburg), *192*

Edmondston-Alston House (Charleston), *161*

Elaine's on Franklin (Chapel Hill), *94*

Elijah's (Wilmington), *150*

Elizabeth on 37th (Savannah), *72*

Elizabethan Gardens (Manteo), *127*

Embassy Suites (Brunswick), *43*

Embassy Suites (Charlotte), *97*

Embassy Suites (Myrtle Beach), *189*

Embassy Suites Buckhead (Atlanta), *20*

Embassy Suites Hotel at Centennial Olympic Park (Atlanta), *20*

Embassy Suites Hotel Columbia-Greystone (Columbia), *174*

Embassy Suites Hotel Greensboro-Airport (Greensboro), *115*

Embassy Suites Hotel Greenville Golf Resort and -Conference Center (Greenville), *179*

Embassy Suites Hotel Raleigh-Crabtree Valley (Raleigh), *137*

Emerald Isle Inn and Bed & Breakfast (Emerald Isle), *129*

Emerald Pointe Resort (Buford), *44*

203

INDEX

★
★
★
★
★

Emerald Village (Little
  Switzerland), *125*
Emory Inn (Atlanta), *21*
Enoteca Vin Restaurant
  and Wine Bar
  (Raleigh), *138*
The Eseeola Lodge At
  Linville Golf Club
  (Linville), *125*
Etowah Indian Mounds
  Historic Site and
  Archaeological Area
  (Cartersville), *46*
Eutaw Springs Battlefield
  Site (Santee), *194*

F
Fairfield Inn & Suites
  Raleigh Crabtree
  Valley (Raleigh), *137*
Fairfield Inn
  (Fayetteville), *111*
Fairfield Inn (Greenville),
  117
Fairfield Inn (Myrtle
  Beach), *189*
Fairfield Inn (Sumter),
  197
Fairfield Sapphire Valley
  Ski Area (Sapphire),
  91
Fairview (Durham), *107*
Fall House and Garden
  Candlelight Tours
  (Charleston), *163*
The Fearrington
  House Country Inn
  (Pittsboro), *135*
The Fearrington House
  Restaurant (Pittsboro),
  135
Fernbank Museum
  of Natural History
  (Atlanta), *17*
Fernbank Science Center
  (Atlanta), *17*
Festival of Houses and
  Gardens (Charleston),
  163
Fire of Brazil
  Churrascaria
  (Atlanta), *30*

First Baptist Church
  (Columbia), *173*
First Colony Inn (Nags
  Head), *131*
First Horizon Park
  (Greensboro), *114*
First Presbyterian Church
  (Columbia), *173*
First Presbyterian Church
  (Fayetteville), *111*
Flat Rock Playhouse
  (Flat Rock), *118*
Florence Stockade
  (Florence), *176*
Flying Biscuit Café
  (Atlanta), *30*
Flying Fish Café (Kill
  Devil Hills), *124*
Flying Frog Café
  (Asheville), *85*
Flying Saucer
  Draft Emporium
  (Charlotte), *100*
Folk Art Center
  (Asheville), *81*
The Food Studio
  (Atlanta), *30*
Foothills Equestrian
  Nature Center
  (Tryon), *145*
Forrest Hills Mountain
  Resort (Dahlonega), *51*
Fort Benning
  (Columbus), *48*
Fort Bragg and Pope Air
  Force Base—82nd
  Airborne-Division
  War Memorial
  Museum (Fort Bragg),
  111
Fort Dobbs State Historic
  Site (Statesville), *144*
Fort Fisher State Historic
  Site (Kure Beach),
  144
Fort Hill (Clemson), *172*
Fort Jackson (Columbia),
  173
Fort King George State
  Historic Site (Darien),
  52
Fort Macon State Park
  (Atlantic Beach), *128*

Fort Watson Battle Site
  and Indian Mound
  (Santee), *194*
Four Points by Sheraton
  (Columbus), *48*
Four Seasons Hotel
  Atlanta (Atlanta), *22*
Four-Square Restaurant
  (Durham), *108*
Fox Theatre (Atlanta), *17*
Francis Beidler Forest
  (Summerville), *195*
Franklin D. Roosevelt
  State Park (Pine
  Mountain), *63*
Franklin Gem and
  Mineral Museum
  (Franklin), *112*
Franklin Hotel (Chapel
  Hill), *93*
Freddie's (Kure Beach),
  150
French Huguenot Church
  (Charleston), *161*
Fritti (Atlanta), *30*
Frog & Owl Kitchen
  (Franklin), *112*
Front Street Inn
  (Wilmington), *149*
Fuel Pizza Café
  (Charlotte), *100*
Fulton Five (Charleston),
  169
Fuse Box (Charlotte),
  100

G
Gabrielle's (Asheville),
  85
Gallery Restaurant & Bar
  (Charlotte), *100*
The Gardens at Callaway
  (Pine Mountain), *63*
Garibaldi's Café
  (Savannah), *72*
Gascoigne Bluff (Simons
  Island), *65*
Gaslight Inn Bed &
  Breakfast (Atlanta),
  26
Gate City Chop House
  (Greensboro), *116*

204

INDEX

Gaulart & Maliclet French Café (Charleston), *170*

Gazebo Café (Franklin), *113*

Georgia Aquarium (Atlanta), *18*

Georgia Grille (Atlanta), *30*

Georgia Mountain Fair (Hiawassee), *56*

Georgia Music Hall of Fame (Macon), *59*

Georgia Southern University (Statesboro), *74*

Georgia State Farmers' Market (Forest Park), *18*

Georgia Tech Hotel And Conference Center (Atlanta), *22*

Georgia's (Greensboro), *54*

The Georgian Room (Sea Island), *74*

Gibbes Museum of Art (Charleston), *162*

Glendale Springs Inn (16, Glendale Springs), *89*

The Glenn Hotel (Atlanta), *22*

Goodbread House Bed & Breakfast (St. Marys), *64*

Governor Charles B. Aycock Birthplace State Historic Site (Fremont), *114*

The Governor's House Inn (Charleston), *167*

Governor's Mansion (Columbia), *173*

Grand Dining Room (Americus), *13*

Grand Dining Room (Jekyll Island), *58*

Grand Hyatt Atlanta (Atlanta), *22*

Grandfather Mountain (Linville), *124*

Grandfather Mountain Highland Games, *125*

Grandover Resort & Conference Center (Greensboro), *115*

The Graystone Inn (Wilmington), *149*

Green Street Historical District (Gainesville), *53*

Greenleaf Inn (Camden), *159*

Green-Meldrim House (Savannah), *68*

Greensboro Historical Museum (Greensboro), *114*

Greenville County Museum (Greenville), *178*

Greenville Marriott (Greenville), *179*

Greenville Museum of Art (Greenville), *117*

Greenville Zoo (Greenville), *179*

Greyfield Inn (Fernandina Beach, Cumberland Island), *49*

The Greystone (Lake Toxaway), *91*

The Grove Park Inn Resort & Spa (Asheville), *83*

Guilford Courthouse National Military Park (Greensboro), *115*

H

Habitat for Humanity—Global Village and Discovery Center (Americus), *13*

Hampton Inn & Suites Oceanfront (Myrtle Beach), *189*

Hampton Inn (Atlanta), *22*

Hampton Inn (Cornelius), *104*

Hampton Inn (Elizabeth City), *110*

Hampton Inn (Fayetteville), *111*

Hampton Inn (Greenville), *179*

Hampton Inn (Hendersonville), *118*

Hampton Inn (Hilton Head Island), *182*

Hampton Inn (Jacksonville), *123*

Hampton Inn (Morehead City), *128*

Hampton Inn (Myrtle Beach), *189*

Hampton Inn (New Bern), *132*

Hampton Inn (Raleigh), *137*

Hampton Inn (Rock Hill), *193*

Hampton Inn (Rocky Mount), *141*

Hampton Inn (Salisbury), *141*

Hampton Inn (Southern Pines), *143*

Hampton Inn (Valdosta), *77*

Hampton Inn (Wilmington), *148*

Hampton Inn (Wilson), *151*

Hampton Inn at Albany Mall (Albany), *12*

Hampton Inn Atlanta-Marietta (Marietta), *60*

Hampton Inn Chapel Hill (Chapel Hill), *93*

Hampton Inn Greensboro-Four Seasons (Greensboro), *115*

Hampton Inn Hickory (Hickory), *120*

Hampton Inn-Downtown Historic District (Columbia), *174*

Hampton Plantation State Park (McClellanville), *177*

Hampton Street Vineyard (Columbia), *175*

Hampton-Preston Mansion (Columbia), *173*

★
★
★
★
★

Hank's Seafood Restaurant (Charleston), *170*

Hanover House, *172*

Harbor Light Guest House (Cape Carteret), *129*

Harbour Town Golf Links, *182*

Harbourmaster's Ocean Grill (Hilton Head Island), *184*

Harmony House Inn (New Bern), *132*

Harry Bissett's New Orleans Café and Oyster Bar (Athens), *15*

Haveli (Atlanta), *30*

Haywood Park Hotel & Promenade (Asheville), *83*

Helen to the Atlantic Balloon Race & Festival (Helen), *55*

Hennessy's (Columbia), *175*

Herons Restaurant at the Umstead Hotel (Cary), *138*

Heyward-Washington House (Charleston), *162*

Hi Life (Roswell), *38*

Hickory Furniture Mart (Hickory), *120*

Hickory Knob Resort (McCormick), *181*

Hickory Museum of Art (Hickory), *120*

Hieronymus Seafood (Wilmington), *150*

High Cotton (Charleston), *170*

High Hampton Inn and Country Club (Cashiers), *91*

High Museum of Art (Atlanta), *18*

Highland Lake Inn (Flat Rock), *118*

Highlands Suite Hotel (Highlands), *121*

Hilton Atlanta Airport and Towers (Atlanta), *22*

Hilton Atlanta and Towers (Atlanta), *23*

Hilton Atlanta Northeast (Norcross), *37*

Hilton Charlotte Center City (Charlotte), *97*

Hilton Durham (Durham), *106*

Hilton Greenville (Greenville), *180*

Hilton Head Marriott Beach and Golf Resort (Hilton Head Island), *183*

Hilton Myrtle Beach Resort (Myrtle Beach), *190*

Hilton Oceanfront Resort Hilton Head Island (Hilton Head Island), *183*

Hilton Savannah De Soto (Savannah), *70*

Hilton University Place (Charlotte), *98*

Hilton Wilmington Riverside (Wilmington), *149*

Historic Brattonsville (McConnells), *193*

Historic Camden Revolutionary War Site (Camden), *159*

Historic District (Elizabeth City), *110*

Historic Edenton (Edenton), *109*

Historic Halifax State Historic Site (Halifax), *140*

Historic Old Salem (Winston-Salem), *152*

Historic Savannah Waterfront Area, *68*

Historic Statesboro Inn (Statesboro), *74*

Hofbrauhaus (Helen), *56*

Hofwyl-Broadfield Plantation State Historic Site (Brunswick), *52*

Holiday Inn (Cartersville), *47*

Holiday Inn (Cherokee), *103*

Holiday Inn (Fayetteville), *111*

Holiday Inn (Forsyth), *53*

Holiday Inn (Lumberton), *126*

Holiday Inn (Norcross), *37*

Holiday Inn (Perry), *62*

Holiday Inn (Rocky Mount), *141*

Holiday Inn (Rome), *64*

Holiday Inn (Salisbury), *141*

Holiday Inn (Statesville), *145*

Holiday Inn (Waycross, 912-283-4490), *79*

Holiday Inn (Williamston), *147*

Holiday Inn (Wilmington), *149*

Holiday Inn (Winston-Salem), *152*

Holiday Inn Athens (Athens), *15*

Holiday Inn Brownstone (Raleigh), *137*

Holiday Inn Chapel Hill (Chapel Hill), *93*

Holiday Inn Express (Atlanta), *23*

Holiday Inn Express (Boone), *90*

Holiday Inn Express (Dublin), *52*

Holiday Inn Express (Elizabeth City), *110*

Holiday Inn Express (Fayetteville), *112*

Holiday Inn Express (Goldsboro), *114*

Holiday Inn Express (Jacksonville), *123*

Holiday Inn Express (Macon), *60*

Holiday Inn Express
  Athens (Athens), *15*
Holiday Inn Lanier Centre
  (Gainesville), *54*
Holiday Inn Morganton
  (Morganton), *129*
Holiday Inn Select
  (Hickory), *120*
Holiday Inn Sunspree
  Resort (Wrightsville
  Beach), *154*
Holly Inn (Pinehurst),
  134
Homewood Suites
  (Alpharetta), *37*
Hominy Grill
  (Charleston), *170*
Hope Plantation, *147*
Hopsewee Plantation
  (Georgetown), *177*
Horace Williams House
  (Chapel Hill), *92*
Horizons (Asheville), *85*
Horseradish Grill
  (Atlanta), *31*
Horton House (Jekyll
  Island), *57*
Hot Fish Club (Murrells
  Inlet), *188*
Hotel Indigo (Atlanta),
  23
Hound Ears Club
  (Blowing Rock), *89*
House in the Horseshoe
  State Historic Site
  (Sanford), *142*
Hsu's Gourmet Chinese
  (Atlanta), *31*
Huntington Beach State
  Park (Georgetown),
  187
Hyatt Regency Atlanta
  (Atlanta), *23*
Hyatt Regency
  Greenville
  (Greenville), *180*
Hyatt Regency Savannah
  (Savannah), *70*
Hyatt Regency Suites
  Perimeter Northwest
  Atlanta (Marietta), *60*
Hyatt Summerfield Suites
  (Charlotte), *98*

I
Il Palio (Chapel Hill), *94*
Imperial Fez (Atlanta),
  31
Indigo Inn (Charleston),
  167
The Inn at Palmetto Bluff
  (Bluffton), *183*
Inn At Ragged Gardens
  (Blowing Rock), *89*
Inn on Biltmore Estate
  (Asheville), *83*
InterContinental
  Buckhead (Atlanta),
  23
International Folk
  Festival (Waynesville),
  146
Irregardless Café
  (Raleigh), *139*

J
J. Arthur's (Maggie
  Valley), *127*
J. Basul Noble's (High
  Point), *121*
J. Betski's (Raleigh), *139*
J. Mac's (St. Simons
  Island), *67*
James Iredell House
  (Edenton), *109*
James K. Polk Memorial
  State Historic Site
  (Pineville), *96*
Jameson Inn
  (Brunswick), *44*
Jameson Inn (Calhoun),
  46
Jarrell Plantation
  State Historic Site
  (Forsyth), *53*
Jekyll Island Club Hotel
  (Jekyll Island), *58*
Jekyll Island Club
  National Historic
  Landmark District
  (Jekyll Island), *58*
Jimmy Carter Library
  and Museum
  (Atlanta), *18*
Joe Weatherly Stock Car
  Museum and National
Motorsports Press
  Association Stock
  Car Hall of Fame
  (Darlington), *175*
Joe's Bar and Grill
  (North Myrtle Beach),
  191
Joël (Atlanta), *31*
John Mark Verdier
  House Museum
  (Beaufort), *157*
John Rutledge House Inn
  (Charleston), *167*
Johnny Harris
  (Savannah), *72*
Jolly Roger (Kill Devil
  Hills), *124*
Joseph Manigault
  House (Charleston),
  162
JuJube Restaurant
  (Chapel Hill), *94*
Juliette Gordon
  Low Birthplace
  (Savannah), *68*
Jump-Off Rock,
  118
JW Marriott Hotel
  Buckhead Atlanta
  (Atlanta), *23*

K
The Kabob House
  (Charlotte), *100*
King And Prince Resort
  (Simons Island), *65*
King Neptune
  (Wrightsville Beach),
  154
King-Keith House Bed
  & Breakfast (Atlanta),
  26
Kings Courtyard Inn
  (Charleston),
  167
Kobe Japanese House
  of Steak & Seafood
  (Cornelius), *104*
Kolomoki Mounds
  State Historic Park
  (Blakely), *42*
Kyma (Atlanta), *31*

207

INDEX

★
★
★
★
★

L

La Fourchette (Charleston), *170*

La Grotta (Atlanta), *31*

La Maison Restaurant & Veritas Wine & Tapas (Augusta), *41*

La Paz (Asheville), *85*

La Quinta Inn (Columbus), *48*

La Quinta Inn (Myrtle Beach), *190*

La Quinta Inn and Suites (Valdosta), *77*

La Quinta Inn and Suites Charlotte Coliseum (Charlotte), *98*

La Quinta Inn Atlanta Marietta (Marietta), *61*

La Residence (Chapel Hill), *95*

La Strada (Marietta), *61*

Lake Lanier Islands (Buford), *44*

Lake Lure Inn (Lake Lure), *119*

Lake Norman, *104*

Lantern (Chapel Hill), *95*

Las Margaritas (Garner), *139*

Latitude 31 (Jekyll Island), *58*

Laurel and Hardy Museum (Harlem), *40*

Laurel Grove Cemetery (South) (Savannah), *69*

Laurel Hill Bed & Breakfast (Atlanta), *26*

LaVecchia's Seafood Grille (Charlotte), *100*

Levine Museum of the New South (Charlotte), *96*

Lion and the Rose (Asheville), *84*

Litchfield Plantation (Pawleys Island), *192*

Little Venice (Hilton Head Island), *184*

The Lodge at Sea Island Golf Club (Simons Island), *66*

Lodge on Lake Lure Bed & Breakfast (Lake Lure), *119*

The Lodge on Little St. Simons Island (Simons Island), *66*

Lois Jane's Riverview Inn (Southport), *144*

Lords Proprietors Inn (Edenton), *109*

The Lost Colony Outdoor Drama, *128*

Lovill House Inn (Boone), *90*

Lowndes County Historical Society Museum (Valdosta), *77*

Lupie's Café (Charlotte), *100*

M

Macon Historic District (Macon), *59*

Madison's Restaurant & Wine Garden (Highlands), *122*

Magnolia (Pinehurst), *134*

Magnolia Grill (Durham), *108*

Magnolia Plantation and Gardens (Charleston), *162*

Magnolia's (Charleston), *170*

Main Street Inn (Hilton Head Island), *183*

Maison du Pre (Charleston), *167*

Makoto (Boone), *91*

Mama Fu's Asian House (Charlotte), *100*

The Mansion on Peachtree (Atlanta), *23*

Maple Lodge (Blowing Rock), *89*

Margaret Mitchell House (Atlanta), *18*

Marietta Conference Center and Resort (Marietta), *61*

Marina (Elizabeth City), *110*

Market Café (Pittsboro), *135*

The Market Place Restaurant & Wine Bar (Asheville), *86*

Marriott (Columbus), *49*

Marriott Alpharetta (Alpharetta), *38*

Marriott Atlanta Gwinnett Place (Duluth), *38*

Marriott Atlanta Norcross-Peachtree Corners (Norcross), *38*

Marriott City Center (Charlotte), *98*

Marriott Downtown Atlanta (Atlanta), *24*

Marriott Durham Civic Center (Durham), *107*

Marriott Greensboro Airport (Greensboro), *116*

Marriott Greensboro Downtown (Greensboro), *116*

Marriott Raleigh Crabtree Valley (Raleigh), *137*

Marriott Research Triangle Park (Durham), *107*

Marriott Savannah Riverfront (Savannah), *70*

Marshes of Glynn, *43*

MARTIN LUTHER KING JR. HISTORIC DISTRICT, *21*

Martin Luther King, Jr. National Historic Site (Atlanta), *18*

Mary Mac's Tea Room (Atlanta), *31*

Massee Lane Gardens (Fort Valley), *62*

Masters Golf Tournament (Augusta), *40*

Matteo's Italian Restaurant (Brunswick), *44*

McCrady's (Charleston), *170*

McKendrick's (Atlanta), *32*

McKinnon's Louisiane (Atlanta), *32*

McNinch House (Charlotte), *101*

Meadows Inn (New Bern), *132*

Meeting Street Inn (Charleston), *168*

Melhana The Grand Plantation (Thomasville), *75*

Memory Lane Motorsports & Historic Automotive Museum (Mooresville), *104*

Mert's Heart & Soul (Charlotte), *101*

Microtel Inn & Suites Charlotte-Rock Hill (Rock Hill), *193*

Mid Pines Inn and Golf Club (Southern Pines), *143*

Middleton Place Plantation (Charleston), *162*

Millennium Hotel (Durham), *107*

Mom & Dad's (Valdosta), *77*

Moon River Brewing Co. (Savannah), *73*

Moores Creek National Battlefield (Currie), *148*

Moose Café at Western North Carolina Farmer's Market (Asheville), *86*

Mordecai Historic Park (Raleigh), *136*

The Morehead Inn (Charlotte), *98*

Morehead-Patterson Memorial Bell Tower (Chapel Hill), *92*

Moses H. Cone Memorial Park (Blowing Rock), *88*

Mount Mitchell State Park (Brunsville Little Switzerland), *125*

Mountain Creek Inn at Callaway Gardens (Pine Mountain), *63*

Mountain Dance and Folk Festival (Asheville), *82*

Mrs. Wilkes' Dining Room (Savannah), *73*

Mrs. Willis (Morehead City), *129*

Museum of the Albemarle (Elizabeth City), *110*

Museum of the Cherokee Indian (On Cherokee Reservation, Cherokee), *102*

Museum of York County (Rock Hill), *193*

N

Nags Head Inn (Nags Head), *130*

Nakato Japanese Restaurant (Atlanta), *32*

Nana's Restaurant (Durham), *108*

Nantahala National Forest (Franklin), *112*

NASCAR Speedpark, Concord Mills (Concord), *103*

Nathaniel Russell House (Charleston), *163*

National Science Center's Fort Discovery (Augusta), *40*

Natural Science Center of Greensboro (Greensboro), *115*

Nava (Atlanta), *32*

New Echota State Historic Site (Calhoun), *45*

New Perry Hotel (Perry), *62*

Nick's (Highlands), *122*

Nickiemoto's (Atlanta), *32*

Nikolai's Roof (Atlanta), *32*

Ninety Six National Historic Site (Ninety Six), *181*

North Carolina Auto Racing Hall of Fame (Mooresville), *104*

North Carolina Botanical Garden (Chapel Hill), *92*

North Carolina Museum of History (Raleigh), *136*

North Carolina Museum of Life and Science (Durham), *106*

North Carolina Shakespeare Festival (High Point), *121*

North Georgia Folk Festival (Athens), *14*

O

O. Henry Hotel (Greensboro), *116*

Oak Hill and the Martha Berry Museum (Rome), *64*

Ocean Creek Resort (Myrtle Beach), *190*

Ocean Room (Kiawah Island), *186*

Oceanic (Wrightsville Beach), *154*

Oconaluftee Indian Village (Cherokee), *102*

Ocracoke Island Inn (Ocracoke), *133*

Okefenokee Heritage Center (Waycross), *78*

★
★
★
★
★

OKEFENOKEE
SWAMP, *62*
Oktoberfest (Helen), *55*
Old Cannonball House &
Macon-Confederate
Museum (Macon), *60*
Old Colleton County Jail
(Walterboro), *197*
Old Dorchester State
Historic Site
(Summerville), *195*
Old Edwards Inn And
Spa (Highlands), *122*
Old Exchange and
Provost Dungeon
(Charleston), *163*
Old Homes Tour and
Antiques Show
(Beaufort), *87*
Old Oyster Factory
(Hilton Head Island),
184
The Old Reynolds
Mansion (Asheville),
85
Old Well (Chapel Hill),
92
Olde Pink House
(Savannah), *73*
Omni Hotel (Charlotte),
98
Omni Hotel At CNN
Center (Atlanta), *24*
On the Verandah
(Highlands), *122*
One Midtown Kitchen
(Atlanta), *32*
Opera House (Sumter),
196
Owens' Restaurant (Nags
Head), *131*
Owens-Thomas House
(Savannah), *69*
Owl's Nest (Candler), *85*

P

Pano's & Paul's (Atlanta),
33
Papa's Grille (Durham),
108
Paramount's Carowinds
(Charlotte), *96*

Paris Mountain State
Park (Greenville),
179
Parizade (Durham), *108*
Park 75 (Atlanta), *33*
Parker's Bar-B-Que
(Greenville), *117*
The Parks at Chehaw
(Albany), *12*
Parkway Craft Center
(Blowing Rock), *88*
The Parson's Table
(Little River), *191*
Patriots Point Naval and
Maritime Museum
(Mount Pleasant), *187*
Pebble Hill Plantation
(Thomasville), *75*
Pecan Tree Inn
(Beaufort), *87*
Pengs Pavillion
(Calhoun), *46*
Penguin Isle (Nags
Head), *131*
Peninsula Grill
(Charleston), *171*
Pepsi Store (New Bern),
132
Petite Auberge (Atlanta),
33
Pilot House
(Wilmington), *150*
Pine Crest Inn (Tryon),
145
Pine Crest Inn Restaurant
(Tryon), *145*
Pine Needles Lodge
(Southern Pines), *143*
Pittypat's Porch
(Atlanta), *33*
Plaza Restaurant
(Thomasville), *76*
Plums (Beaufort), *158*
Poinsett State Park
(Wedgefield), *196*
Poor Richard's
(Gainesville), *54*
Poplar Grove Plantation
(Wilmington), *148*
Port City Chop House
(Wilmington), *151*
Port O' Call (Kill Devil
Hills), *124*

The President's Quarters
Inn (Savannah), *71*
Presto Bar and Grill
(Charlotte), *101*
Presto Kitchen (Hilton
Head Island), *184*
Pricci (Atlanta), *33*
Prime (Atlanta), *33*
Prime Outlets Gaffney
(Gaffney), *177*
Prince George Winyah
Church (Georgetown),
177
Pullen Park (Raleigh), *136*

Q

Quality Inn & Suites
(Durham), *107*
Quality Inn & Suites
(Gainesville), *54*
Quality Inn & Suites
(Hilton Head Island),
183
Quality Inn (Albany), *12*
Quality Inn (Brunswick),
44
Quality Inn
(Fayetteville), *112*
Quality Inn (Goldsboro),
114
Quality Inn (Winston-
Salem), *152*
Quinones at Bacchanalia
(Atlanta), *34*

R

Radisson Hotel High
Point (High Point),
121
Rainbow Café
(Charlotte), *101*
Ramada (Charlotte), *99*
Ramada (Kill Devil
Hills), *124*
Ramada Columbia
(Columbia), *174*
Ranch House (Charlotte),
101
Rathbun (Atlanta), *34*
Raven Rock State Park
(Lillington), *142*

Ray's Killer Creek (Alpharetta), *38*

Ray's on the River (Atlanta), *34*

Red Fish (Hilton Head Island), *184*

Redcliffe (Beech Island), *157*

Reed Gold Mine State Historic Site (Midland), *103*

Regency Inn (Albany), *12*

Regency Suites Hotel (Atlanta), *24*

Renaissance Asheville Hotel (Asheville), *84*

Renaissance Charlotte Suites (Charlotte), *99*

Resaca Confederate Cemetery (Calhoun), *45*

Restaurant Eugene (Atlanta), *34*

Restaurant Muse (Greensboro), *116*

Reynolda House, Museum of American Art (Winston-Salem), *152*

Rezaz (Asheville), *86*

The Rhett House Inn (Beaufort), *158*

Rice Paddy (Georgetown), *178*

Richard Petty Driving Experience (Concord), *104*

Richmond Hill Inn (Asheville), *84*

Ristorante Divino (Columbia), *175*

The Ritz-Carlton Lodge, Reynolds Plantation (Greensboro), *54*

The Ritz-Carlton, Atlanta (Atlanta), *24*

The Ritz-Carlton, Buckhead (Atlanta), *24*

River Forest Manor (Belhaven), 87, *146*

River House (Savannah), *73*

River Park North Science and Nature Center (Greenville), *117*

The River Room (Atlanta), *34*

River Room (Georgetown), *178*

River Street Inn (Savannah), *71*

Riverbanks Zoo and Garden (Columbia), *174*

Roanoke Island Festival Park, *127*

Robert Mills Historic House and Park (Columbia), *174*

Rock Bottom (Atlanta), *35*

Rosehill Inn (Wilmington), *150*

Rosemary Hall & Lookaway Hall (North Augusta), *41*

Roy's Riverboat Landing (Wilmington), *151*

Rudolph's (Gainesville), *54*

Ruth's Chris Steak House (Atlanta), *35*

Ryan's Restaurant (Winston-Salem), *153*

S

The Sanctuary Hotel at Kiawah Island, *186*

The Sanderling (Duck), *124*

Sandhills Horticultural Gardens (Pinehurst), *133*

Sanitary Fish Market (Morehead City), *129*

Santee National Wildlife Refuge (Summerton), *194*

Sarah P. Duke Gardens (Durham), *106*

Savannah History Museum (Savannah), *69*

Savannah National Wildlife Refuge, *181*

Savannah Scottish Games and Highland Gathering (Richmond Hill), *69*

Savannah Seafood Festival (Savannah), *69*

Savannah Tour of Homes and Gardens (Savannah), *69*

Savoy (Asheville), *86*

Scott's Fish Market (Hilton Head Island), *185*

Scottish Highland Games (Red Springs), *126*

Scottish Tartans Museum (Franklin), *112*

Sea Captain's House (Myrtle Beach), *191*

Sea Palms Golf & Tennis Resort (Simons Island), *66*

SeaBlue Tapas (North Myrtle Beach), *191*

Seasons Restaurant (Flat Rock), *119*

Seaview Inn (Pawleys Island), *192*

Second Empire (Raleigh), *139*

Seminole State Park (Donalsonville), *41*

Serenbe Bed & Breakfast (Palmetto), *26*

Serendipity Cottage (Thomasville), *76*

Serendipity Inn (N., Myrtle Beach), *190*

Sermet's Corner (Charleston), *171*

Shaw House (Southern Pines), *142*

Shellmont Inn (Atlanta), *26*

Sheraton Atlanta Hotel (Atlanta), *25*

Sheraton Atlantic Beach Oceanfront Hotel (Atlantic Beach), *128*

Sheraton Hotel (Chapel Hill), *93*

★
★
★
★
★

Sheraton Myrtle Beach Convention Center Hotel (Myrtle Beach), *190*

Sheraton New Bern Hotel And Marina (New Bern), *132*

Sheraton Raleigh Capital Center Hotel (Raleigh), *137*

Shilling's on the Square (Marietta), *61*

Sia's (Duluth), *39*

Siena Hotel (Chapel Hill), *93*

Simpson's (Raleigh), *139*

Sinbad (Hendersonville), *119*

Six Flags Over Georgia (Austell), *19*

Sleep Inn (Morganton), *129*

Slightly North of Broad (Charleston), *171*

The Smith House (Dahlonega), *51*

Smith House (Dahlonega), *51*

Social Wine Bar (Charleston), *171*

SoHo Café (Atlanta), *35*

Somerset Place State Historic Site (Creswell), *109*

Sotto Sotto (Atlanta), *35*

South (Main) Building (Chapel Hill), *92*

South Carolina Artisans Center (Walterboro), *198*

South Carolina Botanical Garden (Clemson), *172*

South Carolina Peach Festival (Gaffney), *177*

South City Kitchen (Atlanta), *35*

Southern Forest World (Waycross), *79*

SPA (Atlanta), *36*

The Spa at Ballantyne Resort (Charlotte), *102*

The spa at old Edwards Inn and Spa (Highlands), *122*

Spa at Palmetto Bluff, *185*

The Spa at Pinehurst (Pinehurst), *134*

The Spa at The Ritz-Carlton Lodge, Reynolds Plantation (Greensboro), *55*

Spa at the Sanctuary (Kiawah Island), *186*

Spanky's (Chapel Hill), *95*

Spencer House Inn Bed & Breakfast (Marys), *65*

Spoleto Festival USA (Charleston), *163*

Spring Tour of Homes (Athens), *14*

Squid's (Chapel Hill), *95*

Squire's Pub (Southern Pines), *143*

St. Helena's Episcopal Church (Beaufort), *157*

St. Patrick's Day Parade, *70*

St. Paul's Episcopal Church (Augusta), *40*

St. Philip's Episcopal Church (Charleston), *163*

St. Simons Lighthouse (St. Simons Island), *65*

State Botanical Garden (Athens), *14*

State Capitol (Atlanta), *19*

State Capitol (Raleigh), *136*

Stax's Peppermill (Greenville), *180*

Steamers Seafood Company (Hilton Head), *185*

Stompin Ground (Maggie Valley), *127*

Stone Mountain Park (Stone Mountain), *19*

Sugar Magnolia (Atlanta), *26*

Sumter County Museum (Sumter), *196*

Sumter Gallery of Art (Sumter), *197*

Sumter Iris Festival (Sumter), *197*

Sunrise Farm Bed & Breakfast Inn (Salem), *172*

Super 8 (Bainbridge), *42*

Super 8 (Dahlonega), *51*

Surf Side Motel (Nags Head), *130*

The Surf Steakhouse (Jekyll Island), *58*

The Swag Country Inn (Waynesville), *147*

Swan Lake Iris Gardens (Sumter), *197*

Sweet Potatoes (Winston-Salem), *153*

Switzerland Inn (Little Switzerland), *125*

Symphony Hall (Atlanta), *19*

T

Table Rock State Park, *179*

Tam's Tavern (Rock Hill), *194*

Tanglewood Park (Clemmons), *153*

Taqueria Sundown Café (Atlanta), *35*

Tarrer Inn (Colquitt), *42*

Taverna 100 (Charlotte), *101*

Taylor-Grady House (Athens), *14*

Thai Chili (Atlanta), *35*

Thomas County Museum of History (Thomasville), *75*

Thomas Wolfe Memorial (Asheville), *81*

Thomasville Cultural Center (Thomasville), *75*

Thoroughbred Racing
Hall of Fame (Aiken),
157
Toulouse (Atlanta), *35*
Town Clock Building
(Georgetown), *178*
Tranquil House Inn
(Manteo), *128*
Trinity Cathedral
(Columbia), *174*
Trustees' Garden Site, *69*
Tryon Palace Historic
Sites and Gardens
(New Bern), *131*
Tubman African-
American Museum
(Macon), *60*
Tupelo Honey Café
(Asheville), *86*
Tweetsie Railroad
(Blowing Rock), *88*
Twelve Hotel &
Residences (Atlanta),
25
Two Urban Licks
(Atlanta), *36*
Tybee Museum and
Lighthouse (Tybee
Island), *76*

U

U.S. Customs House
(Savannah), *69*
U.S. National
Whitewater Center
(Charlotte), *96*
The Umstead Resort and
Spa (Cary), *138*
The Umstead Spa (Cary),
140
Underground Atlanta
(Atlanta), *19*
Unicoi Lodge and
Conference Center
(Helen), *56*
The University of
Georgia (Athens), *14*
University of North
Carolina at Chapel
Hill (Chapel Hill), *92*
University of South
Carolina (Columbia),
174

Unto These Hills
(Cherokee), *102*
Upstream (Charlotte),
101

V

Van Landingham Estate
(Charlotte), *99*
The Varsity (Athens), *15*
The Varsity (Atlanta), *36*
Veni Vidi Vici (Atlanta),
36
The Verandas
(Wilmington), *150*
Victoria House Inn
(Charleston), *168*
The Victorian Villa
(Charlotte), *99*
Villa Christina (Atlanta),
36
Villas by the Sea (Jekyll
Island), *58*
Vineyard (Winston-
Salem), *153*
The Vinings Inn
(Atlanta), *36*
Vinnie's Steakhouse
(Raleigh), *139*
Vinny's on Windward
(Alpharetta), *39*
Vintage House
(Hickory), *120*
Vito's Ristorante.
(Southern Pines), *143*

W

W Atlanta at Perimeter
Center (Atlanta), *25*
Wake Forest University
(Winston-Salem), *152*
War Between the States
Museum (Florence),
176
Washington Duke Inn &
Golf Club (Durham),
107
Water Street
(Wilmington), *151*
Waterworks Visual Arts
Center (Salisbury),
141

Watt's Grocery
(Durham), *109*
The Waverly Inn
(Hendersonville), *119*
The Westin Buckhead
Atlanta (N.E.), *25*
The Westin Charlotte
(Charlotte), *99*
The Westin Peachtree
Plaza (Atlanta), *25*
The Westin Poinsett
(Greenville), *180*
The Westin Resort,
Hilton Head Island
(Hilton Head Island),
183
The Westin Savannah
Harbor Golf Resort
And Spa (Savannah),
71
Weymouth Woods-
Sandhills Nature
Preserve (Southern
Pines), *143*
Whistle Stop Café
(Juliette), *53*
The Whitlock (Marietta),
61
Whitworth Inn (Flowery
Branch), *44*
The Willcox (Aiken),
157
William B. Umstead
State Park (Raleigh),
136
The Wilmingtonian
(Wilmington),
149
Windmill Point (Nags
Head), *131*
The Winds Resort Beach
Club (Ocean Isle
Beach), *142*
Windsor Hotel, *13*
Winston's Grille
(Raleigh), *139*
Wisteria (Atlanta), *36*
Woodlands Resort & Inn
(Summerville), *195*
The World of Coca-Cola
(Atlanta), *20*
The Wreck (Mount
Pleasant), *187*

Wren's Nest (Atlanta),
    20
Wright Brothers National
    Memorial (Kill Devil
    Hills), *123*
Wyndham Peachtree
    Conference Center
    Hotel (Peachtree
    City), *26*

Y

Yellow House On
    Plot Creek Road
    (Waynesville), *147*

Z

Zachry's Seafood (Jekyll
    Island), *58*
Zambra (Asheville), *86*

Zapata (Norcross), *39*
Zebulon B. Vance
    Birthplace State
    Historic Site
    (Weaverville), *82*
Zevely House (Winston-
    Salem), *154*
Zocalo (Atlanta), *36*
Zoo Atlanta (Atlanta), *20*

214

INDEX